Chrétien, Troyes, and the Grail

"We must so bear ourselves in the company of these twelfth-century people as not to spoil with our Arthurian problem their Arthurian entertainment. For them as for us . . . the Grail story was something of a problem; but, keeping its mystery, it remained charming in its form, evocative and stimulating in its symbolism. It was never, in the Middle Ages, ground up with the grit of erudition." (R. N. Walpole, *Romance Philology*, XI [1958], 221.)

>   Toutes les incorporex choses
>   As corporex sunt si encloses,
>   Si couvertes et si obscures,
>   Que par samblance et par figures
>   Faire entendant les nos couvient.
>   (Gautier de Coincy, *Sacristain noyé*, vv. 261-265.)

Thirteenth-century statues of Ecclesia and Synagoga, Portail de l'Horloge, Cathedral of Strasbourg.

Chrétien, Troyes,
and the Grail

By URBAN T. HOLMES, JR.
AND
SISTER M. AMELIA KLENKE, O. P.

1959

Chapel Hill · THE UNIVERSITY OF NORTH CAROLINA PRESS

Copyright, 1959, by
The University of North Carolina Press

Manufactured in the United States of America

The Library of Congress has cataloged this publication as follows:

Holmes, Urban Tigner, 1900—
    Chrétien, Troyes, and the Grail, by Urban T. Holmes, Jr. and Sister M. Amelia Klenke. Chapel Hill, University of North Carolina Press, 1959.

    x, 230 p. illus., map (on lining paper) 23 cm.

    Bibliography: p. 215-223.

    1. Chrestien de Troyes, 12th cent. 2. Troyes, France—Hist.
i. Klenke, Amelia.

PQ1448.H75	841.1	59-8118
Library of Congress		

Preface

When Chrétien, commonly called Chrétien de Troyes, departed this life in the last quarter of the twelfth century, he left behind a mystery so vast that men have never ceased to be intrigued by it. This is the legend of the Grail. Chrétien seemed to know so clearly the thesis that he wished to portray; and yet a careful reading—nay, a dozen careful readings today—cannot make the reader certain of any solution for the *Conte del Graal*. Scholars have looked for this explanation in the "sources"; but there are not many broad possibilities in this direction. The age in which Chrétien lived was profoundly Christian in ideal and practice even when an occasional individual was not sure of his personal theology. Furthermore there was a certain amount of folk narrative which circulated widely, and prominent in this were tales about a leader named Arthur who would one day restore the dignity of the Celtic peoples. There has been considerable dispute over the amount of these ingredients, but source study alone does not explain the treatment and the meaning. An inner sense is always present in any serious production of the Middle Ages. We must seek for the meaning—the cause which rendered the Quest of the Grail the most significant masterpiece of the Middle Ages, before the *Divina Commedia* of Dante. The present authors do not believe that their predecessors have turned sufficiently all available skills towards this essential problem.

In the pages now before the reader our discussion begins at the simplest level, starting with little more than an assertion that there was a man named Chrétien who wrote romances at the

Court of Henry I and Marie de Champagne. Every one can follow at this initial point. Slowly we attempt to build a new framework, not depending upon previous "authority," but bringing together all ancillary information at our disposal. Probably no one will ever have definitive information on the life and work of Chrétien. It is a service to scholarship to open the door a little wider and encourage every one to speculate further. In recent years the Christian, Celtic, and ritualist explanations have been obliged to contend with a negative approach which has been increasing. Certain scholars have renounced all claim to explain the pattern of detail introduced by Chrétien into the Grail Quest and the Gawain Adventures. Details have been dismissed as mere elements of a story. Those who accept this viewpoint abandon all attempt to study the *sens;* they accept the *matière* alone.* When *sens* is explained it is made to seem very trivial. The present authors cannot agree with this over-simplicity. The difficulty lies not in the presence of *sens* but in the fact that it has been sought almost exclusively in a single direction which is now ceasing to yield new results. Surely the coming generation will not hold back and refuse to "dare the unpastured dragon in his den."

In compiling the present volume, we have become indebted to numerous persons whom we wish to thank: both those who have taken a lively interest in our research, encouraging us with their invaluable criticisms and suggestions, and those who made it financially possible for us to travel abroad to visit areas vital to our project. Some of them are Miss Ann Bracken, Mme Y. M. de Coppet, M. René Jullian, M. Louis Grodecki, M. le Curé at Châlons-sur-Marne, and M. T. L. Cazes. And we are grateful to Commander Hampton Hubbard, Medical Corps USN, for the drawing of the map of Troyes. We also wish to acknowledge our indebtedness to the University of North Carolina Research Council for generous aid in the publication of this book, and to

---

* In a recent book M. Jean Frappier has assembled very competently much of what has been written hitherto on Chrétien de Troyes and on the Grail. We do not accept all of Frappier's conclusions, but his book may be used in conjunction with ours. This is *Chrétien de Troyes* (Paris: Hatier-Boivin, 1957). Another recent book also is very helpful, Peter Rickard, *Britain in Mediaeval French Literature* (Cambridge University Press, 1956) which, in its Chapters 3 and 4, gives an outline more moderate but not so full as Frappier's.

the Ford Foundation for a grant under its program for assisting American university presses in the publication of works in the humanities and the social sciences.

         Urban T. Holmes, Jr.
         Sister M. Amelia Klenke, O. P.

Contents

	PAGE
Preface	v

PART I
by Urban T. Holmes, Jr.

1. Troyes and the Counts of Champagne	3
2. Chrétien de Troyes and the Legends of Britain	19
3. Chrétien in Champagne	41
4. The Castle and the Grail Procession	62
5. Summary	83

PART II
by Sister M. Amelia Klenke, O.P.

6. The Prologue of Chrétien's *Perceval*	91
7. Chrétien de Troyes and the Abbot Suger	108
8. Chrétien de Troyes, the Modena Archivolt, and the Otranto Mosaic	123
9. Summary	158

APPENDICES

Note on Reality versus Ideality in Chrétien by Urban T. Holmes, Jr.	165
Partial List of Scholars and Some of Their Views Regarding the *Perceval*	168
Alphabetical Key to the Symbolism of Chrétien's *Perceval* by Sister M. Amelia Klenke, O.P.	195
Bibliography	215
Index	225

Illustrations

Thirteenth-century statues of Ecclesia and Synagoga,
Portail de l'Horloge, Cathedral of Strasbourg *frontispiece*

facing page

Fig. 1. Holograph of Chrétien de Saint-Maclou — 54

Fig. 2. Drawing of an *aumonière* or wallet owned by Henry the Liberal — 54

Fig. 3. Ecclesia and Synagoga, panels from the twelfth-century window of the Cathedral at Châlons-sur-Marne — 55

Fig. 4. Top of portable altar from Stavelot. Twelfth-century Champlevé enamel showing Ecclesia and Synagoga — 70

Fig. 5. The Crucifixion with figures representing Church and Synagogue, from the top of a reliquary — 71

Fig. 6. King Arthur in the Tree of Life mosaic, Cathedral of Otranto, 1166 — 71

Fig. 7. Ecclesia greets a returning Crusader crushing Heresy underfoot, twelfth-century fresco at Cressac — 118

Fig. 8. Two Combats. Jacob wrestles with the Angel; Truth tears out the tongue of Fraud — 118

Fig. 9. The architrave and Arthurian archivolt of the Porta della Pescheria, Cathedral of Modena — 119

Fig. 10. Three Apostles spreading the Truths of the Gospel. Tympanum of western façade, Angoulême — 119

Fig. 11. From the King Arthur Tapestry, about 1385 — 134

Fig. 12. The Tree of Life, twelfth-century window in the Church of Saint-Nazaire, Carcassonne — 135

PART ONE

CHAPTER ONE

Troyes and the Counts of Champagne

THE CITY OF Troyes is about ninety miles southeast by east of Paris. We know from many sources, including the *Itinerary* of Matthew Paris made in 1253, that Troyes was a focal point, the meeting of two principal routes leading to Italy and beyond. It was at the Troyes fairs that Gerald the Welshman and hosts of other travellers bought their Italian currency from the Bologna merchants, money which was to be delivered to them at Faenza and elsewhere. When he returned from Italy in 1203 Gerald had a rendezvous at Troyes with his agents from England. They brought sterling which he had intended to change into parisis and tournois to be used during his stay on French territory; but he had piled up an unexpected debt with the Bolognese and money had to be conveyed to them. These transactions illustrate the importance of Troyes as a financial center in the period around 1200, and we can assume that the exchange was just as flourishing in the last third of the twelfth century.[1]

A theory of research which is dear to the heart of the present writer is that, except in aesthetic criticism, a literary investigator must be thoroughly steeped in the ideas, the physical surroundings, and the realia of the period which concerns him. It is only by comprehending the background in as much detail as possible that one acquires feeling for the psychological reactions of those who lived and died eight hundred years ago. They were not naïve children, as some used to believe in the days of Sir Walter Scott; but neither were their reactions, their hesitations, and their motives

---

1. George Brunner Parks, *The English Traveler to Italy* (Stanford, Calif.: Stanford University Press, 1954), I, 214 ff.

precisely the same as ours in the mid-twentieth century. Many will nod agreement as they read these lines; but some will fall again into the error of assigning to our mediaeval forefathers advertising techniques, tolerance, and perspective in social problems and world affairs, much the same as what we have today. Procedures and concerns which could not be mediaeval are attributed unconcernedly to Geoffrey of Monmouth and to Chrétien de Troyes, not to mention to that legion of copyists who have transmitted the manuscripts to us. We are making an effort to present Chrétien's physical and cultural surroundings in this initial chapter.

Here is a survey of the city of Troyes as it looked after 1150 and before the great fire of July 23, 1188.[2] The reader may follow this with the reconstructed map (endpapers). It is not practical to clutter the map with the names of all the streets. Roughly, there were two sections in the mediaeval town of Troyes. The commercial area was a rectangle surrounded on three sides by a palisade wall, with earth packed between the pales up to wall level. To enter one of the wooden gates one had to cross over two dry moats by small drawbridges. It is important to know the names of these gates to the commercial city. Moving around from south to north they were the Porte de la Tanerie, the Porte de Cronciaus (for those travelling to Italy), the Porte d'Auxerre, known also as the Porte du Mitre—then the Porte de Paris, the Porte de la Madeleine, and the Porte des Prés. (The mediaeval pronunciation of Prés is still preserved at this spot, with the spelling Preize.) This part of the city was closed on the east by a diversion of the waters of the Seine which was begun in 1072. This canal was called the Ru Cordé. One could cross it by a bridge,

2. This description of Troyes is based upon the available material and upon several archaeologizing visits to the city. The references are Théophile Boutiot, *Histoire de la ville de Troyes et de la Champagne méridionale* (5 vols.; Troyes, 1870-80); Gustave Carré, *Histoire populaire de Troyes et du département de l'Aube* (Troyes, 1881); Anne-François Arnaud, *Voyage archéologique et pittoresque dans le département de l'Aube et dans l'ancienne diocèse de Troyes* (Troyes, 1837); Jean-Charles Courtalon-Delaistre, *Typographie historique de la ville et diocèse de Troyes* (3 vols.; Troyes, 1783-84); Corrard de Bréban, *Les rues de Troyes anciennes et modernes* (Troyes, 1857); Charles Lalore, *Collection des principaux cartulaires du diocèse de Troyes* (7 vols.; 1870-90). These references are very difficult to find. The Courtalon-Delaistre and the Corrard de Bréban are apparently not in any American library.

the Pont des Bains, and thus enter the official section of the city, the Cité or Oppidum (of Gallo-Roman times). For centuries this had been an almost square enclosure, surrounded by a stone wall which was much dilapidated by 1173. The gate which led to the enclosure at the bridge was the old Porte d'Artaud.

The Castle of the Counts of Champagne and Troyes was situated at the northwest corner of this Cité. There was a rectangular keep or donjon surrounded by a wide bailey. This tower was destroyed in 1525 but the forbidding gate in the wall that encircled the bailey or courtyard was preserved until very early in the nineteenth century. A sketch was made before its destruction. In the period that Chrétien wrote his romances the Castle was used only for feudal ceremonies, although it may have served as a lodging for guests at the high feasts and at tourney times. The Count and his retainers were housed in the Palace. Let us say in general that there were four groupings of buildings, aside from the old Castle, in this Cité. In the northwest area, adjacent to the Castle and near the canal, was the great Jewish quarter, the Broce as Juis. Side by side with this, in the northeast, was the enclosure of the Abbey of Saint-Loup, a community of Augustinian canons.[3] The mid-line of the Cité was the Rue de la Cité, which ran from the Porte d'Artaud, and the bridge over the canal, to the Porte de l'Evesque in the opposite stretch of wall. South of this line on the west were the buildings pertaining to the Palace; to the east of these were the Cathedral of Saint-Pierre and structures pertaining to it. Granted that Chrétien spent some periods of his life in the immediate service of the Count of Troyes, it is evident that he lived in very close proximity to the Broce as Juis, the Augustinian canons, and the Cathedral and its school.

A minute cataloguing of the streets of the Cité will be of little use for any reader who is impatient to get on with the business of Chrétien de Troyes. However, Chrétien surely knew all these streets, for they were not many. The Jewish quarter had a synagogue in its center, enclosed by lanes on the four sides, making a sort of square. It is only a guess, but a probable one, that the

---

3. The many holdings of Saint-Loup are mentioned in a letter by Innocent III, dated 1202. See J. P. Migne, *Patrologia Latina* (hereafter cited as *P.L.*), vol. 205, cols. 11-13.

Talmud school was at this spot. This area was separated from the Augustinians of Saint-Loup by a celebrated street—once called Rue des Malheureux, then Rue de la Juiverie, and at a later date, Rue du Flacon. Along the west flank of the quarter was the Rue Haute des Bains, so called because the public baths were there along the side of the Ru Cordé or canal. Eventually this was named Rue de l'Arche de Noé. The Viez Rome, or Rue de la Vieille Rome, bordered the south wall of the Castle bailey, and many wealthy Jews lived there. Inside the area of Saint-Loup the principal street was the Rue de Saint-Loup, starting from the Rue de la Cité and ending in a kind of "four points," continuing as the Rue de l'Orme, with the Rue des Carreaux on the left and the Rue des Tournelles going off to the right.[4] The Abbot of Saint-Loup had his house on the Rue des Tournelles. The street which bordered the Abbey, along the wall, belonged to the Cathedral. It was the Rue du Cloistre Saint-Pierre. We have reason to suspect that the Cathedral school, which Peter Comestor and maybe Chrétien knew, was situated in that street, with the crumbling ramparts of the Gallo-Roman period appearing only slightly above the houses.

The Palace of the Counts was speedily rebuilt after the disastrous conflagration of 1188, and it remained in slightly altered style until 1806. A sketch was engraved shortly before its disappearance.[5] The back of the building was toward the canal; it formed an L with the collegiate Church of Saint-Estienne, which was the private chapel of the Counts. This building must be of interest to any true lover of Chrétien, for the right-hand tower and the lower structure look older and they may have survived the great fire, which would make them contemporary with Chrétien. It was similar to most first-floor halls of its date—with the long principal hall set over an undercroft. A straight stairway led up to this from the ground. At the southern end of the hall there was a platform, and we are told that from this point the Count

---

4. Mentioned in Document no. 113, Lalore, I, 155-56.
5. This is illustrated in a steel engraving found in Arnaud. There is an engraving of the interior plan also. P. Héliot, "Résidences princières bâties en France," *Moyen-Age*, LXI (1955), 37-38, mistakenly calls this the nineteenth-century drawing the first building. See too E. Chapin, *Les villes de foire de Champagne* . . . (Paris, 1937).

could hear masses and offices being said in the Chapel of Saint-Estienne. A door at the top of a wooden newel stair led from the platform directly down into the rear of the Chapel. Living quarters, consisting of three rooms and a garde-robe (over the Ru Cordé), could be entered from the other side of the hall. Kitchen service and other domestic needs were brought up by a stair in a tower at the northern end of this long room.

The Chapel of Saint-Estienne had a cloister and outbuildings which overflowed into the suburb south of the old rampart, through the dilapidated Porte des Jaunes. This suburb was the Bourg-Saint-Estienne. Across the road from it was the Bourg-Saint-Denis, for the Church of Saint-Denis lay directly south and over the wall from the Cathedral area.

Counts Hugues (1093-1125), Thibaut II (1125-52), and Henry I or the Liberal (1152-81) were great "ditch diggers." Still another canal branched off from the Ru Cordé, some distance to the south, and washed the foot of the old wall on the east. By 1173 a third one, the Gislart or Jallart, ran still farther to the east. A palisade wall was placed along the west bank of the third canal and thus the Bourg-Saint-Denis, the Bourg-l'Evesque, and the Bourg-Saint-Estienne were enclosed within the recently expanded Cité. On the other side of Troyes, near the Porte de Cronciaus, another digging was in process. A canal to be called the Trevois was being dug to bring Seine water into the commercial quarter. This was to fill the old bed of the Vienne creek, which was unpleasantly filthy and stagnant, passing as it did slowly through the district occupied by tanners and butchers.

Chrétien has depicted for us the commercial area of a prosperous town, observed through the eyes of Gawain:

> He gazes at the whole town filled with attractive people, at the money changers' tables which are covered with gold and silver and with heaps of coins. He sees the market areas and the streets filled with good workmen who are practicing their trades, each one at his own. This fellow makes helmets, that man coats of mail; another manufactures saddles, another shields; this worker makes bridles and his neighbor spurs. Some are polishing swords, others are fulling cloth, and these are weaving while others are dyeing and some are shearing threads. Certain workmen are melting gold and silver, while

some others are shaping cups, goblets and eating bowls, or designing jewels with enamel inlay: rings, belts, and fastenings. One could imagine that there was always a fair in this town, for it was so full of wax, pepper, scarlet dye, expensive furs, and various sorts of merchandise.[6]

It is vain to imagine the town that Chrétien was picturing, but it could have been the streets of Troyes. Those streets, in the commercial area across the Ru Cordé, were a gateway for Italy and for Germany for many men whose names are celebrated in French and English history. They often came in by the Porte de Paris and went out by the Porte de Cronciaus, tarrying long enough to purchase their foreign moneys at the changers' tables. Between the two principal western gates, the Porte de Paris and the Porte d'Auxerre, was the Viscount's tower from which he could supervise easily the maintenance of order. The triangular place close by was the Marché au blé. There was a hostel for the sick there and quite near was another synagogue, perhaps made of wood like the vast majority of all the little houses that jammed the sides of the streets. The Rue de Composte was called also the Rue du Temple because it had houses which were the location of that order.[7] The Rue de Cronciaus led to the gate of that name. We should like to list the myriad of little streets, some not drawn on the map, which filled the market and Change area. There were two long streets: the one from the Porte d'Auxerre toward the Cité began as the Rue de l'Epicerie, continued as the Rue de la Fanerie, and finally was the Rue Nostre Dame as Nonains as it passed the convent of that name. In the Rue and Place Nostre Dame as Nonains there were many booths maintained by the convent. It was in those booths that the disastrous fire began in 1188 and it spread quickly to the Palace across the canal. The other long street, starting from the Porte de Paris, was the Rue du Beffroy, then Rue de Pontigny (later de la Monnaie), Rue d'Etape de Vin, Rue Champeau, and Grant Rue. The narrow lane in the center of the market was the Rue Pipejoy. If the reader is interested he can find on the map the Rue de la Corterie, which

---

6. *Conte del Graal*, vv. 5754-82. Peter Rickard thought London was intended.
7. Boutiot in *Annuaire administratif et commercial du département de l'Aube*, XLI (1866), 32-33.

was prolonged past the Madeleine as the Rue du Bois. The Rue des Testes connected the Corterie with the Rue du Beffroy (or Grant Rue). The reader will note the Bourg Neuf. The area between the Madeleine and the market was honeycombed with little alleys with fascinating names: Rue des Croisettes, Rue du Mortier d'Or, Ruelle des Chats (still there), Rue du Domino, Cour de la Rencontre, Cour de la Foire. The Rue de l'Orfevrerie ran south of the Change. We might well add, with Chrétien: "If you know how to practice your merchant's trade at Bar-sur-Aube, at Provins, or at Troyes, it cannot be that you will not become rich."[8]

At Troyes the principal fairs were the Foire chaude (early in July until September 13) and the Foire froide (November 2 to January 2). There was also the Foire de l'Assomption held at Nostre Dame as Nonains and the Foire du Clos in the Rue de Cronciaus for two weeks after January 22. The Foire chaude and the Foire froide were the big events which drew merchants and bankers from all western Europe and even from the eastern Mediterranean. They came from throughout France and from Genoa, Lucca, Bologna, Florence, Rome, Cremona, Milan, Pistoia, Asti, Siena, Piacenza, Parma, Naples, Venice, and Urbino and from the Low Countries, Hainaut, Brabant, Switzerland, Savoy, Pamplona, Lerida, Barcelona, Castile, Aragon and Portugal. Others travelled far from Sweden, Acre, and Cyprus and occasionally from Greece, Egypt, and Tunis. England and Scotland were not well represented at these fairs; but the London Hansa, an international group with headquarters at Bruges (despite its London name), was very active at Troyes. With so many strangers present, the fairs had to be well policed. The Viscount had his tower at the western edge of the market area, between the Porte de Paris and the Porte d'Auxerre. Undoubtedly there were professional knights and *serjanz* under his command. There were two Masters of the fairs, whose task it was to handle business arrangements. There was also a Provost of the Merchants, aided by a bailiff. Much of the actual trading was on land held by the abbeys and collegiate churches, so we may be sure that there were men at arms employed

8. *Guillaume d'Angleterre:* "A Bar, a Provins ou a Troies Ne puet estre, riches ne soies . . ." (v. 1987).

by these proprietors; and there were professional *serjanz* in the service of the Bishop's court who handled those disturbers who claimed benefit of clergy. Administration of order and justice in a twelfth-century town was complicated. Side by side were places and peoples who were responsible to different overlords. At times, particularly in the summer, vassals of the Count of Champagne and of the ecclesiastical landholders may have done some of the policing, but mostly there would have been *soudoiiers*, men who made a living under arms. Individuals who served in this way were often Flemings and Bretons.

Breton minstrels could have been welcomed at the donjon and at the Palace; but it is our opinion that they were far fewer than some scholars believe. The statistical method is not in honor among mediaevalists, particularly among the devotees of literature. But where we possess a fair sample of evidence, some attention should be paid to it. Bishop Wolfger of Passau was distinguished for many reasons, and very kindly he left posterity the account of his disbursements for a period around 1203. He had a fondness for minstrels of all sorts. Few days passed without his recording one or two hand-outs to people of this class. Walther von der Vogelweide received money from him on two occasions. Bishop Wolfger mentions a Celtic monk to whom he gave largesse, "cuidam monacho schoto lx den.," but he has no reference to minstrels of this kind. To be sure he does not always give the nationality. Here are some sample entries: "cuidam vetulo ioculatori in rufa tunica .v. sol. mezanorum"; "Flordamor ioculatori tal. bon." Perhaps when a minstrel was superior he noted him better. We find: "Cuidam Lombardo istrioni .x. sol. mezan."[9]; "illi francigene cum giga et socio suo dim. tal."[10] Not every *ioculator* was a singer, e.g., "ioculatori cum cultellis."[11] A Goliard is indicated by this: "Ruolando apostate de Enstorf .xxiiij. den."[12] The Bishop usually noted the fact when there was some peculiarity, e. g., "calvo istrioni .xxx. den."[13]

We ask ourselves how many minstrels carried about rudely

9. I. Zingerle, *Reiserechnungen Wolfgers von Ellenbrechtskirchen* (1877), p. 47.
10. *Ibid.*, p. 27.
11. *Ibid.*, p. 48.
12. *Ibid.*, p. 14.
13. *Ibid.*, p. 15.

constructed tales in French. The number who went about singing in the Breton language must have been really minimum. The catalogue of romances and *contes* found in the *Flamenca* is surely more representative of what was really in the repertoire.[14] Chrétien says of the minstrels who attended the wedding of Erec and Enide that they were dancers, enchanters, whistlers, performers on the harp, rote, gigue, vielle, flute, and chalumele—as well as those who sang and narrated.[15] On the other hand, there were individuals from Brittany who could have furnished some tales, such as the professional soldiers mentioned above.

Many people concerned with trade and commerce in Troyes were technically serfs. In 1170 the Count donated to the Cathedral chapter the person of Odee, daughter of Odo the moneyer, who was married to Simon de Bourges.[16] This meant that Odo the father was a serf, and certainly a wealthy one at that. In 1164 the Count gave to maistre Normant the hand of a female serf who had been granted a money changer's table; then he freed them both. This table earned one hundred sous of income a year (which was probably the amount that would be paid to the Count, rather than the "take" earned by the changer).[17] In 1154 the Count granted to the serfs who belonged to the Abbey of Saint-Loup and lived on or near the Abbey grounds the right to pay no duty on their merchandise and freedom from the Count's justice, if the canons so desired. In 1157 Count Henry made a large donation to his collegiate Church of Saint-Estienne, including many customs dues, proceeds from smaller markets and fairs (among which were those of the Foire du Clos of the Rue de Cronciaus), and justice over those living in the Rue de Cronciaus. Many serfs were transferred in this same charter.

So far we have said little about the Jews who formed a large

14. *Le roman de Flamenca* (ed. P. Meyer), vv. 584-723.
15. *Erec et Enide* (ed. W. Foerster), vv. 2036 ff.
16. Boutiot, *Histoire*, I, 214. Furthermore, in the year 1184 Robert Chauceor was mentioned as a serf (Lalore, I, 111). This seems to be the same Robert Chauceor who signed ahead of the knights in a document of 1193 (Lalore, I, 156). See Raleigh Morgan, Jr., "Old French *jogleor* and Kindred Terms," *Romance Philology*, VII (1954), 279-325.
17. Boutiot, *Histoire*, I, 209.

part of the population in the twelfth century.[18] Their principal center, as remarked, was in the Juiverie or Broce as Juis, close to Saint-Loup. Another center was in the Clos de Cronciaus near their synagogue (which was to be replaced eventually by the Church of Saint-Pantaléon). It is to be inferred that Jews had their houses in this market area at an early date, before the palisade was built as a protection. There is a legend that the great Rashi had lived beside the butchers' quarter or massacreries. This Salomon ben Isaac or Rashi (1040-1105) was the greatest Jewish scholar of his day and perhaps he has never been surpassed. His children preferred the fortified town of Ramerupt, where his grandsons, Samuel ben Meir or Rashbam (1085-1158) and Jacob ben Meir or Rabbenu Tam (1100-71), began their teaching. Pupils came to them from places far and near. Following in the steps of his grandfather, Rabbenu Tam became the highest rabbinical authority and he was also a liturgical poet, in the Hebrew language. In 1147, on the second day after Pentecost he was attacked by Crusaders and owed his life to the intervention of a knight whose name we do not know. Soon thereafter he removed to Troyes, probably accompanied by his brother Rashbam, although there is evidence that the connection with Ramerupt was never broken. Rabbenu Tam was obliged to pay thirty pounds for the privilege of moving his books and furniture to Troyes.[19] We have no evidence but we assume that this great scholar took a house in the Broce as Juis, close to the synagogue which was later to become Saint-Frobert. These famous Talmudists added much luster to the Jewish schools already there. Their activity went on in close proximity to the Abbey of Saint-Loup with its hundreds of serf-merchants, manufacturers, millers, and with its canons who were executives, priests, and teachers. It is hard to believe there was little interchange of ideas, stories, and helping hands. As for the Jews in general, "au XIIe siècle on les trouve banquiers des comtes.... Ils sont fermiers des péages, des impôts et des revenus de toutes sortes."[20] We know that Count Henry consulted with

---

18. The principal reference is Heinrich Gross, *Gallia-Judaica, dictionnaire géographique de la France d'après les sources rabbiniques* (Paris, 1897).
19. Gross, pp. 225, 231, 163.
20. Boutiot, *Histoire*, I, 249.

them on knotty problems of the Old Testament. Most of the learned Talmudists engaged also in trade and banking, as one could not make a living in their schools. The synods which met at Troyes were held in the seasons when Jewish leaders could be present, for commercial reasons. Speaking of the third great synod presided over by Rabbenu Tam, H. Gross says, "Ce synode était réuni à Troyes au moment de la foire à laquelle étaient venus assister des marchands juifs de différentes régions. Ce fait avait facilité la réunion des membres du synode et la publication des résolutions prises par l'assemblée."[21]

But the tone of any community such as Troyes was set by the character of its feudal lords. Those who wrote and sang and practiced the arts were greatly dependent upon those who occupied the Palace within the Cité. More often than not it was the patronage of the women of the court which opened the purse strings and suggested motifs and themes to be elaborated. The people of the Palace were closely related to feudal lords and princes of the Church in other areas. An aspiring young clerk who sought advancement in court circles could have his career greatly changed by the external associations of his feudal lord—by whom the lord married, the places where he travelled, and the relatives who came to visit regularly.

Count Hugues of Champagne (1097-1124) made three pilgrimages to the Holy Land and he was admitted to the Order of the Templars a year before his death.[22] Count Thibaut, his successor (1125-52), never went to the East, but he was active at the Council in Troyes in 1128, where the Templars were given their permanent statutes. He wanted to give all his lands to the newly formed Order of the Prémontré, but the founder Norbert would not accept them and persuaded him to marry Mathilda of Carinthia (Kärnten), daughter of Engelbert, Marquis of Istria and Duke of Carinthia. It was in 1126 that this young German girl made the long journey from Klagenfurt in southeastern

21. P. 237.
22. This is standard historical information. See Brial in *Histoire littéraire de France* (1869), XIV, 205-09, and Migne, *P.L.*, vol. 186, col. 1305; also *Dictionnaire de biographie universelle*, XXIV, 136-8. Boutiot, *Histoire*, I, repeats most of this material.

Austria, through Innsbruck, Regensburg, Nuremberg, to Cologne. In her childhood, close to the Balkan area, she must have learned about Thessaly and its long established reputation for witchcraft. After her marriage she seldom left Champagne, where she became the mother of eleven children. Adèle, the eleventh child, was to be the third wife of Louis VII of France and the mother of Philip Augustus. The oldest, Henry, went on the Second Crusade and was knighted in 1147 by the Greek Emperor Manuel Comnenos, on the suggestion of St. Bernard. This Henry became the next Count and was the patron of Chrétien de Troyes. We may be sure that Chrétien knew the old dowager Countess and some of her memories of southeastern Europe, and some of her fondness for the East passed into the romance, *Cligés*, which he wrote for her son. Count Henry had great magnificence. He was a true internationalist, as much as one could be at this period in history. Aside from his Austrian mother and his Byzantine adventure of a chivalric character, he was also the nephew of the late King of the English, Stephen. The wealthy patron in his family was his uncle, Henry of Blois, Abbot of Glastonbury since 1126 and Bishop of Winchester after 1129, who died in 1171.[23] This great churchman played the role of kingmaker in England during the troubles of 1139-52; also a patron of the arts, he brought back antiquities from Rome to England and encouraged such productions as the St. Nicholas baptismal font at Winchester and the Winchester Bible manuscript. Bishop Henry began his ecclesiastical career as a monk at Cluny, and it was to this home retreat that he withdrew on frequent occasions. He spent the entire year of 1154 in residence at Cluny. Troyes lay on his road from Winchester to Cluny, as well as on the way to Rome. For any young man who read Geoffrey of Monmouth and was curious about the legends of Britain, Bishop Henry would have been a fascinating patron. It was at Winchester, according to Geoffrey, that King Arthur closed in on Mordred.[24] Gaimar said in 1139 that a copy of the *Anglo-Saxon Chronicle* had been placed

---

23. There is a fine article on Henry of Blois in the *Dictionary of National Biography*.
24. Geoffrey of Monmouth (ed. Faral), III, 276.

in the Bishop's hall at Winchester by King Alfred. Anyone could read it, provided he did not move it.[25]

Among the Arthurian "idle tales" that floated about were several associated with Glastonbury. It was told that while Gildas lived in that ancient Abbey, a prince of the country carried off Guenevere and lodged her there.[26] It was said also that the Avalon to which Arthur had been taken, as Geoffrey related, could be identified with Glastonbury. At Troyes there were other reasons for interest in Britain. Count Henry was the nephew of the late King Stephen. His father Thibaut, the eldest brother, had been asked to lay claim to the crown, but he had refused to press his claim against Stephen. Apparently there were traditions, gathered by Geoffrey of Monmouth, that a great battle between Arthur and the Romans had been fought near the Aube and that a still greater one had been won near Langres.[27]

The clerical population was unusually numerous in the vicinity of Troyes.[28] There was the huge Augustinian Abbey of Saint-Loup, the Cathedral of Saint-Pierre, and the collegiate Church of Saint-Estienne, all within a stone's throw of one another, within the area which had been the Gallo-Roman Oppidum. Just outside the eastern walls lay the Benedictine Abbey of Saint-Martin-es-aires (St. Martin in the Field), which occupied the original site of the Abbey of Saint-Loup. Troyes looked toward the east and south along the Seine. In the space between the Seine and the Aube rivers was a great forest which was ideally suited for religious orders desiring to remain isolated. Today three principal roads lead to the east out of Troyes, and I presume they were much the same in the twelfth century. There is one that goes to Piney, Lesmont, and Brienne, another farther south to Lusigny, Vandeuvre, Jaucourt, and Bar-sur-Aube, and another, unpaved today, to Ramerupt and to Dampierre just beyond. Luyères, the

25. Gaimar, *Estorie des Englés*, vv. 2334-40: "K'a Wincestre, en l'eveskez, La est des reis la dreite estorie, Et les vies e la memorie. Li reis Elfred l'out en demaine, Fermer i fist une chaaine; Ki lire i volt bien i guardast, Mais de son liu nel remuast."
26. *Vita Gildae* in Mommsen, *Chronica Minora*, III, 107 ff.
27. (Ed. Faral), III, 258, 263.
28. Boutiot, *Histoire*, I.

home of Andreas the Chaplain, is just off this third road.²⁹ South of the route to Jaucourt and Bar-sur-Aube is a town called Montreuil, not far out of Troyes. Many of the small religious communities in the area were granges of Saint-Loup; others were Benedictine priories. Prominent along the Aube River, and slightly beyond, were the Premonstratensian Abbeys of Beaulieu, Basse-Fontaine, and La-Chapelle-aux-Planches. Beaulieu, dedicated to St. Mark, was established in 1112; Basse-Fontaine, in 1143. Beaulieu and, in fact, all these foundations looked toward Troyes as their regional center. Beaulieu was only twenty miles away; the two Jewish centers of Ramerupt and Dampierre were at a distance of only sixteen and twenty-one miles, respectively.³⁰ Such places would be four hours away by a palfrey or mule "bien amblant." Very important was Clairvaux-sur-Aube, which was the great monastery of Saint-Bernard. This lay farther up the river from Bar-sur-Aube, but near enough for frequent communication with the town of Troyes.

Count Henry the Liberal was much concerned with all these communities and others which lay to the west of Troyes, but he cared especially for his home Church of Saint-Estienne, which formed a wing of the Palace. The treasury of Saint-Estienne received many of his valued possessions. Much of this Romanesque art was destroyed in 1793 by the Revolution. Saint-Estienne also fell heir to his books, of which we have a list: the writings of St. Augustine, the sermons of St. Bernard, the commentaries of St. Jerome on the Bible, a beautiful Psalter (still preserved), Alcuin on the virtues, the *Ecclesiastical History* of Eusebius, Isidore on the Sovereign God, Biblical manuscripts, and a Josephus.³¹ The presence of this last indicates some interest in the history of the Jewish people.

---

29. The identification of Andreas Capellanus can be virtually proved from certain documents in Lalore. John Mahoney has published an article on this subject, *Studies in Philology*, LV (1958), 1-6. In any case there is no doubt that Andreas, the compiler of the worldly *De arte honeste amandi*, was a chaplain and therefore in priest's orders. This is one answer to those critics who insist that Chrétien's romances were too worldly to be the work of a priest. Luyères was a fief of the Abbey of Saint-Loup. See n. 3 above.

30. Gross, pp. 160 ff.

31. Arnaud, pp. 34-41. M. Arnaud collected engravings and documents on early Troyes at a date when many could be found in private hands.

So far we have made little mention of the Cathedral Chapter of Saint-Pierre at Troyes. The Bishop maintained a school devoted to the Seven Arts and to elementary training in theology. The Dean of the Chapter from 1147 to 1164 was the famous Peter Comestor, and such a man would be active in the school. Much of his best work was completed after his call to Paris and even after his withdrawal to Saint-Victor, but the inception of his ideas and a considerable amount of his omnivorous reading belonged to his long years at Troyes. He was the author of "Commentaries on St. Paul," *Allegoriae in Vetus et Novum Testamentum*, and above all of a *Historia Scholastica* which sketched religious history from the Garden of Eden to St. Paul's presence at Rome. It is exciting to realize that the poet Chrétien, during his formative years—if spent at Troyes—would most likely have attended classes under Peter.[32]

Count Henry was long remembered as a patron without an equal; his wife, Marie, was a patron in her own right. She held her own "court" from her marriage (1159?) till her death in 1198. Our readers are aware that she was the eldest daughter of Louis VII of France and of Eleanor of Aquitaine. She undoubtedly possessed much of the sprightliness and vigor that characterized her famous mother. All that we have of her today is the portrait on her seal, made in 1184.[33] She is not pretty there; yet the resemblance to the portrait on the seal of her half-brother Philip Augustus is so close that we are tempted to believe the likeness is not too false. She had four children: Henry II and Thibaut III (who married a princess of Navarre) and the daughters Scholastique and Marie. For a considerable time her personal chaplain was Andreas de Luyères, who is mentioned so often today as Andreas Capellanus; he was the author of the *De arte honeste amandi* which summarizes and embellishes in some measure a theory of love cultivated in the Count's Palace. Marie undoubtedly had other chaplains and a number of chancellors who served

---

32. The "Commentaries on St. Paul" are in Paris MS. B. N. lat. 15,269, still unpublished. The *Allegoriae* have only recently been recognized as Peter Comestor's work. Migne, *P.L.*, vol. 177, cols. 194-284.

33. This is seal D-567 of the Archives nationales at Paris.

in the capacity of scribes and notaries. But for the disastrous fire of 1188, we might still have access to many precious documents which would obviate the necessity of ceaseless speculation on the identity of Chrétien de Troyes and on the associates and activities of Henry and Marie.

Most important for the dating of romances in the third quarter of the twelfth century is the year of Countess Marie's marriage to Henry of Troyes. Critics have been accepting for a long time the date 1164, which has been established on insufficient evidence. There is a charter which should be cited.

> In nomine sancte et individue Trinitatis. Ego Henricus Trecensium, comes palatinus, existentium memorie et futurorum posteritati notum fieri volo, me sanctimonialibus ecclesie sancti Petri de Avenaio, amore Dei et precibus Aelesdis de Marolio, magistre comitisse sponse mee, /.viii. sextarios annone in molendinis meis de Alba Ripa, scilicet .iiii. sextarios frumenti et .iiii. sextarios grosse annone, singulis annis infra octavam sancti Remigii in elemosinam dedisse, et perpetuo possidendos concessisse. . . . Hujus rei et confirmationis testes sunt Maria Trecensis comitissa, Ansellus de Triangulo, Guillelmus marescallus, Guillelmus notarius. Actum est hoc anno Incarnati Verbi M. C. L. VIIII, Ludovico rege Franchorum regnante, Sanxone Remorum archiepiscopo existante. Traditum apud Virtutum per manum Guillelmi cancellarii.[34]

From this document it is apparent that Marie was already Countess of Troyes in 1159, at the age of fourteen. As her *magistra* is mentioned, it is probable that her marriage was recent at that time. Maybe she had been educated at the Convent of Saint-Pierre d'Avenay, which lay between Epernay and Châlons-sur-Marne.

---

34. This was copied by M. Loriquet, conservateur of the Bibliothèque de Reims, from fol. 26 r-v of the Cartulaire de Saint-Pierre d'Avenay. It was a thirteenth- or fourteenth-century manuscript. This item is printed by Louis Paris, *Histoire de l'Abbaye d'Avenay* (Paris, 1879), p. 82. I owe the reference to John Benton of Reed College.

CHAPTER TWO

Chrétien de Troyes and the Legends of Britain

THE POSITIVE information which we have on Chrétien is little, and all of it, except the statement of his death, is found in his own writings.

In the *Erec et Enide* he observes:

Therefore, says Crestiens de Troies, it is right that one should think and be intent upon speaking well and doing well, and he takes from a mere adventure tale a very fine combination of plot and meaning.... Now I shall begin a story which will last as long as Christianity; of this does Crestiens boast.[1]

This gives us little information except that the poet has embellished with higher meaning a simple adventure plot. In the *Cligés* there is more:

He who wrote of Erec and Enide, and composed the Commands of Ovid and his Art of Love in the vulgar tongue, and wrote the Shoulder Bite—about Mark and blond Yseut, and about the transformation of the hoopoe, the swallow, and the nightingale, he now begins once more a new tale.... This story which I wish to retell we found written in one of the books on the shelves of My Lord Saint Peter at Beauvais. The plot was got from there out of which Crestiens has made this romance. The book is very old....[2]

---

1. "Por ce dit Crestiens de Troies, Que reisons est totes voies Doit chascuns panser et antandre A bien dire et a bien anprandre, Et tret d'un conte d'avanture Une mout bele conjointure..." (*Erec*, vv. 9-14); "Des or comencerai l'estoire Qui toz jorz mes iert an memoire Tant com durra crestiantez; De ce s'est Crestiens vantez" (vv. 23-6).

2. "Cil qui fist d'Erec et d'Enide, Et les Commandemanz Ovide Et l'Art d'amors an romanz mist Et le Mors de l'Espaule fist, Del roi Marc et d'Iseut la blonde, Et de la Hupe et de l'Aronde Et del Rossignol la Muance, Un novel conte recomance..." (*Cligés*, vv. 1-8); "Ceste estoire trovons escrite, Que conter vos

The *Lancelot* has an interesting preface:

> Because my lady of Champagne wants me to undertake a romance I will do it very willingly, since I am hers completely for all that I can do in this world. . . . Crestiens begins his book; the Countess transmits to him the plot and the allegory, and he sees to it that he adds nothing else except his effort and his intention, now he begins his argument. . . . Godefroi de Laigny, clerk, has closed the Tale of the Cart, but let no one blame him because he has added to Crestien, for he has done this with the consent of Crestiens who began it. He has added that part which begins where Lancelot was emprisoned behind the wall.[3]

This informs us that Godefroi de Laigny started his conclusion to the tale at v. 5106. The *Yvain* offers fewer details:

> Crestiens ends in this way his romance of the Knight with the Lion. He has never heard more told of him, nor will you hear any more [dear reader] unless one wishes to add what is false.[4]

The *Guillaume d'Angleterre* is a bit more generous:

> Crestiens wishes to begin without adding or removing anything. . . . If anyone would care to look for English tales, he would find at Bury-Saint-Edmund's one which is quite trustworthy, because it is charming and true. If one wishes proof of this, let him go there to find it, if he desires. Crestiens is speaking, and he is used to speaking. . . .[5]

Surely at this time our poet was a prominent man of letters, so

---

vuel et retreire, An un des livres de l'aumeire Mon seignor saint Pere a Biauvez. De la fu li contes estrez, Don cest romanz fist Crestiens. Li livres est mout anciiens. . ." (vv. 18-24).

3. "Des que ma dame de Champaingne Viaut que romanz a feire anprainge Je l'anprandrai mout volantiers, Come cil qui est suens antiers De quanqu'il puet el monde feire. . ." (vv. 1-5). "Comance Crestieens son livre; Matiere et san l'an done et livre La contesse, et il s'antremet De panser si que rien n'i met Fors sa painne et s'antancion; Des or comance sa raison" (vv. 25-30). "Godefroiz de Leigni li clers A parfinee la Charrete: Mes nus hon blasme ne m'an mete Se sor Crestiien a ovré, Car ç'a il fet par le buen gré Crestiien qui le comança: Tant an a fet des la an ça, Ou Lanceloz fu anmurez" (*Lancelot*, vv. 7124-49).

4. "Del Chevalier au Lyon fine Crestiens son romans ansi. N'onques plus conter n'en oï; Ne ja plus n'en orroiz conter S'an n'i vialt mançonge ajoster" (*Yvain*, vv. 6817-22).

5. "Crestiiens se viaut antremetre Sanz rien oster et sanz rien metre" (vv. 1-2). "Qui les estoires d'Angleterre Voldroit ancerchier et anquerre, Une, qui mout fet bien a croire Por ce que pleisanz est et voire, An troveroit a saint Esmoing. Se nus m'an demand tesmoing, La l'aille querre, se il viaut. Crestiiens dit, qui dire siaut. . ." (*Guillaume d'Angleterre*, vv. 11-8).

we place this composition later in his career. But it is in the *Conte del Graal* that he is most explicit:

> Crestiens sows and scatters the seed of a romance which he now begins—and he sows it in so favorable a place that it must be to great advantage, for he does this for the finest gentleman who is subject to Rome: this is Count Philip of Flanders.... Then Crestiens will have spared himself trouble, Crestiens who undertakes to rhyme the best story which can be told in a king's court, by order of the Count. This is the Narrative of the Grail, for which the Count has furnished him the book, and you will hear how Crestiens acquits himself of this.... Know that the gifts come from Charity which the good Count Philip bestows, for nothing bids him do it except his noble, kindly heart.[6]

Some critics, and I am one of these, are sure that Chrétien's tale about the transformation of the hoopoe, the swallow, and the nightingale survives in a *Philomena* which has this signature: "This is told by Crestiens li Gois" (v. 734).

Last of all, in his continuation of the *Conte del Graal* another poet, Gerbert de Montreuil, has this to add:

> Crestiens de Troie, who began the story of Perceval, told us this—but Death overtook him and did not let him bring it to an end.[7]

These known facts can be summed up very quickly. There was a Chrétien de Troyes who had written adaptations from Ovid's *Ars amatoria*, his story of Philomela in the *Metamorphoses*, as well as an adaptation of the Pelops tale from some source, a complete or an episodical poem on the Tristan theme, and an *Erec et Enide*. The *Cligés* had its beginning from a very old manuscript in the cathedral library of Beauvais; the *Lancelot* was outlined to Chrétien in both *matière et sens* by Countess Marie

---

6. "Crestiiens seme et fet semance D'un romanz que il ancomance, Et si le seme an si bon leu Qu'il ne puet estre sanz grant preu, Qu'il le fet por le plus prodome Qui soit an l'empire de Rome: C'est li cuens Phelipes de Flandres..." (vv. 7-13). "Donc avra bien sauvé sa painne Crestiiens, qui antant et painne A rimoiier le meillor conte Par le commandemant le conte Qui soit contez an cort real: Ce est li contes del Graal, Don li cuens li bailla le livre, S'orroiz comant il s'an delivre" (vv. 61-68). "Donc sachoiz bien de verité Que li don sont de charité Que li buens cuens Phelipes done, Qu'onques nelui n'an areisone Fors son franc cuer, le deboneire" (*Conte del Graal*, vv. 51-5).

7. "Ce nous dist Crestiens de Troie Qui de Percheval commencha, Mais la mors qui l'adevancha Ne li laissa pas traire affin" (vv. 6984-7).

and it was completed on Chrétien's own suggestion by Godefroi de Laigny. The source for the plot of the *Guillaume d'Angleterre* can be read in manuscript at the monastery of Bury-St.-Edmund's. At the close of his life Chrétien was engaged upon a very long poem, the *Conte del Graal*, for which he owed the suggestion, or *livre*, to Count Philip of Flanders. This Philip, he says, was noted for his charity, and we receive the impression that charity was to be the theme throughout the tale. Chrétien says he has sowed this good seed abroad, referring, no doubt, to the Parable of the Sower. This romance is to be something special, the best that has ever been told in courts of kings.

It is at this point that a few hypotheses must be suggested before we can proceed further as investigators. There are three matters which present themselves. Was Chrétien the poet clerk or layman? Did he gather most of his Arthurian themes from the Continental Bretons or from the Celtic peoples in Britain? Lastly, was his baptismal name sufficiently rare so that one can make some progress towards identifying him from surviving documents? The answers to these questions are essential for further study. They determine the direction in which we will look in all Arthurian research.

Mediaeval education was acquired in three stages, on the average. Boys, sometimes together with girls, began in the Psalter school, conducted by a local clerk, where they learned to read and write and recite their psalter. This was lay education. For boys who went beyond this stage it was necessary to be received by the Bishop and be given simple tonsure. From then on they were technically clerks although they were not bound by ecclesiastical obligations. The next school was the Grammar school, where the *Disticha Catonis*, Ovid etc., were read, with emphasis upon the elements of Latin grammar, very little rhetoric, and perhaps an introduction to the methods of dialectic—because debate was the normal way to display one's progress in letters. It was the examination system. By the age of twelve, more or less, a youth might secure enough financial support to enable him to go on to a *Studium generale*, which we will call university (although the term was not yet in use). From then on, whether the young man

Chrétien and the Legends of Britain 23

remained a simple clerk, took the four minor orders (which still permitted marriage etc.) or was received into the major orders (subdeacon, deacon, priest) depended upon his appointment or upon the use which the Bishop might have for his services. To us it seems impossible to assume that Chrétien was not a clerk. We could argue the case by listing his mentions of the Seven Arts and more recondite Latin writers, but this is hardly necessary. It is true that some clerks slipped over into other fields—many became travelling minstrels and some even devoted themselves to the military (like Guillem de Nevers in *Flamenca*); and an occasional stray sheep might take up trade. Chrétien informs us outright that he was not a minstrel.[8] We must make our decision on whether he had the family connection to warrant his passing over to the handling of arms. We say no. It is to be assumed then that he continued in the schools, seeking for eventual employment as accountant, copyist, chancellor, or teacher. Whether he ever became a chaplain and therefore a priest will require a further decision on our part.

In view of the presence of Bretons in so many places outside of Brittany and because there is absolutely no suggestion or evidence that our Chrétien ever visited Brittany, we are disposed to believe that Chrétien spent a little time in England. Many scholars, from Gaston Paris to Peter Rickard, have thought this very likely. The argument was countered by Wendelin Foerster.[9] Those who disagree hold that relations in the mid-twelfth century between Welsh and English were not sufficiently warm for tales and social contacts between the two peoples. This is odd reasoning. Some of Chrétien's romances display an acquaintance with English (and even Scottish) places which some critics think he obtained by interrogating friends and chance visitors who passed through Troyes. This was hardly in conformity with mediaeval practice. There are even more details given by Chrétien which, if examined sensitively, mightly argue positively for his stay in England. In the *Cligés* Alixandre lands at Southampton; there he learns that Arthur is in residence at Winchester. Between dawn

---

8. *Erec et Enide*, vv. 19-22.
9. *Kristian von Troyes: Wörterbuch zu seinen sämtlichen Werken* (Halle, 1914), p. 40.

and the first hour of the day he rides on to Winchester which is in fact some thirteen miles away. After a summer in Brittany the court returns to England early in October to oppose the rebellion of Angrés of Windsor, a rebellion which follows the pattern of the Mordred episode in Geoffrey. Angrés slips away from London and goes to his better fortified position in Windsor. Arthur and his army, including Alixandre, take position across the Thames, looking up at the Castle. I should like to think that their posts were on the meadows which are now "the playing fields of Eton," but it is more probable that the Windsor in question was Old Windsor, which is at Runnymede. (It was because King John was staying at Old Windsor that he signed Magna Carta at Runnymede.) Angrés again steals away in the night with all his men, hoping to flank the army of the king camped across the Thames. He leaves Windsor by a postern gate where his exit will not be visible across the river. The gate is "vers la galerne," on the north side.[10] This specific expression of direction on the part of Chrétien is evidence that he knew first-hand the directions at Old Windsor. The river takes a bend to the north at that spot and so the postern "vers la galerne" would have allowed Angrés to slip away without heading directly into the river and Arthur's camp. The *Cligés* has other mentions of English place names. Alixandre leaves for Constantinople from the port of Shoreham-by-Sea. This was a minor port town; it is not mentioned by either Geoffrey or Wace.[11] John landed there in 1199 when he wished to get to England as quietly as possible. When Cligés, the son of Alixandre, lands in England he goes immediately to Wallingford and participates in a general tourney of knights. The King's party is based at Oxford (which is actually twelve miles from Wallingford). The tourney is held between.

If Chrétien travelled in the company which Bishop Henry, brother of Count Thibaut of Troyes, brought back with him to England in 1155, he could have met Geoffrey of Monmouth. Documents published by H. E. Salter make it evident that Geoffrey of Monmouth was a longtime resident of Oxford, prob-

---

10. *Cligés*, v. 1689.
11. Roland Blenner-Hassett, *A Study of the Place-Names in Lawman's Brut* (Stanford, Calif.: Stanford University Press, 1950), pp. 109-13.

ably as one of the *clercs lisants* on Catte Street and perhaps as a canon of the collegiate Church of St. George, between the years 1129 and 1152. He was then chosen to be Bishop of St. Asaph, a district in North Wales which was not suitable for episcopal residence at that time. This nomination was owed, no doubt, to Count Ranulf of Chester. In 1153 Bishop Geoffrey was present with others at an agreement between King Stephen and young Henry Plantagenet, signed at Winchester. He died in 1155.[12] A young cleric curious and interested in the arts could have found no better opportunity for experience than to pass a season or two in the entourage of the great patron Henry of Blois, at Winchester and at Glastonbury. If we could assume such a stay it would be easy to comprehend how Chrétien received his initiation to Celtic themes and to the topography of southern and western Britain. Breton families (from the continent) had been settled in the west since the Conquest, and some say that Geoffrey was the son of such a family—which might account for his un-Welshlike name, *Gaufridus* or *Geoffrey*, as well as for his sympathy toward the Bretons rather than toward the Welsh.

Before we make any acceptance or rejection of possible sources for Chrétien's themes we should examine briefly the background with which William of Malmesbury and Geoffrey of Monmouth must have been acquainted, near as they were to the Celtic peoples in the west.[13] As already hinted, it is a strange argument to insist that Welsh and Anglo-Normans had little communication with one another at this time because of campaigns and revolts in Wales. The upper crust of twelfth-century society lived in an atmosphere of defiance and rivalry in combat. This was no total war. Among the lower reaches of society, legends and tales were transmitted by captives, servants, traitors, and above all by women. Mediaeval warriors had a distressing habit of appropriating the

12. H. E. Salter is quoted by Sir John Lloyd, *English Historical Review*, LVII (1942).
13. This is well-known history. See A. L. Poole, *From Domesday Book to Magna Carta* (Oxford, 1950), pp. 283-301.
A remarkably interesting book is R. S. Loomis's *Wales and the Arthurian Legend* (Cardiff, 1956). We are unhappy that despite all this material Professor Loomis still supports the thesis that Chrétien got his Arthurian sources through Brittany.

women of their adversaries. How many Anglo-French boys and girls must have heard stories of Arthur, Taliessin, and Myrddin from their mothers and their nurses, despite the fact that Norman knights and Welsh chieftains were laying traps for one another! Hue of Chester (formerly of Avranches), helped by his cousin Robert of Rhuddlan, secured possession of North Wales by 1098, and Gruffydd ap Cynan was kept a prisoner at Chester. When released, this Welsh prince stirred up revolt against the Normans, and in 1098, thanks to a chance descent of the Norwegians, who sided with them, the Welsh were victorious once more. They gave only nominal submission to Henry I of England. Gruffydd died in 1137, feeble and blind but unconquered. In South Wales the Normans were settled in Gwent, at Caerleon, Monmouth etc., along the border. After the death of Rhys ap Tewdwr in 1093 the south Welsh fell to feuding among themselves, and the Normans marched into Pembroke, Cardigan, Brecknock, Radnor, and Glamorgan. However they were immediately driven out of Cardigan and Carmarthen by Cadwgan and his followers. In 1108 a colony of Flemings was permanently established in Pembroke. The Anglo-Normans continued a piecemeal infiltration into the whole of South Wales, without organized fighting. It will be seen from this brief sketch that William of Malmesbury and Geoffrey of Monmouth were active in decades where Welsh influence was particularly strong among French-speaking neighbors. The troubles between Stephen and Matilda greatly altered the balance of power in western England. The Welsh were once more independent, except for the Flemish colony, between 1139 and 1167, when Owein Gwynedd, son of Gruffydd ap Cynan, ruled in the north and Rhys ap Gruffyd, grandson of Rhys ap Tewdwr, was lord in the south; but this was only a matter of feudal independence. Henry II of England reestablished nominal submission of the Welsh in 1157, although unable to enforce it for another ten years.

While we are stressing these relationships between Welsh and Anglo-Normans, in which we have been preceded by Jean Marx, it would be well to bear in mind the criticism of our predecessors which ensued at the symposium on "Les Romans du Graal" held at Strasburg March 29-April 3, 1954.[14] In a paper by the eminent Celticist of Edinburgh, Kenneth Jackson, on "Les sources celtiques du Roman du Graal," we find this:

> J'ai souvent pensé, en lisant les ouvrages de certains arthurisants traitant de choses celtiques, que s'il me fallait mettre un point rouge dans la marge chaque fois que l'auteur commet une erreur grave, une "fâcheuse bévue," en fait de philologie ou d'histoire celtiques, le livre aurait l'air d'avoir la scarlatine.

The story-tellers of the Welsh were the *cyfarwddion*, who wandered about narrating their prose tales from memory, with some momentary additions and embellishments. The few interspersed lyrics were memorized strictly because of their rigid system of metrics, which did not facilitate changes. In addition to these prose reciters there were bards or poets who chanted verse of a reflective rather than a narrative kind. Some of the bards who had sung long ago—supposedly in the spirit of prophecy—continued in people's memory, even though most of their actual verse was lost. These were the Cynfeirdd (early bards) of the late sixth century: Taliessin, Aneurin, who served Mynyddawg of Gododdin around the year 600, and Myrrdin in the service of Gwenddoleu ap Ceidiaw, who was defeated around 575. Myrddin or Merlin is mentioned as a prophet in the *Armes Prydein Fawr* (ca. 935), "Omen of Great Britain." Merlin is a poet in the *Gododdin*, a poem by Aneurin. The *Gododdin* is little more than a eulogy of the Britons killed by the Angles at the Battle of Catterick in Yorkshire. This poem gives us our first mention of Arthur. A warrior is cited who "glutted the black ravens on the wall of the city, even though he was no Arthur." By the close of the eleventh century some of the prose story-tellers began to record in writing a few of their tales. Thus, around 1100 the story of *Kulhwch and Olwen*, in which Arthur appears as a tribal leader, took substantial form. Kulhwch goes to Arthur asking for the hand of Olwen—but many adventures must be accomplished first. With Arthur are two knights, Kei and Bedwyr, who accompany

---

14. Editions du Centre National de la Recherche Scientifique (1956), pp. 215-27. The quotation given is from p. 214. See Loomis in *Romania*, LXXIX (1958), 68-75.

the young man on his bride quest. The character of Kei is most interesting. He can hold his breath for more than a week; he can grow as tall as a high tree, and he possesses a fatal sword. The *Dream of Rhonabwy* is a tale which took its present form around 1159 and which, it is now believed, shows considerable influence from French romances. It is most likely, however, that it has a hard core of Welsh tradition. One of the characters is Ederyn, son of Nudd, who leads the men of Denmark. Another is Owein, the son of Urian. This would be the Owein in Strathclyde who aided Riderch Hen at the Battle of Armterid in 573.[15] We readily grant the existence of the core of this tale previous to Geoffrey. From such a narrative Geoffrey could have drawn Ider, son of Nuth, and Iwenus, son of Urian. From the *Kulhwch and Olwen* and other similar material could have come Arthur, Keu, and Beduerus. The legend of the "Coming of Arthur" was almost indigenous among the Celts of western Britain.

On the subject of Welsh versus Breton influence again we can do no better than cite Kenneth Jackson: "On répond généralement par l'intermédiaire de récitateurs et d'auteurs de lais armoricains. Je dois avouer que je ne vois pas la force probante des arguments sur lesquels repose cette théorie.... En tout cas pas sous cette forme que les intermédiairies étaient exclusivement armoricains" (p. 225). We have already acknowledged that influence from continental Brittany was current in England. It is true also that Marie de France has Breton names. But the reader should not forget that Marie laid claim to Continental origin: "si sui de France" (*Fables*, Epilogue, v. 4). Marie drew also upon Geoffrey and Wace. Her Eliduc must be the Aliduc of Geoffrey.[16] This Eliduc lands first at Totnes, which reminds us of the landing of Brutus at that same spot.[17] William of Malmesbury says of the Bretons:

> ... they are a race ... poor at home, and seeking abroad to support a toilsome life by foreign service. Regardless of right and affinity, they decline not even civil war, provided they are paid for it; and, in pro-

---

15. *Ibid.*, p. 87. The article is by Maurice Delbouille.
16. (Ed. Faral), III, 263: "Aliduc de Tintagol."
17. *Ibid.*, p. 90.

portion to the remuneration, are ready to enter any service that may be offered.[18]

This description fits very exactly the character Eliduc of Marie de France, who goes to England as a *soudoiier*.

As evidence of the prevalence of tales about Arthur which circulated in Britain we can cite Ailred, later Abbot of Rievaux, who was writing in 1142. He spoke of a young novice who remembered the tears he had shed over the stories "quae vulgo de nescio quo finguntur Ar(c)turo."[19] This young man must have heard tales capable of stirring the emotions—probably in the 1130's. As Ritchie says, tears could hardly have been inspired by the dry text of Geoffrey of Monmouth.[20] We have reason to believe that Wace was writing in England shortly before 1155, just prior to the date we postulate for Chrétien's stay in that country, when he said:

... the adventures in verse which are told so often of Arthur, which are decked imaginatively, neither completely false nor altogether true—not all silliness, not all seriousness. The tale-tellers have told so much, and the imaginative writers have spun so many fables to embellish their yarns, that they have caused it all to seem imaginative.[21]

This is the sort of milieu into which Chrétien, the young cleric, could have been initiated during a stay in England. But first we must estimate how it influenced Geoffrey of Monmouth and Wace.

On three occasions Geoffrey cites his indebtedness to an Archdeacon Walter for the material of his *Historia Regum Brittaniae*. He says:

18. (Ed. Hardy), II, 629. "Est enim illud genus hominum egens in patria, aliasque externo aere laboriosae vitae mercatur stipendia: si dederis, nec civilia, sine respectu juris et cognationis, detrectant praelia, sed pro quantitate munerum ad quascumque voles partes obnoxium...."
19. R. L. Graeme Ritchie, *The Normans in Scotland* (Edinburgh: Edinburgh University Press, 1954), pp. 299-300; *Crétien de Troyes and Scotland* (Oxford, Eng., 1952), p. 16.
20. *Crétien and Scotland*, p. 16.
21. "...les aventures truvees Ki d'Artur sunt tant recuntees Ke a fable sunt aturnees. Ne tut mençonge, ne tut veir, Tut folie ne tut saveir. Tant unt li cunteur cunté Et li fableur tant flablé Pur lur cuntes enbeleter, Que tut unt fait fable sembler" (*Brut*, ed. Arnold, vv. 9791-8).

... Walter, Archdeacon at Oxford, a man learned in Rhetoric and in strange histories, offered me a very old book in the British language....[22]

... as he found it in the above-mentioned British account and as he heard from Walter of Oxford, a man most learned in many histories....[23]

... [William of Malmesbury and Henry of Huntingdon] I bid be silent about the kings of the Bretons, because they do not possess that book in the British language which Archdeacon Walter at Oxford brought from the British which I have endeavored to translate thus into Latin from their version truly presented, in honor of the already mentioned princes....[24]

We make no effort to identify this famous book of Walter. This could have been a goodnatured bit of manufactured evidence trumped up in order to confound the veracity of William of Malmesbury and Henry of Huntingdon. In later years Beneëit de Sainte-More doubted the veracity of Homer, citing the book of Dares which, however, we do possess.[25] We know that Archdeacon Walter was an associate of Geoffrey's over many years, not just an acquaintance of the moment.[26] Surely we do not have to agree with Zimmer that Brittania could mean only Continental Brittany.[27] Throughout the text of Geoffrey the term "Brittania" has reference to the Celtic-speaking sections of Great Britain.[28]

In addition to names and situations which appear to have been current in Welsh traditions, Geoffrey drew elements of his Arthurian narrative from other areas. He places certain of his principal characters in Scotland and in northern England. In Chapter 152 of the *Historia Regum Brittaniae* there is mention

---

22. "...mihi...obtulit Walterus, Oxenfordensis archidiaconus, vir in oratoria arte atque in exoticis historiis eruditus, quemdam britannici sermonis librum vetustissimum..." (ed. Faral; III, 71).

23. "...ut in praefato britannico sermone invenit et a Waltero Oxenfordensis in multis historiis peritissimo viro, audivit..." (*ibid.*, III, 275).

24. "...quos de regibus Britonum tacere jubeo, cum non habeant librum illum britannici sermonis, quem Walterus, Oxenefordensis archidiaconus, ex Britannia advexit, quem de historia eorum veraciter editum, in honore praedictorum principum hoc modo in latinum sermonem transferre curavi..." (*ibid.*, II, 303).

25. *Roman de Troie* (ed. L. Constans), vv. 45-128.
26. Sir John Lloyd, p. 208.
27. *ZFSL*, XII (1890), 253-6.
28. See *Britannia* in Faral's index to his edition, III, 379.

of the three brothers Lot, Urianus, and Anguselus.²⁹ We assume that Urianus is derived from the chieftain of the sixth century; but Lot and Anguselus are Scottish. To Anguselus (< *Angus?*) King Arthur restores his kingdom of Scotland; Lot receives back his kingdom of Lothian or Londonesia. Lot had previously married Arthur's sister Anna, and the royal pair have for sons Walguanus or Gawain and Mordred. Urianus was given the *sceptrum Murefensem*, which we translate as Moray. It becomes apparent from Chapter 149 that this Moray is thought of as being close to the *stagnum Lumonoi*, Loch Lomond.³⁰ The men of Moray take refuge in the sixty islands of this lake. But another source also, in the ninth century, spoke of Loch Lomond and its sixty islands. In addition this early author located Arthur's great battles in northerly territory.³¹ In 1905 Anscombe identified rather successfully some of these battle grounds. Arthur's second, third, and fifth battles are placed on the Douglas River, which must mean the Douglas in Lancashire. The eighth battle was at Vinovia, now known to be Binchester near Bishop Aukland in County Durham. The ninth battle was at Chester, and the eleventh was at Bravonia or Leintwardine (Shropshire).³² Iwenus, the son of Urianus, becomes the Scottish king on the death of Anguselus. Here again the character was originally Welsh. Professor Ritchie suggests that Geoffrey may have been acquainted with some Augustinian canon who knew traditions at Carlisle or at St. Andrews among the Augustinians there. Geoffrey speaks of a Mons Dolorosus, a Mons Agned or Castellum Puellarum, of Alclud, and Catenesia, which can be identified with Melrose, Carlaverock Castle, Dumbarton Rock, and Caithnesshire.³³

There is something else in Geoffrey's account of Arthur which is neglected. We have in mind the references to areas in France. After slaying the giant at Mont-Saint-Michel, Arthur takes his army towards Autun, where he expects to encounter the forces of the Roman emperor. He camps on the banks of the Aube River (Alba Fluvius) and soon his men defeat Lucius Hiberus there.

29. (Ed. Faral), III, 237.
30. *Ibid.*, p. 235; Nennius, *Historia Britonum* (ed. Faral), III, 59.
31. Nennius, III, 38.   32. *ZCPh*, V (1905), 103 ff.
33. Ritchie, *The Normans in Scotland*, p. 300, n. 3.

The principal battle occurs outside of Langres (Lengrias) in the Valley of Sessia, Siesia, or Soesia, which I identify with the valley of the Suize River just below the Langres plateau.[34] The original name of this stream was *Segusia* or *Segucia*, which results in *Suise* or *Seuise* (*Soesia* is a Latinization of the French form). As Faral has said, this journey made by Arthur from Mont-Saint-Michel to Autun is not by any normal route—passing through Langres.[35] There must have been a definite reason for locating this fictitious battle of Britain against Rome in the region which, strange to relate, was close to the home of the man who was to be the great Arthurian poet—Chrétien de Troyes. I suspect the source for this was Henry, Bishop of Winchester and Abbot of Glastonbury. As a former monk of Cluny he may have had some reason for exploiting the fame of this area—with the help of Geoffrey's pen.

Kaius, the Duke of Anjou, is fatally wounded at the Battle of Suize and is buried near Chinon, his capital city. This character is the Keu of Welsh tradition. When Latinized to Kaius the name resembled *Caino*, the traditional Latin name for Chinon, and this surely influenced Geoffrey in associating the two.[36] As Wace expresses it:

> Keu who was mortally wounded was buried within Chinon—a town which he had founded and encompassed with walls; from Keu it received its name.[37]

Geoffrey introduced also the Beduerus of Welsh tradition, whom he designated as Duke of Normandy and butler of King Arthur.

Hardly to be taken seriously are the identifications of the

---

34. (Ed. Faral), III, 258, 263.
35. *Ibid.*, II, 292.
36. This name *Caino* is found first in Gregory of Tours in the late sixth century. It may seem far-fetched but we call the reader's attention to the coins of Chinon from about 1000. They have *Cainoni Castro* on the reverse and a most forbidding head on the obverse, probably of St. Martin. Could a mediaeval man, holding one of these early coins in hand, have imagined that the head was of Kaius? See A. Dieudonné, *Manuel de numismatique française* (Paris, 1936), pp. 365, 367.
37. (Ed. Arnold), vv. 13403-06: "Kex, qui estoit a mort navrés, Fu dedens Chinon enterrés, Qu'il fist et compassa Chinon, Et de Kex reçut il le non."

name *Ganhumara* or *Guennevera* with Findabair, the daughter of Ailell and Medb of Connaught, and the attempts to see parallels between the character of Arthur and that of Finn mac Cumall, leader of one group of the Fenians. Those who believe these things are inclined to see a reflection of the standards required of the Fenian warriors in the requirement of the Knights of the Round Table (first mentioned by Wace).[38] Kenneth Jackson says: "Je n'irai pas jusqu'à affirmer que les romans arthuriens ne tirent aucun de leurs motifs de sources irlandaises, mais j'hésiterais tout autant à dire que certainement ils en tirent une grande partie de leurs motifs.... L'hypothèse celtique impliquerait l'existence d'un ensemble vaste et dense d'histoires d'origine irlandaise circulant en Grande-Bretagne, et il n'a pas la moindre preuve qu'il y ait eu quelque chose de ce genre.... Les plus audacieux d'entre eux ne semblent connaître aucune limite à leurs hypothèses."[39]

We may assume that the oral legends about Arthur and his knights received a tremendous boost from Geoffrey and from Wace and that they continued to circulate in prose and verse, apart from Chrétien's romances. Gerald the Welshman, writing in the last quarter of the twelfth century, had no sympathy for these false tales. When he describes, somewhat erroneously, the circumstances of the discovery (?) of the tombs of Arthur and Guenevere at Glastonbury in 1191, he has an explanation to offer for Morgan la Fee:

> Wherefore Morgue, a noble lady and overlord of those parts and related to King Arthur by blood.... This is clear also how Morgue has been called a fairy [*dea phantastica*] by the minstrels.... For they had told him often as the King had heard from the history of the Britons and from those who had sung their tales.... Furthermore, since many things are told about Arthur and his fate and imaginary things have been composed, and because the British peoples contend foolishly that he is still alive, and because tales are blown up and false things are stated to be true, in order that the true may be very evident

---

38. *Ibid.*, vv. 10459-62, for the Table. Again we make the excuse that much has been written on suggested Irish parallels. Brief statements about these comparisons are in Myles Dillon, *Early Irish Literature* (Chicago: University of Chicago Press, 1948), p. 39.

39. Pp. 222, 225.

we have intended to add what has been found to be completely true....[40]

Thus it was Gerald's contention that Morgan was a respectable relative of the historical Arthur who had been distorted into a *dea phantastica* by the silly minstrels. Elsewhere Gerald speaks of the man formerly possessed of the demons at Caerleon, who had a relapse when the lying book of Geoffrey of Monmouth was brought near him.[41]

If Chrétien visited at Winchester, Glastonbury, and various other places in England some time in the interval 1155-60, as we suggest, his curiosity was quickly stimulated by all these legends. All that we can say is mere conjecture—but we hazard the guess that he soon got possession of a crude form of the Tristan story. His attempt to improve upon this would have been an experiment. It did not survive. Then he gathered names and possible episodes from the materials that came to hand, reaping a bit generously, having in mind what was to become the *Erec et Enide*. The plot, as was often the case in his later work, had two parts. In the first the knight Erec is riding unarmed with Guenevere. A strange knight rides by, accompanied by a lady and a dwarf. Both knight and dwarf are oddly rude when asked for their identity. Erec follows them and finds himself in a town where a beauty tourney is to be held. A knight who can prove by combat that his lady is the fairest will win a hawk. Erec is befriended by a lovely girl and her father, an impoverished knight. She accepts him as her champion and Erec wins the hawk. They go to Arthur's Court and there the two are married. The lady's name is now known to be Enide (v. 2031). Werner Ziltener thinks that postponement in giving the name, in this particular case, has special

---

40. *De principis instructione* (ed. George Warner, Rolls Series), p. 128: "Unde et Morganis, nobilis matrona et partium illarum dominatrix atque patrona, necnon et Arthuro regi sanguine propinqua.... Patet et hoc quoque, quo pacto dea phantastica Morganis a fabulatoribus nuncupata.... Dixerunt enim ei pluries, sicut ex Gestis Britonum et eorum cantoribus historiis rex audierat.... Porro, quoniam de rege Arthuro et ejus exitu dubio multa referri solent et fabulae confingi, Britonum populus ipsum adhuc vivere fatue contendentibus, ut, fabulosis exsufflatis, et veris ac certis asseveratis, veritas ipsa de cetero circiter haec liquido pateat, quaedam hic adjicere curavimus indubitata veritate comperta...." Cf. also *Speculum Ecclesiae*, Dist. II, chap. 9.

41. *Itinerarium Kambriae, Opera* (ed. Dimock; London, 1868), VI, 58-59.

significance.⁴² (We have no suggestion for the source or meaning of the name *Enide*. Some see it as *eneid* "soul, life" in Welsh, but the association is not obvious.) In the second division of the story Enide bewails Erec's failure to continue as a brave knight. Marriage has hurt him. He rises in anger, having overheard her early morning lament, and insists that she accompany him on a journey, where he demonstrates his prowess and tests her love in a series of adventures. This is the outline of the narrative with which Chrétien launched his new "Comédie humaine" of King Arthur's Court and the Knights of the Round Table.

Just as Geoffrei Gaimar in 1139 asked his patron Dame Custance of Scampton (Lincs.) to aid in collecting and borrowing worthy books of reference,⁴³ we can imagine that Chrétien too did not neglect any written sources. He would have had a copy of Wace's *Brut* (just completed and dedicated), the *Historia* of Geoffrey, and other titles. For the Round Table he was indebted to Wace or maybe to Wace's source. All of this was *matière*. It is entirely probable that the poet was already planning a *sens*, or demonstration on a higher level of meaning, which was quite plain to even the thickest-headed listeners of his day but which is now lost to us eight centuries after. We might have a key if we could explain the *Erec*. For those who are very literal-minded there is only a childish picture of knights in shining armor who cannot be visualized as men with social and individual problems.

In the *De arte honeste amandi* of Andreas Capellanus (Andrieu de Luyères) there is narrated under the Rules of Love a strange tale of a knight of Britain who is riding through a forest. He comes upon a lovely lady binding her hair, who says he cannot obtain what he desires—the love of a lady, for whom he must procure a hawk on a golden perch in Arthur's court—unless in order to get this hawk he can establish by combat that he already enjoys the love of a girl more beautiful than anyone else at the court. The Briton admits this and asks that this girl be his love. She lends him the wonderful horse on which she is riding and

---

42. *Chrétien und die Aeneïs* (Hermann Böhlaus Nachf.; Graz-Köln, 1957), p. 51.

43. This information is given at the beginning of Gaimar's *Estorie des Englés*.

gives him necessary instructions. In somewhat disparate adventures which suggest vaguely that of the underwater bridge in the *Lancelot* and that of the guardian of the Ford and the Palace (on the other side) in the Gawain adventure of the *Conte del Graal*, the young man secures the hawk. He discovers a parchment attached to the perch, with the Rules of Love which have been pronounced by the god himself. He returns the horse to the lady of the forest, kisses her thirteen times, and makes the Rules known to all lovers. The relation of this poorly connected and badly motivated story to the "beauty contest" theme in the *Erec et Enide* is a matter for dispute. Does this represent the sort of Celtic tale on which Chrétien could have been drawing? Andreas was writing some ten years after the *Erec* and, we believe, after the *Lancelot*. He was, beyond any doubt, an associate with Chrétien of the court circle at Troyes. Whatever his reason for introducing such a hodge-podge—*mal à propos*—in order to expound the Rules of Love, we may assume that the tale was secondary and that it does not represent a lucid narrative that could have been a source for the *Erec et Enide*.

Professor R. L. Graeme Ritchie has emphasized Chrétien's acquaintance with ancient Strathclyde and with Scotland proper, over and above what we noted in the work of Geoffrey.[44] He claims that the tale of Tristan and Iseut circulated in its primitive form in these areas, and this we can believe if it was Pictish in origin. (The surviving fragments of Thomas and Beroul show Cornish place names.) In the *Erec et Enide* there are stray references to things Scottish. Take this passage: "Ot Guivrez fet deus robes feire ... de deus dras de soie divers ... Et l'autre [fu] d'un bofu roiié, Qu'an presant li ot anvoiié D'Escoce une soe cousine."[45] This is surely a mention of Scottish plaid. In the same romance Erec's father is King Lac of Estregales, the land beyond Wales proper which is in our opinion Cumbria and Strathclyde—represented today by Westmorelandshire, Cumberlandshire, and parts of Kirkudbrightshire, Dumfries, Lanarkshire, Ayrshire, and Renfrew. The principal strongholds there were

---

44. *The Normans in Scotland*, pp. 359-60.
45. Vv. 5227-33.

Dumbarton Rock and Carlisle. The Solway could be forded at its narrow part—witness the extension of Hadrian's Wall as far as Bowness and then for some further protection out into the water beyond. Cumbria was for a long time menaced by the Scots and the Picts, wild clansmen who inhabited Galloway, i. e., Wigtonshire and parts of Kirkudbrightshire and Ayrshire. (The incursion of these Picts and Scots was responsible for Vortigern's invitation to the Jutes in 447.) Ritchie is probably correct in believing that the residence of David I (1124-53) at Carlisle, where he knighted Henry Plantagenet, the future Henry II of England, on Whitsunday 1149, is echoed in the Cardueil of Chrétien.[46] A Whitsunday celebration is in progress there at the opening of the *Yvain*. King David continued his status as Earl of Huntingdon and Northampton. He sat in court at Woodstock during Eastertide in 1130.[47] He was with the Empress Matilda at Winchester in 1141 from May until September. David was succeeded by his grandson Malcolm IV in 1153. The latter wished to be knighted by Henry at Carlisle in June, 1158, in the course of a journey which the English king was making from Malmesbury to Carlisle; but Henry refused and did not knight the young Scottish king until the following year, at Périgueux, when Malcolm had attended him in the Toulouse campaign.[48]

In the *Erec et Enide* the poet gives two long lists of names. Werner Ziltener suggests that in these lists Chrétien was seeking to produce an exotic sound effect, stimulating to his listeners.[49] This may be so, although I should add that if he was aware of initiating a new subject matter, this multiplicity of names gave a certain air of authenticity. These two catalogues are the names of the Knights of the Round Table (vv. 1691-1750) and those of the guests at the wedding (vv. 1932-2024). Some of these were repeated from Wace or Geoffrey, namely, Keu, Gauvain, Beduere, Angusel, Yvain the son of Urien, Ider the son of Nut, and King Lot. The other names came from many sources and, I insist, there is no evidence that they were all obtained from Celtic tales.

46. For Estregales see *Crétien and Scotland*, p. 11. For King David see *The Normans in Scotland*, pp. 144, 348-50.
47. *The Normans in Scotland*, p. 228.
48. *Ibid.*, pp. 349-50.
49. Pp. 94-96.

Some of the knights mentioned are never referred to again in the romances, such as Garravains d'Estrangot, Vaslez au Cercle d'Or, Brun de Piciez, Grus l'iriez, Caverons de Robenic.[50] There are three Iders, two individuals named Keu, and four Yvains. Some of the knights are mentioned once again in another listing, of those who attend the tourney in the *Lancelot* (vv. 5793-5844).[51] A few names were destined to be picked up again in the later romances and given important roles: Lancelot, Perceval, Sagremor, and Yvain, the son of Urien. There is no necessity for assuming that the name *Erec* was Celtic. It could easily have been reminiscent of Erec the Wild, who is mentioned in both Geoffrey and Wace. Morgue la Fee is designated as a sister of Arthur (*Erec*, v. 4220), a fact not found elsewhere except in the passage cited above from Gerald the Welshman. Where did Chrétien find this name? In *Erec et Enide* (vv. 1954-7) he says that she was the love of Guigomar, lord of Avallon. It will be recalled that in Marie de France's *Lanval* the hero is carried to Avallon by a fairy who must have been Morgue. Guigemar is the protagonist of the preceding *lai*. Perhaps Marie copied from the *Erec et Enide*.

"Hiderus filius Nun [*sic*]" is in Geoffrey, and he must be the same as Ederyn, the son of Nudd, of the Welsh *Dream of Rhonabwy*.[52] This Ider is in the *De antiquitate Glastoniae ecclesiae* which William of Malmesbury wrote at Glastonbury, presumably in 1129-35, for Henry of Blois (Chrétien's patron of twenty years later?). William's episode begins with "Legitur in gestis illustrissimi regis Arturi" and continues with a narrative of how at a Christmas feast in Caerleon King Arthur knighted a valiant youth named Ider, son of Nuth. Arthur tests him, mentioning two frightful giants at Mons Ranarum or Brentnecol. Ider goes to find them, ahead of Arthur, but in slaying them is overcome by exhaustion. The King arrives and believing the youth dead, he

---

50. These names vary with the manuscripts of Chrétien's work. The edition published by Mario Roques does not include all the names which are found in the Foerster edition.

51. Here, in the *Lancelot*, shield devices are described which should be studied further. There are no authentic lists of arms preceding 1240; but it is possible to make comparisons which show heraldry in its early stages.

52. III, 260.

sends a vehicle for the body. In penitence for his tardiness in reaching the spot he established an obit for the young man, at Glastonbury.[53] Although Chrétien mentions Ider in another connection, he transfers the salient points of this story to his hero Erec. In the sixth adventure of the wandering Erec he fights against giants. After his victory he faints and is believed to be dead by Oringle de Limors, who carries him away in a cart.[54] Furthermore, in the early part of the *Yvain* the knight is told of an adventure which Arthur is about to undertake. He goes ahead of the King, with success. It is quite probable that this very tale, perhaps read in a forged document at Glastonbury, was twice a direct source for Chrétien.

A matter of special interest is the emergence of Keu as a character with a mean disposition. In Geoffrey and Wace, Kaius is amiable enough. In the *Erec et Enide* Gronosis, the son of Keu, is mentioned as the one "qui mout sot de mal."[55] Keu is not used in the *Cligés*. It is in the *Lancelot* that he is developed as the unfortunate champion, and this may have been only imagination on the part of Countess Marie or of Chrétien.

The *Erec et Enide* shows an acquaintance with the Tristan theme: "La ou Tristanz le fier Morhot An l'Isle saint Sanson vainqui."[56] It reflects also the *Roman d'Eneas* and some version of the Alexander story.[57] There is influence from certain *chansons de geste*. We fail to understand why Fernagu, Thibaut l'Esclavon, and Ospinel are cited as outstanding examples of ferociousness. Fernagu is in *Floovant*, and Thibaut is the first husband of the lady who was to become Guibourc in *Aliscans*. Ospinel does not occur in any surviving epic, unless identified with Otinel in the poem of the same name. The Old Testament was a definite source.

---

53. Edmond Faral, whose arguments are usually clear, endeavors to prove that all mentions of Arthur were interpolated later into William's *De antiquitate Glastoniae ecclesiae*. The second version of his *Gesta* does not repeat this story featuring Iderus; but this is no evidence that William did not use it originally in his history of Glastonbury. Even Faral admits this (*La légende arthurienne* [Paris, 1929], II, 408). Faral thinks the story is contradictory: Iderus is mentioned as reaching Glastonbury ("cum demum Glastoniae adveniret") when it had been specifically stated before that he was carried dead in a cart (*ibid.*, II, 456-7). Such argument is ridiculous and is based upon a bad reading of "cum demum adveniret," which refers to Arthur.

54. Vv. 4729 ff.   55. V. 1740.
56. V. 1248-9.   57. Vv. 5537-53; vv. 2270 *et al.*

On one occasion Absalom, Solomon, and Samson are mentioned in one breath.[58] The episodes which feature Guivret le Petit and his *Irois* (episodes 5 and 6) remind the reader of the appearance of King Auberon, the little fairy king, and his men in the later *Huon de Bordeaux*. It is not impossible that there is some association in the minds of Chrétien's informants between the Gaels and the little men of the mounds. This idea could have filtered down from Scotland.[59]

58. Vv. 2266-8.
59. Readers may ask why I continually show scepticism over relations with Ireland. One reason is the evidence from coin hoards. D. F. Allen remarks that from the Scrabo Hill hoard "Trade with Europe must have been negligible," *Numismatic Chronicle*, 6th Ser., II (1942), 80. There are only two English coins in this twelfth-century Irish hoard. In the early thirteenth century, trade with England and Scotland picked up rapidly. See W. A. Seaby in *Numismatic Chronicle*, 6th Ser., XV (1955), 161-71. We have always thought that the Irish sent trading vessels to Bristol and that tales and other evidence of contact must have been exchanged. Apparently if vessels made this voyage in considerable numbers they did not bring back money. Why? On the other hand the Gaels in Scotland spoke a variety of Middle Irish, and they preserved the traditions as well as the language.

CHAPTER THREE

Chrétien in Champagne

It is to be assumed that the *Cligés* was composed at Troyes, for the delectation of Henry the Liberal and for his patron's mother, Mathilda of Carinthia. This romance is somewhat flattering for both Germany and Byzantium. It contains an interesting statement on the growth of chivalry, which began in Greece, passed to Rome, and then to France—and that is why Alixandre, the son of the Greek emperor, wished to go to Arthur's Court to be knighted —for as Chrétien adds, "now is it [the peak of chivalry] come to France. May God grant that it be retained there... so that it will never leave...."[1] We are a little surprised that Arthur, the traditional leader of the British Celts, is considered equivalent with France in this connection. There is probably an allusion to Count Henry's own reception of knighthood, but in reverse. Henry was knighted in Greece. Perhaps a touch of humor was involved.

The basic plot of the *Cligés* is the Romeo and Juliet tale of the lady who escapes from her husband (or an unwanted suitor) by taking a drug which causes her to appear dead. In the *Cligés* three physicians from Salerno guess this ruse by remembering that such a thing had been practiced by one of Solomon's wives.[2] We judge that this was the substance of the story which Chrétien read in the ancient manuscript at the cathedral library of Beauvais. (It should be borne in mind that Beauvais was a regular stopover point at a day's distance from Paris for those who were travelling to or returning from the Channel ports.) The manuscript may

1. Vv. 35-8. See Appendix, "Note on Reality versus Ideality."
2. Vv. 5815-6050.

have contained a version of the *Solomon and Marcolfus*. Chrétien built his romance of *Cligés* into a vigorous anti-Tristan theme. Iseut had belonged to two men at the same time; Fenice, with the aid of her clever nurse Thessala, would have only one lover. Some of Chrétien's best lines in the *Cligés* have to do with a social problem—that of the serf Jehan. Chrétien is always concerned with social matters. The obligations of Jehan as a serf are explained twice, as well as his loyalty and his desire for freedom for himself and his family.³ These lines ring true and make us reflect upon such serfs at Troyes as maistre Normand, and Odee and her husband, whom we mentioned in the first chapter.⁴ To distinguish oneself at Arthur's Court was the highest badge of chivalry, so Chrétien digresses from his principal theme long enough to enlarge on the honor paid there to his two Byzantine heroes, Alixandre and Cligés.

The *Lancelot*, or *Chevalier de la Charrette*, was not a composition of Chrétien's own planning. He explains that "Plot and allegory were both given to him by the Countess, and he sets about planning it so that he adds nothing save his own labor and his exertion."⁵ It is not likely that we will find here Chrétien's personal thought, except his admiration and affection for the young Countess. He praises her highly, with genuine emotion: "By my faith I am not the kind who flatters his lady ... but all this is true in spite of myself."⁶ He is so charmed by her that he has agreed, perhaps unwisely, to versify a series of motifs in which she is interested. It is the kind of language that a poet would use towards a new female patron who is endowed with feminine appeal. The present writer receives this impression so strongly that he cannot understand how Gaston Paris and many others have insisted that the *Lancelot* was composed some time after Countess Marie became Chrétien's patron. For this they give an argument which is certainly no more cogent or provable than our general impression. They say that a young bride (she was nineteen years old in

---

3. Vv. 5491-5512.
4. See p. 11.
5. "Matiere et san l'an done et livre La contesse, et il s'antremet De panser si que rien n'i met Fors sa painne et s'antancion" (vv. 26-9).
6. "Par foi, je ne sui mie cil Qui vueille losangier sa dame.... S'est il veoirs...."

1164) would not have been concerned with an adulterous motif such as courtly love, which is the essence of the *Lancelot*.[7] It is very hard indeed for some of us to understand the "prudery" which some modern critics attribute to individuals in the twelfth century. It is even less understandable how this can be cited as valid argument. The marriage of Marie and Henry of Champagne was not a love match; it was the usual political *mariage de convenance*. Have we any evidence that Marie, the daughter of Eleanor of Aquitaine, was reared strictly? Last of all, the sophisticated defense of adultery that can be inferred from the *De arte honeste amandi* of Andreas Capellanus is not what is stressed in the *Lancelot*. It is true that Lancelot loves Guenevere, the wife of Arthur, but that was a relationship that would hardly have brought a blush to a young lady of fourteen, married or unmarried, in the mid-twelfth century. That kind of situation was already a conventional motif in the poetry of the troubadours. In the romance which we call *Lancelot* it is the hardships which a knight is willing to endure for love—not agitation for a "low single standard between man and woman"—which is uppermost with both Marie de Champagne and Chrétien. There is little reason for assuming that this romance could not have been a sort of belated wedding present to the new Countess; in fact, this is even a likely supposition.

It can be assumed that the *Lancelot* (or *Chevalier de la Charrette*) has to do with the struggles of a true and worthy knight who seeks the solace of his lady, who has been snatched beyond his reach. This is a quest of a faithful lover who obeys the rules of what we term courtly love and is rewarded accordingly. A haughty knight presents himself at Arthur's Court and promises to free the many prisoners that he has from Arthur's people if a knight can defeat him in solitary combat; otherwise he will be permitted to carry off the queen. Keu demands the battle and loses. Gawain follows after to rescue the queen. He meets a knight (not named until v. 3676) who is on the same quest. When this knight loses his horse, he endures disgrace by riding in a peasant's cart. The two spend the night at a lady's castle,

---

7. Foerster, pp. 35 ff.

where the adventure of the Dangerous Bed occurs. The lady mocks the unknown quester; but his worth is tested in the Bed by the lance and the burning banner.[8] The two men separate. The unknown hero, who persists with his thoughts upon his beloved Guenevere, withstands the temptation from a girl who takes him to her manor on the promise that he will sleep with her. The temptation is heightened when the knight rescues her from a supposed ravisher (rescued ladies were fair booty, with no moral stigma attached).[9] The knight and the girl ride forth together; they come to a stone by a spring and see the ivory comb and a handful of hair which had belonged to Guenevere. Then is the episode in which they meet a knight who loves the girl who is with the hero. They see the suitor's father, who tells his son to let her alone. The people mock the hero. Next comes the visit to a cemetery where the knight (who will be named Lancelot) reads the names of knights of the Round Table on the tombs: Gawain, Yvain, Louis, and others. One tomb slab is especially heavy. Only he who can lift it will rescue Arthur's imprisoned people. Our protagonist lifts it with ease and learns it will eventually be his own tomb. He goes on alone. He is lodged by a knight who has two daughters and five sons, who are kept in captivity, away from their native land of Logres (which is Lancelot's mother land). They recognize him as the one who seeks to free the queen; they tell him of the sword bridge and of the stony passage through which he must pass. The guards at the stony passage let him through. He enters a fortress where men from Logres are fighting and helps them win. The second day thereafter he is obliged to fight a rude, impetuous knight who insults him. He overcomes the man and is disposed to let him live when a girl appears, mounted on a tawny mule which she drives with a scourge.[10] She pleads with the hero to slay this man because he is Treachery. She then promises to help him some day. Next comes the sword bridge to the land of Gorre[11] and

---

8. Vv. 402 ff.   9. Vv. 1314 ff.
10. Vv. 2793 ff.
11. Vv. 3021 ff. The name Gorre is mentioned twice: "A knight strong and tall, son of the king of Gorre, has taken her" (vv. 642-3), and "For near to Gorre near here" (v. 6141). Meleaganz (of Gorre) is positively identified as the character who is holding Arthur's people in confinement (vv. 6203-04).

his meeting with King Bademagu and his son Meleaganz (the ravisher of Guenevere). Bademagu befriends the hero, who is now identified as Lancelot del Lac, and arranges for him to fight Meleaganz. Bademagu interrupts the combat. The queen is now free, but not Lancelot. She gives him the solace he desires. After this night of love he genuflects before his lady's bedchamber "Con s'il fust devant un autel."[12] This may have been the end of the story as supplied by Countess Marie, for the remainder of the romance, with its celebrated tourney at Arthur's Court, is an anticlimax. After the tourney Lancelot returns to prison. He is finally freed by the girl who had come to him on the tawny mule, asking for the head of the treacherous knight.[13] She is the daughter of Bademagu. Once more at Arthur's residence Lancelot fights Meleaganz and cuts off his head.

Our interpretation of this romance was made before we had the opportunity to read a discussion published very recently by Mario Roques. M. Roques emphasizes that throughout the *Lancelot* the protagonist is struggling step by step to win the heart and affection of Guenevere. There is no suggestion that they were lovers before the quest. M. Roques says that the knight Lancelot finally triumphed over the "coeur altier d'une dame souveraine, ... triomphant de sa légitime et naturelle réserve...."[14] In contrast, we assume the "heart" of the lady has been carried away to the land of Gorre, which means "pomp and vanity" in Old French, by an unworthy lover, Meleaganz, making her frigid until she succumbs once more to the persistence and devotion of her perfect lover, Lancelot. This would be the basic theme which was proposed by Countess Marie. Other unfortunate people also had been carried away to this land of Gorre and were held captive there until Lancelot included them also in his "general delivery." We are in agreement with M. Roques that

12. Vv. 4734-6.
13. Vv. 6588 ff.
14. *Cahiers de civilisation médiévale*, I, 151. M. Roques is one of the scholars who seek to date Chrétien's romances ten or twelve years later than we believe is necessary. Nur-ed-Din of Aleppo is referred to as "alive" in the *Yvain* (v. 596). He died in 1174. Since every one agrees that the *Yvain* shows knowledge of the *Lancelot*, we cannot agree in placing the *Lancelot* around 1177. This problem of dating is only incidental and has no bearing upon our interpretation.

Guenevere is not interested in Lancelot when he first arrives to rescue her—but that is before his constancy has again touched her heart. The girl on the tawny mule who is recognized, eventually, as the daughter of King Bademagu of Gorre has a suggestion of the Hideous Damsel on a similar mount in the *Conte del Graal*.[15] Lancelot's quest for his love foreshadows somewhat the concept of the lady which was to appear in the *dolce stil nuovo* school of Florence in the mid-thirteenth century. Lancelot genuflects before the chamber in which he has experienced physical love with the queen. It should not be forgotten too that *bade* (used by Chrétien in the *Guillaume d'Angleterre*) means "that which is worthless." The king of Gorre is Bademagu. Other scholars have compared Gorre with *voirre* "glass" and Meleaganz with a Celtic character Melwas. We do not have to go so far afield to discover an interpretation. We assume that after the perfect knight, Lancelot, had received the solace of his lady he too was held captive in that land of Vanity (Gorre) from which he was freed at last by the girl upon the tawny mule, because he had slain her faithless lover.

The development of the character Lancelot and of his name is a considerable problem. The name first occurs in *Erec et Enide*. Chrétien says:

Devant toz les buens chevaliers, Doit estre Gauvains li premiers, Li seconz li fiz Lac, Et le tiers Lanceloz del Lac. Gornemanz de Gohort fu quarz.[16]

Gauvains was drawn from Wace and Geoffrey *(Galvaginus)*. Gornemanz was to appear no more until in the *Conte del Graal*.[17] The second appearance of the name Lancelot is in *Cligés*, where he is one of three knights unhorsed by Cligés at the tourney held between Oxford and Wallingford. On the first day, Cligés, in black armor on a black horse, defeats Sagremors li Desreez; on the second day, wearing green armor and astride a tawny steed, he vanquishes Lancelot; on the third day, clothed in red mail, with a sorrel mount, he overthrows Perceval.[18] There should be color symbolism in all this, which we are unable to explain. However, there is one detail which has value. Chrétien says of Lancelot:

---

15. Vv. 4610 ff.   16. Vv. 1691-5.
17. Vv. 1548 ff.   18. Vv. 4828 ff.

"Cligés gives him such a blow on his golden shield painted with a lion."[19] A member of the College of Heralds in London tells me that there are no formal lists of devices preserved which antedate 1240; but he admits that devices were becoming fixed by the mid-twelfth century. He agrees also that the shield mentioned by Chrétien resembles the red lion rampant on a gold field (with tressure) which is the royal arms of Scotland.[20] The King of Lothian in Geoffrey and in Wace is Lot, father of Gawain and Mordred. I cannot with certainty determine Chrétien's notion of a connection between Lancelot and the family of Lot. The reader should recall, nonetheless, that Mordred was the lover of Guenevere. Chrétien never mentions him, by this name. If the association with Scotland is acceptable, one thinks at once of Loch Lomond, celebrated in Nennius, Geoffrey, and Wace, as inspiration for the appellation *del Lac*. In the Old French prose Tristan the protagonist is Tristan li Lohenois.

Much has been written about Chrétien's *Yvain*, or *Chevalier du Lion*. This poem was composed shortly after the *Lancelot*, although I can see no basis for the argument, freely advanced nowadays, that the *Lancelot* and the *Yvain* were written concurrently by our poet.[21] In Geoffrey, Iwenus is the son of Urien, King of Moray, but Owen of Chester and Urien of Bath are names that go back to Welsh bardic times. In Geoffrey, Iwenus succeeds Angusel to the throne of Scotland and thereafter wins great renown for his prowess in the wars.[22] The earliest occurrence of the name in Chrétien is in that list of Knights of the Round Table in *Erec et Enide*. Four Yvains are listed as sitting together:

And Yvain the son of Urien, beyond was Yvain de Loenel, and on the other side was Yvain li avoutre. Beside Yvain de Cavaliot was Garravains d'Estrangot....[23]

It is possible that Chrétien was aware of the identity of *Yvain* with *Owen*, and that he recognized *Owen* as a very common Welsh

19. Vv. 4794-5.
20. Our correspondent has been the Richmond Herald, Mr. Anthony Wagner.
21. So Frappier in *Chrétien*, p. 12; Martín de Riquer in *Filologia Romanza*, IV (1957), 147.
22. (Ed. Faral), III, 276.
23. *Erec et Enide*, vv. 1706-09.

name. There may have been some thought of humor in this passage. Yvain, the son of Urien, is not mentioned in the *Cligés*, but he is one of the knights whose tomb is seen in the cemetery of future prophecy in the *Lancelot* (v. 1878).

The higher level of meaning of the Magic Fountain episode, experienced first by Calogrenanz and then by Yvain, which includes Yvain's winning of the hand of Laudine de Landuc, widow of Esclados the Red, still has us guessing, despite the attempts to explain it as a Celtic otherworld theme and as a story of classical origin. Professor Ritchie identifies the Lady of the Fountain with Sybilla, wife of David of Scotland.[24] He suggests that the *Voyage of St. Brendan*, which was translated for Matilda, Henry I's second queen and aunt and sister-in-law of Sybilla, was the inspiration for the birds' singing over the magic fountain. Who were the vavassor and his daughter who seem to be at the gateway to the Magic Adventure? Who was the weird herdsman? A hanging sheet of metal, used in place of a bell at the death of one of the monks, existed at Bury St.-Edmund's.[25] This type of "bell" was used by the vavassor. The theme of the weird herdsman was apparently mocked in *Aucassin et Nicolette*, at a date when Chrétien's meaning may still have been understood.[26] Whether it be Celtic or not (and it may be), the main episode could be a courtly version of an old tale well known to us of the young hero who attacks the giant's castle, first violating the giant's taboo and then slaying him. Here he departs with the "giant's" wife. There is another common motif also, the adventure that is tried by others, usually two, before the true hero makes his successful attempt. Elements of this tale are common in Celtic (notably Irish) sagas, but there is no precise analogue which we can say was known to Chrétien. We can find best parallels in the fairy books edited by Andrew Lang and his wife, which are based on folk material.

The second part of the *Yvain*, the lion story, has some parallel in an object which once belonged to Henry the Liberal and which

---

24. *Crétien and Scotland*, pp. 5-6.
25. Jocelyn, *Life of Abbot Samson* (ed. L. C. Jane), pp. 167-8.
26. (Ed. Suchier), p. 24.

passed to his collegiate Church of Saint-Estienne.[27] This is a red silk wallet or *aumonière*, with green tassels. It has a raised design in white, showing a man in Byzantine dress presenting a tame lion to a lady who is seated on a formal chair. She is, in turn, holding a victory apple of some kind (see *Chanson de Roland*, v. 392). On the flap of the wallet is this same Byzantine knight, in armor of *cuir bouilli* with a phial in his hand. We can imagine, but only imagine, that Chrétien was familiar with this *aumonière* worn by his patron on special occasions and that he asked for the story. The Count, who had brought it from Constantinople, may have explained it by a tale of the Androcles and the Lion type which charmed and interested Chrétien.

In the *Yvain* the author continues to be interested in social and economic questions. There are the scenes with the maidens who are doing needle work for a minimum wage. We learn from them what such a minimum wage was for a woman of the time.[28] Then there is the quarrel between the younger and the older sister which is actually a conflict between Roman law and German custom law on the subject of inheritance. Eventually Arthur decides for the Roman.[29]

The *Guillaume d'Angleterre* is a retelling of the Divided Family tale of Placidas-Eustathius. It is a frequent theme in the Middle Ages, including among its variants the *Jourdains de Blaivie* and the Spanish *Caballero Cifar*. Especially interesting is the fact that Chrétien places his setting in Scotland. Guillaume as king of England lives in Bristol, a reminder of the period when the Empress Matilda and her brother Robert of Gloucester had their headquarters there, in the war against Stephen. But the family, when separated, goes north. The king is carried to Galveide, which is certainly Galloway. The two sons go separately to Quatenasse or Catenaise, which is Caithness. The mother is taken to Sorlinc, which, along with Miss Elizabeth Francis, I identify as Stirling, on the Forth River, between the other areas.[30] Per-

---

27. A careful drawing of this is in A. F. Arnaud. See Fig. 2.
28. *Yvain*, vv. 5314-5.
29. This is my interpretation of the dispute between the two sisters. In Roman law the children inherit equally; in common law there was primogeniture.
30. In *Studies Presented to R. L. Graeme Ritchie* (Cambridge, Eng.: Cambridge University Press, 1949), pp. 68-70.

haps Chrétien did not know that Caithness lies far to the northeast, for he seems to identify it with the Fifeshire peninsula which would be adjacent to Stirling.

So far in these chapters we have been discussing possible inspiration and sources that lie behind the works of Chrétien. We are hazarding a guess about his earlier life, that as a young cleric in simple tonsure he went to England, possibly in the entourage of his patron's close relative, Henry of Blois, and that he returned to be attached in some way to the court of Henry the Liberal and later to Henry's wife Marie de Champagne. We have no indication and no need to assume that at Troyes he was immediately in the capacity of chaplain with the cure of souls. More likely he remained for some years a secretary or chancellor, where his real duty was to scintillate brightly in court society as a man of letters. He was not unfamiliar with the pangs of love or at any rate with literary pangs:

> Before I thought to yield to her I was hard and mean. Now I am pleased to surrender without any excuse, that she may do as she wants with me.... I know of no escape from love, nor need any one tell it to me. My feathers can moult in that coop all my life: my heart will not change, if I may have an understanding with her; I fear she may slay me, but my heart remains constant.... never do I cease, never do I tire of wooing my sweet lady. I beg and plead again without success, as one who cannot serve Love jokingly or full of flattery.[31]

Such love protestations were commonplace, and I suspect these words were addressed to Marie de Champagne, but they are the words of Chrétien speaking of personal affection. There is punning here on *plume*, "feather" or "pen," and *muer*, "moult" or "change." Perhaps Chrétien never changed his literary mood until his last, greatest work, the *Conte del Graal*. But in his

---

31. W. Foerster, pp. 205-09, vv. 29 ff.: "Ainz que m'i cuidasse prendre, Fui vers li durs et sauvages. Or me plest sanz reson randre, Qu'an son preu soit mes damages.... D'amor ne sai nule issue, Ne ja nus ne la me die. Muer puet an cest mue Ma plume tote ma vie: Mes cuers n'i muera mie, S'ai en celi m'atandue, Que je criem que ne m'ocie, Ne por ce cuers ne remue....onques ne fin, onques ne las De ma douce dame proiier. Pri et repri sanz esploitier, Come cil que ne set a gas Amors servir ne losangier."

literary prime no one knew so well as he how to express a heart full of sentiment:

> But to tell the truth, Crestiens de Troies spoke better of the wounded heart, of the dart, of the eyes, than I could tell you.

This last is from the *Tournoiement* of Huon de Méry, written around 1235.[32] In all this Chrétien was a disciple of Ovid, an influence which permeates his romances, except perhaps the *Guillaume d'Angleterre* and the *Conte del Graal*. We leave to others the tracing of this influence.[33]

Ten years ago I mentioned in passing that Chrétien, because of the meaning of his name and because of the possibility that he had drawn interpretations from the *Midrashim*, could have been a baptized Jew.[34] Troyes and the vicinity were filled with individuals in the twelfth century who had this history. I have been astounded to find that there are some critics who think my whole interpretation of the meaning of the Grail is based upon this assumption. This is far from the case. Jews and Christians lived in close proximity and, one might even say, in fellowship of a kind in certain areas, and there were frequent exchanges of views and background. A typical community was the little town of Dampierre-sur-Aube, twenty-five miles northeast of Troyes, beyond Ramerupt. It could not have been more than a large bailey surrounding a castle. Today this village has only two hundred and fifty inhabitants, and there is no indication that it was larger in the past. The present layout shows vividly how the streets came into being, extending around a central feudal keep. After the mid-twelfth century Isaac ben Samuel and his son Elhana were leaders of the Talmud school there. Gross says of the town, "Il existait à Dampierre une communauté juive assez

---

32. "Mes qui le voir dire en vodroit, Crestiens de Troies dist miex Du cuer navré, du dart, des ex, Que je ne vos porroie dire" (vv. 2583 ff.).

33. In this study of ours we are not presently concerned with the literary influences that left their mark upon Chrétien's romances. Virgil, Ovid, and the *chansons de geste*, as well as the *Roman de Thèbes*, were prominent in suggesting the evolution of plot, the style, and the psychology. See, in particular, Werner Ziltener on this; and also Foster E. Guyer, *Romance in the Making* (New York: S. F. Vanni, 1954).

34. This was in my "A New Interpretation of Chrétien's *Conte del Graal*," *University of North Carolina Studies in the Romance Languages and Literatures*, VII (1948).

importante, qui comptait des gens riches parmi ses membres."[35] The chief activity of the tiny community must have been these schools, and Count Guy de Dampierre, whose movements are notable in the records of the time, doubtless drew considerable revenue from the Rabbis. Many forced conversions were made in Champagne, as elsewhere, at the period of the Second Crusade (1147). Rabbenu Tam was nearly killed, and he decided to move to the protection of Troyes.[36] Some documents in the Archives of Troyes bear witness to interesting situations. In one of these, Thibaut "miles, quondam Judaeus" and his son Walter forgive debts owed to them by the Abbey of Saint-Loup from the time when they were money-lenders.[37] Here is a usurer turned knight! Because of the frequent exchange of ideas between Christian and Jew at Troyes and nearby, our conclusions are not influenced in the slightest by the question whether Chrétien de Troyes was a converted Jew. At the same time we are interested in the truth. If the reader should form an opinion from information that we give, this might lead him to further speculation.

The name *Chrétien* can be examined scientifically, from what we know of medieval onomastics. Every one received his legal name at baptism—and this was a single name. But inevitably there was so much repetition of common names that appellations qualifying the individual were added immediately and often unconsciously. The commonest kind was the patronymic, e. g., Gautier fius Gui or, in Latin, Gualterus Christiani (where the genitive case designates the patronymic). If a person had a physical peculiarity he was soon labelled with it. When an individual was residing away from his home district, even for a limited space of time, he would often designate himself as coming from there. Chrétien called himself Chrétien de Troyes only in the *Erec et Enide*, which is good indication that this romance was composed when he was living elsewhere.[38] It would hardly be worthwhile for a person to add *de Troyes* when he lived in that town or in the

---

35. P. 161.   36. *Ibid.*, p. 636.
37. Lalore, I, 205-6.
38. His residence abroad must have been for study or some other specific purpose. He was no travelling minstrel. He says of this particular early romance: "D'Erec, le fil Lac, est li contes, Que devant rois et devant contes Depecier et corronpre suelent Cil que de conter vivre vuelent" (vv. 19-22).

immediate neighborhood, except when witnessing legally as a local citizen. But those who knew the poet and his work, at some distance from Troyes or at a much later date, would be apt to crystallize his identity as Chrétien de Troyes, like Huon de Méry, quoted above.

One variety of appellation is that which describes the nationality or the spiritual condition of a subject, e. g., Pierre l'anglois, Gautier li batisiez. It is evident that this second example designates a converted Jew (or possibly a Saracen). Professor Robert L. Reynolds of the University of Wisconsin, although not concerned with Chrétien de Troyes, has given me a number of examples from documents of Genoa (dating from the close of the twelfth century) where Daniel Baptizatus, Johannes Baptizatus, Gerardus Christianus, Carlus de Bapizato, and several cases of Cristinus and Christianus are accepted as indicating converts—perhaps some from Islam. St. Thomas Becket, when he was fleeing to France from the wrath of Henry of England, assumed the name Christianus.[39] Did he call himself Thomas Cristianus or did he attempt to give the impression that he had been baptized Cristianus? Similarly Lambert d'Ardres records that the Countess of Ardres was commonly called Cretiene because of her piety.[40] In this last instance it was definitely an appellation and known as such to every one.

In studying the use of Cristianus or Chrétien, we should like to be able to make a differentiation between its frequency as a qualifying designation and its use as a single baptismal name, legally designating its owner from baptism till death. Such differentiation can be made, within reason, but it will always be open to sweeping denials and demands for proof. Following good onomastic procedure and statistics, name lists should be studied—lists produced in normal activity or relationship of the time, where there is no arbitrary selection by us today. An early list of this kind is the table of moneyers who struck the silver pennies of King Alfred the Great (reigned 871-900). There are fifty-eight names, of which all but four are as Anglo-Saxon as they could be. I will

39. *Guernes de Pont Sainte-Maxence*, vv. 2060, 2095.
40. MGH SS, XXIV, 573.

not repeat them all.⁴¹ The four "foreigners" are Samson, Simon, Chrestien, and Stefanus. The first two were surely Jewish. Note that Chrestien is not Cristianus, which we might expect. It is French in form and has the inserted -*h*- which would suggest a slightly learned person. Was this man a converted Jew from France? This much can be said for Stefanus. It is the Latin form of a Saint's name (a notable martyr), which is odd in the midst of Aethered, Beagstan, Beorhmer, etc. It is fortunate for onomastics that the moneyers in England signed their coins. Among the 306 mint masters who struck in England from 1150 to 1190 one had the name Cristien.⁴² We know further, from Reginald of Durham, that this same Cristien operated a mine for Bishop Hugh de Puiset of Durham.⁴³ We have on record from the eleventh century that Bishop Waso of Flanders converted a Jewish physician and gave him the baptismal name of Christianus. This was in 1037.⁴⁴

There is another fine list of some 1500 names which we have analyzed, without publishing the results. This is the roster of the garrison of Dublin Castle around 1184.⁴⁵ The men involved were adventurers, vassals etc. brought together for the expedition by their English leaders, a typical sample of men of the non-clerical class—knights and *serjanz*. Some came from Flanders—Isaac, Marcus, Norber, Arnaldus; some bore the designation from Brittany—Robertus de Dinaunt, Walterus Britun, Willielmus le Bretun; a considerable number came from Bordeaux, Saint-Omer, Toulouse, and France in general. There were a few very interesting appellations—Walterus diei Ueneris ("Walter Friday"), Reginaldus Inferni, Baldewinus le poete, Walterus devand le mast, Adam de la More, Osbertus Wace, Alfredus le Puca. There was not a single Crestien among this rough gang.

41. George C. Brooke, *English Coins* (London, 1932), p. 53.
42. D. F. Allen, *A Catalogue of English Coins in the British Museum, the Cross and Crosslets . . . Type of Henry II* (London, 1951), pp. cxxii, cxxxi, etc.
43. *Regnaldi Monachi Dunelmensis Opera*, Surtees Society, I (1835), p. 210.
44. Jean d'Outremeuse, *Ly Mireur des histors*, IV, 238: "Waso concludit li juys et li quitat son doit a coupeer; et ilh prist baptesme et fut nommés Xristoiens." See also MGH SS, VII, 216.
45. J. T. Gilbert, *Historic and Municipal Documents of Ireland* (Rolls Series, 1870), pp. 3-48.

Fig. 1 (top). Holograph of Chrétien de Saint-Maclou. In the fourth line from the bottom, Xristianus, chaplain at Saint-Maclou, states that this is his handwriting (From a charter at Troyes dated 1179). Fig. 2 (bottom). Drawing of an *aumonière* or wallet owned by Henry the Liberal. At bottom, a Byzantine knight presents a tame lion to a seated lady, who holds a victory apple. Perhaps this wallet and tales by Count Henry suggested the lion story of Chrétien's *Yvain*.

FIG. 3. Ecclesia and Synagoga, panels from the twelfth-century Crucifixion window of the Cathedral at Châlons-sur-Marne (Archives Photographiques, Paris).

Chrétien in Champagne 55

It is time we pass to names found in the vicinity of Troyes. In a list of holders of fiefs at Aiguizy (Champagne) there is a "Girardus filius Christiani. Foedum est apud Aguissi." The date is 1172.[46] This district is in the present Département de l'Aisne, between Rheims and Château-Thierry. We have culled the names mentioned by Boutiot in his history of the region, taken from many charters and documents. It would be interesting to cite these as examples of what names were prevalent in Champagne in the twelfth century. They are: Acharie, Adam, Alain, Alart, Albert, Amatrius, André, Anseau, Archambaut, Belin, Bernart, Bernarade, Bonel, Boscus, Busil, Chardon, Clerembaut, Colon, David, Dodon, Dominique, Engenoul, Erart, Eude, Eustache, Faucon, Foulque, Fulbert, Gaillart, Galeran, Garin, Garnier, Gautier, Geoffroi, Gervin, Gillon, Girart, Gislebert, Godefroi, Gui, Guillaume, Haice, Henri, Hervee, Hilduin, Hubert, Hugue, Humbert, Ingelmer, Jacques, Jehan, Mathieu, Miles, Morin, Musnier, Nicolas, Normant, Odbert, Odon, Osmont, Othon, Pasquier, Payen, Philippe, Pierre, Rainaut (Renaut), Raoul, Robert, Rolant, Roscelin, Roulin, Simon, and Thibaut. Among women we find: Aceline, Alix, Anne, Blanche, Constance, Jehanne, Marie, Marion, and Odee.[47] Names specifically indicated as Jewish, taken from both Boutiot and Gross, are: Abraham, Bandin, Cresselin, Biel-li-Vaingne, Deuaye, Dieudonné, Eliezer, Haquin, Helie, Isaac, Jacob, Joseph, Juda, Matatia Yohanan, Meir, Menahem, Moïse, Moxe, Oschaya Hallevi, Schemaya, Simeon, Simson, Solomon, and Vivet Herbouth.[48] There is no Chrétien anywhere here.

We believe that the poet Chrétien's baptismal name was Christianus—whether this was given to him shortly after birth or as a result of conversion later in life. Probably at this date the name was not given lightly, even to an infant. Philippe de Harveng, the Premonstratensian abbot who was associated with both Henry of Troyes and Philip of Flanders, speaks explicitly about the individual who bears the imprint of the name of God. "Him that

---

46. A. Longnon, *Documents relatifs au comté de Champagne et de Brie* (Documents inédits), I, 27, no. 761.
47. Boutiot, *Histoire*, I, 158-328.
48. *Ibid.*, and Gross, pp. 226-43.

overcometh will I make a pillar in the temple of my God, and he shall go out no more: and I will write upon him the name of my God" (Apocal. 3:12). Philippe explains this with "Et nomen... meum novum est Christus"—that is, Christianus.[49] When we do not encounter the name Christianus as a frequent baptismal name in the vicinity of Troyes in the latter half of the twelfth century, we cannot continue to say sweepingly that Chrétien was a common name. And yet this is precisely what some of the critics are doing today in order to deny that Chrétien, the great poet of romance, was the author of the extant *Philomena* or of the *Guillaume d'Angleterre*, and that he can be identified with any of the few individuals who did bear this name in the Champagne region.[50] I ask of these critics, before they generalize further, that they take the pains to prove their contention from evidence as specific as my collection of the individual occurrences of the name.

I have omitted so far an episode in William of Malmesbury's *Historia Novella* where he describes the council held at Winchester in 1141, when it was planned to elect Empress Matilda to replace King Stephen. William of Malmesbury observes: "In the meantime a certain person, whose name, if I remember rightly, was Christian, a clerk belonging to the queen, as I have heard, rose up and held forth a paper to the legate."[51] The clerk was attached to the wife of Stephen of Blois, and the legate was Bishop Henry of Blois—but the date is probably too early for this Christian to have significance for us. The next appearance of the name is in a charter of the Premonstratensian abbey of La-Chapelle-aux-Planches near Troyes, dated 1173 and signed in the Bishop's palace at Troyes. The signatories to this were Girardus the abbot of Montier-la-Celle, Guiterus the abbot of Saint-Loup, Vitalis the abbot of Saint-Martin-es-aires, Johannes the abbot of Beaulieu, Harduinus the abbot of La Rivour, Rainaudus of Provins, Magister Bernardus Archdeacon, Alexander (Bishop's Chaplain), Magister Guiardus of Beaufort (today, Montmorency), Canon Petrus Bugre of Troyes, Everardus deacon of Dierrey-Saint-Pierre, Girardus priest of Gigny, and three canons of Saint-Loup: Poncius,

---

49. "De Continentia Clericorum" in Migne, *P.L.*, vol. 203, cols. 824-6.
50. J. Frappier, *Chrétien*, p. 9.
51. *Historia novella*, Bk. III, 47 (ed. Hardy; III, 748).

Johannes, and Christianus.⁵² The name Poncius holds our attention at once. It must represent the penitential name of a converted Jew. No Christian mother would have baptized her child with the hated name of Pontius Pilate. Critics are aware of this document. Some dismiss summarily the possibility that this could be our Chrétien with the statement that Chrétien the poet could not have been a priest, because of the worldly nature of his romances.⁵³ This statement is completely gratuitous, again assigning a kind of "prudery" to the twelfth century which simply did not exist at that time. Furthermore, there is no need to assume that a canon regular of Saint-Loup was necessarily in priest's orders—if that would make any difference. Thirdly, this argument is based upon an assumption, by no means proved, that Chrétien wrote most of his romances after 1172.⁵⁴

Several other documents have not been noticed by our colleagues. There was a deed drawn in 1188 in which Manasses, Bishop of Langres, gives the church at Jaucourt to the Premonstratensian Abbey of Beaulieu.⁵⁵ Jaucourt is a tiny village just across the Aube River from Bar-sur-Aube. The signers of this particular document were very few: Petrus the dean at Bar-sur-Aube, Magister Jacobus the notary of the Bishop, Magister Galterus, and dominus Christianus. We are concerned only with Magister Galterus and dominus Christianus, who were doubtless related in either employment or parentage. How else can we explain their presence together with the two officials on this very small witness list? In another charter, of 1193, the Monastery of Saint-Loup gives to Gui de Dampierre (the village with the Jewish school) for the remainder of Gui's life the use of a house within their enclosure at Troyes—a house that had belonged to Reine, daughter of Gautier the granarius.⁵⁶ This deed is drawn up by Galterus Christiani "Walter the son of Chrétien." He is the last to sign, and it was common practice for the chancellor who copied out the document to affix his name the last. This transfer in

---

52. Lalore, IV, 22-4, and L. A. Vigneras in *Modern Philology*, XXXII (1934-35), 341-2.
53. J. Frappier, *Chrétien*, p. 9.
54. Frappier repeats this from Stefan Hofer and A. Fourrier, p. 12.
55. Lalore, IV, 283.
56. *Ibid.*, I, 155-6.

favor of Gui was ratified shortly thereafter by Marie, Countess of Troyes, and the paper was drawn by Galterus the chancellor of Marie. A year later this same Gui de Dampierre got by exchange from La-Chapelle-aux-Planches the grange of Lavalle-le-Comte.[57] Here the notary was again Galterus, chancellor of Marie de Champagne. The name Galterus is very common, but M. Georges Bernard, archiviste en chef at Troyes, authorizes us to say that he has examined these charters and he thinks it extremely likely, from the handwriting, that the same Galterus was concerned in all three.

Speculation about the dominus Christianus has now been greatly increased by a recent find made by John Benton of Reed College. Professor Benton has examined all the acts of the Counts of Champagne preserved at Troyes and most of those at Chaumont, and he states most emphatically that the name Christianus is rare—non-existent except for the few documents that we are now considering. He has discovered two additional charters.[58] They are both signed by Xristianus, chaplain at Saint-Maclou, a collegiate church established at Bar-sur-Aube by Henry I of Champagne. Xristianus states specifically that one of these documents is in his own handwriting (dated 1179).[59] The other act is earlier (1172). Even our critics who persist in thinking of Chrétien as a common name will certainly allow us to claim that this Chrétien de Saint-Maclou is the same as the dominus Christianus who signed the charter for Jaucourt just outside Bar-sur-Aube in 1188. We may assume that at this time he was just dominus, retired from his active post as chaplain. In this case we can postulate that he had a son Galterus, who was chancellor of the Countess Marie de Champagne. Such posts as chancellor were assigned through privilege, through close personal association. By a short step we may claim that dominus Christianus, former chaplain of Saint-Maclou, was closely associated with Marie de Champagne. Bar-sur-Aube was, of course, within active range of Troyes, about twenty-five miles away.

57. *Ibid.*, IV, 39.
58. These acts are in the Archives at Troyes in *liasse* Aube. 4 bis H 256. I have examined these personally at Troyes.
59. This document is reproduced as Fig. 1.

It remains to consider whether Christianus the canon at Saint-Loup could be the same as dominus Christianus the chaplain of Saint-Maclou. This was indeed possible, ecclesiastically speaking. The canons of Saint-Loup, an Augustinian foundation, were extremely active in the Troyes region—operating granges and filling many posts. There is no question but that Count Henry could have presented a canon from Saint-Loup to be chaplain at Saint-Maclou.

If the reader is willing to grant the possibility of this identity of Chrétien the poet with dominus Christianus of Saint-Loup and Saint-Maclou, perhaps we should stop here. But there is the temptation to continue the thumbnail sketch which we began a few pages back. After writing the *Yvain* and the *Guillaume d'Angleterre,* Chrétien may have decided to withdraw from worldly employment and think of other things. Perhaps he had been married while in lower orders; or he could have had a son Galterus out of wedlock. Admitted at Saint-Loup, he could soon have been presented at Saint-Maclou, which would demand that he be ordained to the priesthood. He may even have regretted his former attachment to the Lancelots and Erecs of this world as he labored at Bar-sur-Aube, in close proximity to the Premonstratensian canons at Beaulieu and La-Chapelle-aux-Planches. It was not difficult to secure a transfer from the Augustinian Order to the Premonstratensian. A frequent visitor in Champagne, particularly after 1181, was Philip of Flanders. As the fierce and brutal currents which preceded the Third Crusade (1191) grew stronger, we assume that Count Philip thought incessantly of growing social problems—the "sores" that lay at the heart of Christendom, at home. Many others were concerned with the problem of the Jews, who were close to and yet so far from their Christian brethren. Chrétien, in his *Lancelot* of years before, had presented a special quest: a perfect knight who was destined to free "Arthur's people" of Logres from blind folly, which Chrétien had called Gorre, "vanity." This same quest—by a still more perfect knight who could labor to convert the folly of the blind people of Synagoga (the Isles) through the Grace of God—was a subject which could bring even the old Chrétien out of retirement. So Philip gave Chrétien his text or *livre* and the result was the *Conte del Graal*. If some of our readers prefer to accept that Chrétien wrote his earlier romances after 1172, we can claim that throughout his early "religious" life he kept an active interest in people and in worldly things—and what harm was there in his doing this?

The use of the name Christianus, both as an appellation and apparently as a baptismal name, increased a little in the thirteenth century, particularly in documents later than 1250. A Jehan Chrétien owned a house on the Marche de Provins in about 1252.[60] Cretiennet de la Routière was a landowner near Bar-sur-Aube in 1269.[61] In the baillie de Chaumont, in 1276-78, there was a Crestienne feme l'Aveugle.[62] Jehan Chrestien was provost of Troyes in 1252.[63] We find a Crestien d'Avelli near Provins in 1288,[64] and Crestien le Tissier was at Aunoy near Chaumont in 1338.[65] At Courcelle (Chaumont) a collector of the *taille* in 1338 was Perrinet filz Crestien.[66] In 1319-20 at Provins, there is mention of a "place en la foire as chevaus que Crestiens Lombart tient par an."[67] At Saint-Cristophle (Chaumont) in 1338 there was a Crestien filz Colin;[68] near Dampierre in 1338 lived a tax collector with the name Crestien le Maire.[69] Perrenet fil Jaquinet le Crestien is found at Vertuz in 1340-41;[70] note Li clers Crestienné.[71] Crestiennet de Poulangi occurs in 1287.[72] Crestiennot du Val is a tax collector at Ferté-sur-Aube in 1338.[73] At Nogent-en-Bassigny (Chaumont) are found in 1340-41 Crestiennote suer dou dit Wauterin and Crestiennette fame Jehan Hannequin.[74]

There is also the Tax Roll of Paris from the year 1292.[75] Here also the names Crestien and Crestienne do occur. We find Crestien de Meleun, Crestien le crieeur, Crestien le coutier, and Crestien le mareschal. Among the women listed are Crestienne fille de Robert de Massi, Crestienne la couturier, Crestienne la

---

60. See note 46 (*Foeda Campanie*, I, no. 225).
61. *Foeda Campanie*, II, 502 OP.
62. *Ibid.*, II, 181 F.
63. *Ibid.*, III, 12 F and 14 A.
64. *Ibid.*, III, 78 M.
65. *Ibid.*, III, 245 M.
66. *Ibid.*, III, 241 J.
67. *Ibid.*, III, 173 M, 294 M.
68. *Ibid.*, III, 249 J.
69. *Ibid.*, III, 253 J.
70. *Ibid.*, III, 318 F.
71. *Ibid.*, III, 251 N.
72. *Ibid.*, III, 60 F.
73. *Ibid.*, III, 240 N.
74. *Ibid.*, III, 372 P.
75. *Paris sous Philippe le Bel* (Documents inédits, 1837). The names here cited are on pp. 128, 51, 147, 42, 161, 121, 158, 81, and 16 respectively.

chapeliere de soie, Crestienne la boucliere, and another young girl with this name. But there are some 11,000 individuals in this Tax Roll; so the name Crestien and its feminine equivalent do not appear with any frequency. One is tempted to attribute this rise in frequency partially to the popularity of the romances of Chrétien de Troyes. If we are correct in assuming that converts were given the name, there also may have been an increase of these.

CHAPTER FOUR

The Castle and the Grail Procession

THE *Conte del Graal* is much different from the other romances of Chrétien in the over-all impression which it conveys. Rickard, following Sir John Rhys, has commented upon the strange flavor of its proper names and upon its realism.[1] We may assume there was a compelling purpose behind this story:

> Crestiens... is resolved and takes pains to put into rhyme the best of stories which can be told in court of king. This he does by order of the Count.[2]

Count Philip of Flanders provided the text or *livre*. Count Philip was a frequent visitor in the Troyes area during the 1180's. For a time it was his intention to marry Marie, who had been widowed in 1181. Chrétien devotes some forty lines to praise of this patron, claiming that he is superior to Alexander the Great. Philip does not care for crude joking, silliness, nor evil gossip; he gives freely, for he has the greatest of all virtues—Charity—which is God Himself. Chrétien quotes from Matt. 6:3, "But when thou doest alms, let not thy left hand know what thy right hand doeth." For still another twenty lines Chrétien extolls this charity which Alexander did not have, but which Count Philip practices—a charity that works in secret.[3] It is not difficult to realize that charity is the theme of the *Conte del Graal*. There are two threads to the development of this theme: the coming of

---

1. Peter Rickard, *Britain in Mediaeval French Literature* (Cambridge, Eng., 1956), p. 80, n. 1.
2. *Conte del Graal* (ed. Hilka), vv. 62 ff.: "Crestiens... antant et painne A rimoiier le meillor conte Par le commandement le Conte, Qui soit contez an cort real."
3. Vv. 21-59.

the young hero to Arthur's Court (before he knows that he is Perceval), followed by the Grail adventure, and the Quest by Gawain, which is so reminiscent of the *Lancelot*. It is virtually certain that these two threads deal with Charity in two manifestations.[4]

The sermons of Saint Bernard were popular at Troyes. Count Henry had them in his library.[5] One of these sermons, No. 79, is concerned specifically with charity. Here is a paragraph from this:

> The great Charity of the Church, which does not wish to withhold its delights from the rival Synagoga.... What can be more charitable than when one is prepared to communicate to an enemy that which your soul loves. This is marvellous, that salvation is from the Jews. The Savior has returned to the place whence He came forth that the remnants of Israel may be saved. The branches are not ungrateful to the root nor the sons to the mother.... The Church preserves salvation until all the people may come to it, and so may all of Israel be saved.[6]

This may be paraphrased as meaning that conversion of the Jews is entirely possible. It can be accomplished by the great Charity of the Church.

The adventures of the young man who was to be called Perceval have so long puzzled the readers of Chrétien de Troyes that it is a relief to turn first to the Gawain adventures in the *Conte del Graal*, where the meaning is phrased more clearly. We seek to

---

4. Professor Martín de Riquer believes that because of certain inconsistencies in the expression of time between the two sections, the Perceval adventures and the Gawain Quest were two distinct poems on which Chrétien was working during his last days. The two parts were united later at verses 4688-4746, the episode of the Hideous Damsel with the tawny mule. As much as the present writer admires the work of Martín de Riquer, he cannot agree with him here. One argument against his view is that the two parts of the story are together in all manuscripts. See Martín de Riquer, "Perceval y Gauvain en Li Contes del Graal," *Filología Romanza*, IV (1957), 119-47.

5. See above, p. 16.

6. Migne, *P.L.*, vol. 183: "Magna Ecclesiae charitas, quae ne aemulae quidem Synagogae suas delicias invidet. Quid benignius, quam ut, quem diligit anima tua, ipsum communicare parata sit et inimicae. Hec mirum tamen, quia salus ex Judaeis est. Ad locum unde exierat, revertatus Salvator, ut reliquiae Israel salvae fiant. Non rami radici, non matri filii ingrati sint.... ipsa [salutem] apprehendit donec plenitudo gentium introeat, et sic omnis Israel salvus fiat."

find contrast there that will enable us to speculate better on the meaning of the Grail Castle and the Procession.[7]

Gawain is challenged by Guingambrezil to appear before the King of Escavalon to answer an accusation of murder, the slaying of the King's father. Agrevains li Orgueilleus, "he of the hard hands," a brother of Gawain, says that he will settle the matter. (We have not heard of this brother before.) Gawain refuses help and undertakes to go in person. Next he is at Tintagel, where he is called a coward because he avoids the complications of combat, wishing to continue on his journey without delay. He suffers the taunts until a little maid, younger daughter of the lord of Tintagel, is maltreated by her offensive older sister because of him. Gawain makes himself champion of the little maid, is victorious, and continues on his way. At Escavalon he is not recognized at once during the absence of the King and of Guingambrezil. The King's sister receives him with embraces, but he is soon recognized and attacked by the mayor and members of the commune. The King and Guingambrezil return and save him from the commune. Although they hate him, he is technically their guest. He promises also that in the next year he will attempt the Quest of the Bleeding Lance, which, it is written, will some day destroy the whole realm of Logres. He continues on his way, presumably seeking for the Lance in the direction of Galloway (which in the Britain of Chrétien's time was a home of "strange" people). He comes upon a badly wounded knight (Greoreas) who lies with his head in the lap of his lady. This man was hurt at the ford where one passes over to Galloway.[8] Gawain feels his pulse, like some one skilled in medicine, and finds it *raide*. He knows the knight will recover. When Greoreas is sufficiently restored to recognize his benefactor he calls Gawain his greatest enemy and rides away with Gawain's horse. There follow several episodes shared by Gawain with a pathologically disturbed young lady called the Orgueilleuse de Logres. She reviles him mercilessly,

---

7. Vv. 4814-6216, 6519-9234.

8. The Solway that separates Cumberlandshire from Galloway was certainly fordable in Roman times, since the Roman Wall stretched to Bowness and then for a short distance into the water. We are not proposing that Chrétien knew any such details, but this is evidence of the actual use of the Solway.

but he turns to her again and again with kind and cheerful words. There is a wonderful palace across the water. A hospitable ferryman *(notonier)* carries him across and lodges him in his own place.[9] He does not want to take him to the palace. Gawain insists. They pass before a one-legged man with a richly adorned silver stump who sits on a bundle of thatch before the palace stair, whittling a stick of ash wood. Regretfully the ferryman permits him to enter and recline upon a miraculous bed. Trial now begins: first, showers of bolts and arrows, and then, attack from a dreadful lion. Gawain wards these off successfully and is informed that he is now master of the place. No knight could pass this test who was not free of envy, slander, avarice, and vice and was not truthful and brave. He is greeted by two queens and many other ladies and men of all condition and of all ages. They are all unhappy and waiting for their deliverer; but they are carefully protected by the necromancy of a certain "clers sages d'astrenomie," who is surely the one-legged man outside the gate. Gawain learns later that the Castle is called Roche de Champguin and that the two queens are his grandmother Yguerne (the mother of King Arthur) and his mother, Anna.[10] He has a young sister there whom he has not seen before. He is admitted as lord because of his virtue; but he is commanded never to leave the place. The people who live on the outside are dreadful folk—all except the ferryman who is Yguerne's contact with the region. But Gawain is more than a virtuous knight; he yearns to go among the forbidden folk, in perfect charity. First he renews acquaintance with Orgueilleuse and fights her champion, Orgueilleus de la Roche a l'Estroite Voie. Then she tells him of another knight—apparently the lord of this strange land which does not recognize Arthur. Gawain's horse carries him over the Perilous Ford to meet this man, Guiromelant de Orqueneseles.[11] At first Guiromelant is friendly. He speaks of Orgueilleuse as a

9. The ferryman remarks that strange things happen along this shore and offers Gawain a haven; v. 7464.
10. Roche de Champguin maintains itself by cloth manufacture; vv. 8816-20. Champguin could be translated as "white field," mixed French and Welsh, but this does not explain anything further.
11. The names *Orgueilleus* and *Orgueilleuse* are self-explanatory. The Orqueneseles may be reminiscent of the Orkneys.

former love; he displays his fear of those who live at Roche de Champguin, but he now loves Gawain's sister, while admitting that he hates Gawain and his father Lot. Gawain proclaims his identity and agrees to fight this man of fear and hate in twenty-four hours, in which time he hopes to have Arthur and Guenevere present on the field of combat. After he has recrossed the Perilous Ford the girl Orgueilleuse confesses to him her fault and says that Guiromelant had made her that way. Gawain returns to Roche de Champguin for a merry evening, but sends his messenger to Arthur at Orcanie. Arthur and his Court are sad, having had no news of Gawain for a long time. Dame Lore (who is she?) speaks of this to Guenevere, and it is at this point that Chrétien lays down his pen—forever.

To the present writer it appears quite clear that Gawain did not end his Quest when he was admitted to be lord of the manor of Roche de Champguin. His mission was greater than that. Queen Yguerne established her oasis, in the midst of violence, immediately after the death of Utherpendragon, her husband. She has remained isolated and still thinks of Arthur as a mere child, not more than a hundred years old.[12] She has been joined by many who have no husbands, are disinherited, or are orphan girls with no marriage prospects. Protected by enchantment, they wait for a truly virtuous man who will set their little "kingdom" right. But Gawain's "kingdom" is far larger than that. The Orgueilleuse de Logres learned to understand his heart, and we surmise that the other violent folk whom he entrusts to the ferryman after their defeat, and Guiromelant himself, are destined to know him better. Arthur's protection will be brought over all this violent land, and the ladies and gentlemen of Roche de Champguin will return to the larger court. The Bleeding Lance is not in Gawain's mind at this time. That is a greater quest, destined for Perceval, although it is likely that Chrétien intended to bring the two protagonists and their Quests together at the end. When Lancelot freed the men and women of Logres who were captives of Meleaganz de Gorre, he was the perfect lover, showing other lovers how to be free from pomp and false pride. But Ga-

---

12. V. 8170.

wain has a higher mission. By his charity he will bring to Arthur from across the Ford those who are self-sufficient and those who are violent to their neighbors, except when prevented by fear. Perceval's task—the Quest of the Bleeding Lance in the Grail Castle—is even more significant. We will now summarize that section of the *Conte del Graal.*

The protagonist is a youth, still unnamed, who lives with his mother in the depth of a great forest. They came from the Isles de Mer. The father, who was lame, and the brothers have all fallen in knightly combat. The mother wishes to shield her son from knighthood. One morning the boy encounters a troop of knights from Arthur's Court who inflame him with a desire to go there. Against his mother's fervent wishes he sets out for the Court. He sees a lady in a tent which, at first, he takes for a church. He insists upon kissing the girl twenty times (in all innocence) and he removes her emerald ring. (When the lady's male companion returns he believes she has been unfaithful and says that henceforth he will treat her ill.) The youth goes on his way. A charcoal burner gives him the route to Carlisle and informs him that Arthur has just defeated Rion, the king of the Isles. He rides his horse into the King's hall and knocks off the King's cap in his awkwardness. A red knight from Quinqueroi has just insulted the King and taken away his golden cup. The boy proposes to get this man's armor and he is permitted to leave, in some derision. He passes by a maid (who has not laughed for six years) who proclaims that he will be the greatest knight. Keu slaps her down. The boy sees this and thereafter considers himself the champion of this girl. (There is a faint suggestion here of the maid of Tintagel whom Gawain champions.) The Red Knight is killed with a javelin, and Yonet, who stands by, aids in the removal of the armor. The boy rides on. He sojourns at the castle of an elderly knight, Gornemanz, who instructs him in the use of arms and gives him advice, especially to refrain from quoting his mother at every turn; Gornemanz knights him. Next, the young knight, who still has no name, stops at Belrepaire, where he is welcomed by Blancheflor, the niece of Gornemanz. Her town is in sore distress because of a siege maintained by Clamadeus des Isles and his seneschal Anguingueron. She goes to the youth in the night, asking for help. For some of us there is every indication that this visit was chaste. Chrétien states specifically:

> That she came to weep upon his face for no other reason than that she might make him disposed—that she might put into his heart that he should undertake battle for her, if he dared....[13]

Previously the poet had remarked:

> All the ease and all the pleasure that one could devise in bed did the knight have that night except pleasure with a girl, or if he wished, with a lady, if that were possible. But he knew nothing about that, nor did he think of it at all....[14]

Furthermore, Blancheflor observes when she comes into his presence,

> For God's sake and for His Son I beg of you not to hold me more vile because I have come here—because I am almost naked. I have not had in mind anything foolish or evil or low....[15]

The embrace which ensues is symbolic, not sexual.

The young man defeats Blancheflor's enemies. Then he travels on and sees two men fishing in a boat on a river. One of them tells him that a castle is near and that he may spend the

13. "Qu'onques cele por autre chose
Ne vint plorer desor sa face,
Que que ele antandant li face,
Fors por ce qu'ele li meist
Au corage qu'il anpreist
La bataille, s'il l'ose anprandre...." (vv. 2040-45)

14. "Trestot l'eise et tot le delit
Qu'an seüst deviser an lit,
Ot li chevaliers cele nuit
Fors que solemant le deduit
De pucele, se lui pleüst,
Ou de dame, se lui leüst;
Mais il n'an savoit nule rien,
N'il n'i pansoit ne po ne bien...." (vv. 1935-42)

15. "Por Deu vos pri et por son fil
Que vos ne m'an aiiez plus vil
De ce que je sui ci venue;
Por ce que je sui presque nue
N'i pansai je onques folie
Ne mauvestié ne vilenie...."

The Castle and the Procession 69

night there. He climbs a hill and gazes, "Et ne vit rien fors ciel et terre." He exclaims over the barrenness before noting, "devant lui an val le chief d'une tor qui parut; L'an ne trovast jusqu'a Barut Si bele ne si bien assise...."[16] (The concept of a building in the wasteland of the Middle East is thus suggested.) When he draws near he finds a square-shaped hall with a porch before it. This is described as *loges*. Within the hall he sees curious bronze columns—strong, thick, and high—which support the smoke opening *anmi la sale*. An older man lies on a bed beside the fire, dressed in black garments lined or fringed with purple, and the knight is urged to sit beside him. A young man enters with a wonderful sword sent by the Blonde Maid, who is a "niece" (perhaps we should translate *niece* "descendant") of the Fisher King. The latter is the same individual as the fisherman who was in the boat. We are told that this sword blade will fail in only one peril and that it was forged by a smith who made only three of its kind.[17] The King may give the sword to whom he will. It is then given to the heroic guest, who learns later from a lady outside the Castle that when the blade does break it must be sent to Trebuchet, the smith who made it, beside the lake called Cotoatre.

A young man enters bearing aloft a white lance; from the tip of it blood drips upon his hand. Two servitors follow who are "mout bel," carrying golden candlesticks each with more than ten candles. Then there comes a lovely damsel carrying in both hands a grail. It is surrounded by a brightness which puts to shame the light from candles, just as stars lose their light when the sun or

---

16. Vv. 3050-53. Manfred Gsteiger, *Die Landschaftsschilderungen in den Romanen Chrestiens de Troyes* (Bern: Francke, 1958), p. 122, has noted this bit of detail. Because he does not interpret the Grail Castle as we do, for him the passage strikes an unusually jarring note: "Die banale rhetorische Formel des Vergleichs mit einer andern Stadt—wobei Barut wohl des Reimes wegen gewählt worden ist—bildet einen unschönen Missklang in der dichten Stimmung des Ganzen."

17. In *Jehan de Lanson*, vv. 270-72 (an edition made as a University of North Carolina dissertation by John Myers, which we have at hand) there is this passage: "Cez .iij. espeez furent de la forge Gallant; Il n'en fist que cez .iij., ce trouvons nous lisant. .iij. bons vassaulz les portent, hardis et combatant." The three heroes are Rolland, Ogier, and Oliver; the three swords are Durendal, Courtain, and Hauteclere. Gallant is Wayland the Smith. This text is much later than the *Conte del Graal*.

moon rises. There follows another feminine figure with a *tailleor d'arjant*, a flat tablet or plate of silver. The Procession passes between the fire and the couch and vanishes into an inner chamber. The young knight is mystified by what he sees but he refrains from asking because of the counsel of Gornemanz. Dinner is served. A haunch of venison is carved and the servings are placed each upon a whole *gastel* (strangely enough and not in an *escuele* or dish). The Grail reënters the hall. Again the knight asks nothing, putting off his questions until the morrow. Fruit, nuts, and wine are served before retiring. The lame King is carried to his chamber and a bed is set for the knight in the hall. When he wakes in the morning the Castle is deserted.

As he rides forth he sees a lady with a headless knight in her lap. (The reader will recall that Gawain met a lady holding in her lap the badly wounded Greoreas.) She reproves the young man for not having asked the questions by which the Fisher King could have been restored to health and tells him that his mother died of grief at his leaving. She asks him:

"What is your name, friend?" He who did not know his name makes a guess and says that he was called Percevaus li Galois, nor does he know that he spoke the truth and did not know it.[18]

When the lady hears this she exclaims, "Your name is changed, dear sir." It will be very evident to all who read this that the young man does not deserve his true name of Perceval at this particular moment—because he did not do what the name implies. The name must therefore have special implication. Perceval, as he is now called, continues on his way and overcomes Orgueilleus de la Lande, who, it seems, was the companion and oppressor of the girl whom he had once kissed and from whom he took the emerald ring. At this point Arthur and several of his knights set forth from Caerleon to find the young man and persuade him to return. Eventually they find him as he muses over a patch of snow spotted by the blood of a wild goose. The red and white

---

18. "Comant avez non, amis? Et cil qui son non ne savoit Devine et dit qu'il avoit Percevaus li Galois a non, N'il ne set s'il dit voir ou non; Mes il dist voir, et si nel sot" (vv. 3572-7).... "Tes nons est changiez, biaus amis...."

Fig. 4. Top of portable altar from Stavelot. Twelfth-century Champlevé enamel showing, at center, figures of Ecclesia with processional cross and chalice and Synagoga with instruments of the Passion (Copyright A. C. L. Bruxelles).

Fig. 5 (top). The Crucifixion with figures representing the Church and the Synagogue, from the top of a reliquary in the form of a portable altar. Champlevé enamel on gilt copper. North German, late twelfth century (Phot. Victoria and Albert Museum, Crown Copyright).

Fig. 6 (bottom). King Arthur in the Tree of Life mosaic, Cathedral of Otranto, 1166 (Phot. Alinari).

The Castle and the Procession

pattern reminds him of the face of Blancheflor. He defeats Sagremor and Keu, who try to bring him in. Only Gawain is successful with him. They all return to Caerleon. Next comes the visit of the Hideous Damsel on the tawny mule. "Teus con li livres les devise" is their only description. She upbraids Perceval for not having asked the questions about the Bleeding Lance and the Grail which would have freed the Fisher King and his lands. She says she must return that night to the Chastel Orgueilleus where there are 566 knights each with his lady. Girflot and Gawain accept adventures that she suggests; Perceval continues the Quest of the Grail. For five years he wanders without thinking of God. Then he meets a group of penitents, three knights and ten women. One of the knights asks why he is travelling armed on Good Friday. As Perceval seems not to know the significance of this day, the knight gives him a life of Christ in thirty-five lines. In speaking of the Crucifixion and Resurrection he says:

The wicked Jews through their envy, who should be slain like dogs, did ill to themselves and great good to us when they raised Him upon the Cross. They damned themselves and gave us salvation.[19]

These lines should hardly be taken as Chrétien's bitter personal feelings toward all Jews, which is an opinion some critics seem to hold. Of course, if he had been a convert himself such bitterness would be explainable; but this is rather conventional language of the age, in a passage spoken by a fictitious character.

Perceval is shown the way to the hermit's cell and makes his confession there. He admits that since he failed to ask the Grail questions he has fallen from Faith. The hermit replies that he *could* not ask them because he was in mortal sin as a result of the death of his mother. The Being in the inner room, served only by the Grail, was brother to the hermit and to Perceval's mother. The Fisher King is the son of this Being. The hermit absolves Perceval, who remains with him for two days.

19. "Li fel Gïu par lor anvie
Qu'an devroit tüer come chiens,
Firent lor mal et nos granz biens
Quant il an le croiz le leverent;
Aus perdirent et nos sauverent." (vv. 6292-6)

Even for us today who read this tale but imperfectly, the narrative has great depth and dignity. It gives the impression of having been composed by a man "auques d'aé"[20] who has reflected much upon life. There are some details which come to the eye immediately. Those individuals who live on the outer fringe, outside of Arthur's jurisdiction, are said to be from the Isles de Mer, or simply from the Isles.[21] Orgueilleus de la Lande, another bad man with Pride in his name, observes of Perceval: "In all the Isles de Mer I have never heard a knight named who is better . . ."[22] than Perceval. It is evident that he comes from there. Arthur has just slain Rion (Ritho), the giant king of the Isles.[23] Most interesting of all, the father and mother of the young man who is to be Perceval are natives of the Isles—which means that Perceval himself had similar origin.[24] His eldest brother had been sent to the King of Escavalon to be knighted, which would suggest that Escavalon also is within the Isles. The reader will recall that the King of Escavalon's son accused Gawain of having murdered his father. It may be safely assumed that the people of the Isles were those beyond the pale of Arthur; and Arthur like Charlemagne was a symbol of Christendom. More of this later. The Hideous Damsel comes from the Chastel Orgueilleus where there are 566 knightly couples—held, undoubtedly, by force—and we assume that this Chastel was in the Isles, although we cannot be certain.[25] She recalls to us the damsel on the tawny mule who was the daughter of Bademagu of Gorre, who persuaded Lancelot to kill the faithless knight.

There are vague outlines of similarity in the Quests of Gawain and Perceval, as we have been hinting. It is a little maid who recognizes the hero's worth in each case, at the outset. Gawain is received warmly (but not lewdly) by the sister of the young king of Escavalon; and there is the future Perceval's reception at Belrepaire. In the Perceval section there is the lady with the

20. We have borrowed this expression from *Lancelot*, v. 1661.
21. *Conte del Graal*, v. 4091: "Qu'an totes les Isles de Mer N'ai oï chevalier nomer...."
22. Vv. 850-2. Geoffrey (ed. Faral), III, 257.
23. V. 2005.
24. Vv. 418-26.
25. Vv. 4688 ff.

headless knight in her lap; in the case of Gawain Greoreas lies wounded in his lady's lap. Gawain in every situation displays kindliness and perfect charity toward those who affront him; but it is a personal virtue called forth by his own will. The protagonist in the Grail adventures—Perceval, if you will—is also a person of goodness and charity; but he is this more by the Grace of God than by struggle within himself. He seems to move as an instrument of God in the course of what is his own development and his own coming to maturity. Like many instruments he can fail at times—and fail hard—but in each case he springs back to his original purpose. I see in the Gawain and Perceval sections two representations of the practice of Charity—but Charity at different levels, with different achievement.

It is now my intention to outline our explanation of the Grail Castle and of the Grail Procession, according to what we are now calling the Judaeo-Christian interpretation. This is not a mechanical repetition of what was said in 1948. Since then both Sister Amelia and Mario Roques have discovered simultaneously, unknown to each other at the time, the identification of the Grail Procession with the Church Triumphant in the Synagoga-Ecclesia motif.[26] We have felt obliged to modify our own viewpoint accordingly. We no longer yield to the temptation to impose an explanation of all minor details in Chrétien's narrative. Such explanation in most instances should be entirely possible; we are now examining only the larger phases of the problem.

26. Sister Amelia Klenke, "Chrétien's Symbolism and Cathedral Art," *PMLA*, LXX (1955), 266 ff.; Mario Roques, "Le Graal de Chrétien et la demoiselle au Graal" (Paris, 1955). For the time being we pursue no further certain parallels which we saw between the Grail theme and Jewish *Midrashim*. However, very recently, M. Pierre Ponsoye in his *L'Islam et le Graal* (Editions Denoël, 1957) has found similarities in Wolfram's *Parzival* and Chrétien's *Conte del Graal* to Oriental themes. In each case M. Ponsoye decides for Islam when, in our opinion, a better case can be made for Jewish tradition. This tendency to trace the situations and themes of the Grail narrative in the East is spreading. Because we feel that there is a kernel of truth in some of this it is hoped that those who attempt it will weigh carefully their assertions. It is not enough to make general comparisons. Likelihood of transmission must be studied. Chrétien was not an electrode attracting particles from every conceivable direction. As far as we know he was a clerk making his living in the vicinity of Troyes. For the latest attempt of this kind see Arthur U. Pope, "Persia and the Holy Grail," *The Literary Review*, I (1957), 57-71. He says he was assisted in this by Dr. Phyllis Ackerman.

In 1948 I thought I was the first to recognize in Chrétien's description of the Grail Castle a portrayal of Solomon's Temple at Jerusalem. I have noted since that the distinguished Hebrew scholar Moses Gaster observed this many years ago. We quote from a collection of his writings that was published in 1925-28. The article is entitled "The Legend of the Grail."

> ... I wish to go straight to the question of the Grail itself. I have already stated at the beginning, that the temple of the Grail in the poem is the temple of Jerusalem, and the Grail is in double character a certain sacred stone in the Holy place.... some light may be thrown upon Flegetanis the Jew, to whom, according to Wolfram, Kyot owed the original of the Grail legend....[27]

The essential for us is that Gaster, an eminent Jewish scholar, recognized the resemblance which the Grail Castle has to the Temple of Solomon. It is unfortunate that Gaster did not carry on with this. He preferred to elaborate on the dependence of the Grail legend upon the Alexander theme, in which we cannot follow him.

Chrétien's description of the Castle has already been presented. In Solomon's Temple there was a lofty tower which covered the outer portico (which was not separate as in Chrétien), flanked by smaller towers, one on each side.[28] (Chrétien also has the two *tourelles*.) From the outer portico or *loges*, one entered the Holy Place, where there were two bronze columns. (Chrétien has four, but he needed a support for the smoke-exit in his great mediaeval hall and Solomon did not.) The inner room is the Holy of Holies. Chrétien made his hall a perfect square, which was the shape of the Holy of Holies. The main hall or Holy Place of Solomon had a table for the shew bread. The Fisher King had his magnificent table, and the food in each instance was set upon a *gastel* which, despite some of the errors of Hollywood, is not a mediaeval practice in serving. Mediaeval food was placed in *escueles* or plates which resembled small shields with turned-up edges. There was much candlelight in both the Grail Castle and Solomon's Temple.

27. *Studies and Texts* (London, 1925-28), II, 898, 895.
28. The description is in III Kings 6 and 7.

In a previous article[29] I quote from the twelfth-century chronicler Lambert d'Ardres, who says of the Counts of Guines and Ardres that Arnould the Elder in 1114 ornamented the chapel in his new donjon to resemble Solomon's Temple. These words are there for all to read, no matter how incredible they may seem. Chrétien does not picture the Temple with complete accuracy, nor could the Counts of Guines and Ardres have copied minutely the details as given in the Bible. Mediaeval man achieved the spirit of a thing much more than the letter. The Counts of Guines and Ardres were intimately associated with the entourage of the Counts of Flanders; Philippe d'Alsace was in the Holy Land in 1177-78; Henry the Liberal made his second journey there in 1179-81, dying shortly after his return. The pilgrims in the East had various guide books for Jerusalem, of which *The City of Jerusalem*, written probably around 1187, is typical of its kind; it repeats information that could have been available to all in the period 1177-81. Here is a paragraph:

> In the midst of the Temple [of the Lord] is the great Sacred Rock, where was the ark of Our Lord in the time of David, and there were the Old Testament and the rod of Aaron, and the seven candlesticks of gold, and the pot of manna which came from Heaven, and the fire which used to devour the sacrifices they made there, and the tables of the Old Covenant, and the oil which dropped wherewith kings and prophets were anointed. On this rock slept Jacob, and saw the angels ascend to Heaven and descend by ladder.[30]

Within the Temple enclosure were two buildings which were designated as the Templum Domini and the Temple of Solomon. (The Kubbet es-Sakhra and the El-Aksa Mosque are the present names of these structures.) It is well known today that the original building of Solomon's Temple was destroyed in 586 B. C. and that its successor was burned in 77 A. D. by the Romans. The Crusaders of the twelfth century were not informed about this. They knew only that Solomon's house of worship was described in the Biblical text and that the contents of the Holy

---

29. *Speculum*, XXV (1950), 100-02.
30. *City of Jerusalem* (trans. Conder), Palestine Pilgrims Text Society, VI, 53.

of Holies were listed in the Epistle to the Hebrews.[31] The Temple took a preëminent position in the imagination of many: in *Huon de Bordeaux* the evil brother claimed to have tested Huon on his voyage to the East: "I asked him about Solomon's Temple; he could not tell me yes or no."[32]

Despite the fact that there were not more than two hundred Jews in the Jerusalem known to the Crusaders,[33] this Temple stood for the Jewish people, and Jacob was their eternal high priest. The building had been constructed, so they thought, on the spot where he had wrestled and received the Lord's Grace. But Synagoga was represented in iconography by the twelfth-century men of France as a lady who is accompanied, in some way, by a lance. The Romanesque cathedral at Châlons-sur-Marne has a magnificent glass panel (Fig. 3) portraying the triumph of the Church over the Synagogue. (This was removed in 1872 but has now been replaced, after restoration.) In this panel the Church has a banner, a cross, and a chalice; the Synagogue has a lance and a sponge attached to a long shaft, symbols of the Passion. Directly over the cross there is an inscription which begins with the word S A L O M O N.[34] Châlons-sur-Marne is forty-six miles north of Troyes, on the road which goes through Arcis-sur-Aube. Ramerupt is only thirty miles from Châlons-sur-Marne. In this area where Jewish schools and Jewish students were so plentiful, the people must have comprehended very well the conflict of Ecclesia and Synagoga. The window was made around 1155. Contemporary with it is the decoration of a portable altar at Stavelot, perhaps carved by Godefroid de Huy[35] (Fig. 4), now preserved at the Musée de Bruxelles. The design is very similar to that of the Châlons-sur-Marne window. Perhaps the theme of Ecclesia versus Synagoga in art can be traced to a window planned by Abbot Suger at Saint-Denis, although the ivories at Metz show the same

---

31. Chapter 9. See note 43 below.
32. (Ed. Guessard et Grandmaison), p. 282: "Demandai lui dou temple de Salemon; Ainc ne m'en sot dire ne o ne non."
33. Benjamin of Tudela is our authority that he found only two hundred Jews in Jerusalem *(Itinerary)*.
34. Musée des Arts Décoratifs, *Vitraux de France* (23d ed. rev. et corrigée; 1953), p. 43.
35. Emile Mâle, *L'art religieux du XIIe siècle en France* (Paris, 1928), p. 161, Fig. 127.

subject as early as the tenth century.³⁶ Suger was an innovator, a creator of symbolism. In his window there is a medallion in which Christ crowns the New Law with one hand and with the other removes a veil from the face of the Old Law: "Quod Moyses velat Christi doctrina revelat." Von Simson says of this:

> For St. Paul, as for Suger, the veil of Moses denotes the dullness of the senses of those not yet illuminated by Grace; and the denuding of Moses, far from being an offense, signifies that the "veiled" truth of the Old Testament has been replaced by the revelation of the New....³⁷

At this point we are asking our readers to take the first two steps with us in our interpretation of the Grail Castle. We say that the Castle is a representation in mediaeval fashion of the Temple of Solomon. In that case we propose that the Fisher King, with his purple fringed garment, with his lameness, is the high priest of the Jews, Jacob. He symbolizes the Jewish people, enthroned in Solomon's hall. Next we believe that the dominant idea represented is the conversion of the Old Testament into the New—Solomon's Temple into Ecclesia. There is much testimony of this hope for conversion in the writings of the time. The *Tractatus contra Judaeos* of Gautier de Châtillon-sur-Seine compares the wait for the Messiah of the Jews to the senseless waiting for the coming of Arthur by the Celts.³⁸ Gerald the Welshman also phrases this, saying of the Celts and Arthur, "... propter quod ipsum exspectant adhuc venturum, sicut Judaei Messiam suum, majori etiam fatuitate et infelicitate, simul ac infelicitate decepti."³⁹ The major theme of the Procession in the Grail Castle must represent the Conversion of Synagoga to Ecclesia, an event so warmly urged in the Epistle to the Hebrews. This Conversion could be realized best by Charity, which "is God" and can bring everything good to pass, in the end:

> Charity does not boast of her good works; instead she conceals so that none will know save God, and God is named both God and

---

36. *Ibid.*, p. 166, Fig. 130. See also chap. 7 below.
37. *The Gothic Cathedral* (Bollinger Series XLVIII; 1956), p. 121.
38. Migne, *P.L.*, vol. 209, cols. 419-58.
39. *Speculum Ecclesiae*, Dist. II, cap. 9.

Charity. God is Charity and he who lives by her, as St. Paul has said —and I have read it—dwells in God and God in him.[40]

These steps represent the basic belief of those of us who profess the Judaeo-Christian theory for the origins of the meaning of the Grail story. The Grail hall is the Temple; Jacob is enthroned there, and Charity has the power to change all this Old Law into the New. By this much sorrow and bloodshed can be avoided. However it was presented, whatever the *livre* may have been, this, we say, was the burden of the theme given to Chrétien by Philip of Flanders. Death took Chrétien when he was well warmed to his task, and many of those who liked his tale in later years failed to understand it. I am not sure that all misunderstood. The author of the *Parzifal*, either Wolfram or one of his immediate sources, had some idea with his mention of the Jew Flegetanis and with his description of the Grail altar made from a "sun stone," an essonite garnet. It is possible that the first continuator, Gerbert de Montreuil, also knew, but these people had other themes which they allowed to hide Chrétien's purpose, like autumn leaves falling upon a marker.

We insist upon these two premises—the Temple and the Conversion theme—but other interpretations, hosts of them, have fitted beautifully into an understanding of the Grail. Like most interpretations applied to mediaeval literature, their proof depends upon the direction in which one is looking, upon a sense of proportion, and upon knowledge of the background. Since it is unlikely that we shall ever discover documents that will furnish us with complete evidence, convincing to all, on the genesis of the Grail story, we must continue to grope intelligently. We must

---

40.   "Charité, qui de sa bone oevre
Pas ne se vante, einçois se cuevre
Si que nus nel set se cil non
Qui Deus et charitez a non:
Deus est charitez, et qui vit
An charité, selonc l'escrit,
Sainz Pos le dit et je le lui,
Il maint an Deu, et Deus an lui."

(*Conte del Graal*, vv. 43-50)

There is actual record of an important conversion in the year 1124 attributed by the convert to the allegory of the Old and New Testament and to all the writings of St. Paul. This was Judas le Juif, who took the name Herman. See his *Opusculum de sua conversione*, Migne, *P.L.*, vol. 170, cols. 803-35.

possess ourselves of the learning and knowledge of life as they were in Chrétien's time. Some attempt to understand society in detail, an adequate knowledge of the political and feudal movements, a thorough understanding of the writings and liturgy of the Church as they would be known to the average intelligent cleric, acquaintance with substratum thought and writings (notably Celtic, Jewish, and Arabic)—all these and more must be brought into play. By such synthesis it will be possible to proceed. We understand also that there were different levels of meaning and interpretation in almost every mediaeval work. In speaking of Alain de Lille, Richard H. Green has said:

> Alain echoes the customary levels of Scriptural interpretation, but with a difference which I shall point to in a moment: the literal meaning engages the senses and imagination and appeals to the pleasures of recognition; the figurative meaning informs the intelligence with truths which lie beneath appearances; the moral instruction excites the will to the love and practice of virtue; and beyond all this lies the final aspiration, the intuition of the divine mysteries which are the ultimate goal of man's knowledge and desire.... Once his poetry is placed in the tradition of mediaeval philosophical poetry, not merely by recognizing its sources and analogues, but by taking seriously the poetic theory of allegorical representation and the use of fabulous narrative, the burden of his carefully managed theme can be discovered and followed in the texture of the verbal tapestry.[41]

C. S. Lewis has spoken of the variations in Chrétien:

> Wherever Chrétien became psychological he became allegorical.... Chrétien combined two methods in his work because he combined two different appeals. He wished to satisfy the taste for marvellous adventure... but he also wished to satisfy the taste for refined emotionalism.... It was inevitable, therefore, that a story by Chrétien must have appeared in very different lights to different members of his audience.[42]

41. *Speculum*, XXXI (1956), 651, 655, 673.
42. *The Allegory of Love* (Oxford, 1948), pp. 113-4. Erich Köhler, in his *Ideal und Wirklichkeit in der höfischen Epik—Studien zur Form der frühen Artus- und Graaldichtung* (Tübingen, 1956), has constructed an elaborate study of Idealism versus Actuality (see first Appendix). If Chrétien were capable of elaborating such inner meaning as this he was a different man from what we have thought him to be. However Köhler agrees with us somewhat in seeing that Gawain, Lancelot, Bohors, Perceval, and Galahad represent different levels of

Believing as we do that the Grail Procession represented Synagogue in the Temple of Solomon before her conversion to the Church, we can make some attempt to identify the figures in the Procession. They pre-figure what will ultimately be the Church Triumphant—Ecclesia leading the way with her Chalice, followed by unblinded Synagoga with the Lance and the Law. As it is, the characters within the Temple are still playing Synagoga, but some of them are "dressed" for the second act. As long as the elements of the Procession are still in the Temple of Solomon they must continue to suggest the mysteries of the Holy of Holies. The Chalice at this stage is the vessel containing manna; the Bleeding Lance is the rod of Aaron carried in the Temple still unredeemed. This rod had a tremendous mystical history in later traditions and became everything from lance to cross. The *tailleor* or flat plate represented the tablet of the Law. I propose that the fire on the hearth, between the curiously wrought columns of bronze, could suggest the fire which devoured the sacrifices in the Temple. The two feminine figures, later to be Ecclesia and Synagoga, were now the two Cherubim who watched over the relics of the Holy of Holies.[43]

When the present writer was speaking on this subject recently, a scholar who is by no means a partisan of the Judaeo-Christian theory observed that the term *Isles* was used by the Jews in France to designate Britain, in the Middle Ages. Perhaps this could ex-

---

virtue (pp. 186, etc.). We are also in agreement over the importance of the Bleeding Lance. Köhler thinks (p. 207) that the King of Escavalon needed it in his war against Arthur. We hold that Escavalon was already in alliance with the Lance and that by forcing Gawain to make an attempt to conquer it the king of Escavalon hoped to send Gawain to certain destruction.

43. So often in following the points of an argument the reader is tempted to skip the fine print. There is a treatise which *must* be considered in this connection. Adam Scot, a Premonstratensian who died before 1180, wrote a sermon called *De fide sanctae ecclesiae et de vocatione Synagogae ad fidem* (Migne, *P.L.*, vol. 198, cols. 133-41). Most striking is his *De Tripartito Tabernaculo*. This is an exposition of the details of the Tabernacle and the Temple, examining the descriptions from Pentateuch, Bede, and Josephus. (It may be recalled that a copy of Josephus was among the books of Henry the Liberal.) In chap. xxv, Pars Prima (col. 676), Master Adam says: "Posita est ibi urna aurea plena manna in testificationem quod panem dedisset eis et de coelo. Tabulae in testificationem quod in legem naturalem sopitam in cordibus suscitaverat in scripto. Virga Aaron in testimonium quod omnis potestas a Domino Deo est. . . . Ex utraque vero parte oraculi, scilicet in duobus angulis anterioribus, positi sunt duo Cherubin aurei . . . ."

The Castle and the Procession

plain why for Chrétien the practicing Jewish communities adjacent to Logres, the land of Arthur, received the designation of *Isles (de Mer)*.

There is undoubtedly need for a study of Chrétien and his possible association with the Premonstratensian Order, as figured in the *Conte del Graal*. There were many monks and abbots of that order who bore the name Chrétien in religion. A Christianus was a Premonstratensian at Cappenberg in 1155-72.[44] Christianus of Mainz served Philip of Flanders in 1167 and became a bishop shortly thereafter.[45] Chrétien d'Overheim was probably a canon at Saint-Lambert.[46] Christianus of Wevelinghoven founded an abbey at Lanwaden in 1168.[47] Christianus was Abbot of Tron around 1200.[48] John L. Johns is preparing a list of the names of Premonstratensian abbots. He has found eighteen with the name Chrétien, but most of these are later than the twelfth century. Aside from the Premonstratensian charters which we have already cited, there is another possible *rapprochement*. This is the association of Philippe of Harveng, Abbot of Bonne Espérance, with both Henry the Liberal and Philip of Flanders. Much of the writings of Abbot Philippe is extant, and he has many pages which show an interest in Jewish thought, particularly in the *Song of Songs*. Some evidence can be advanced that Gerbert de Montreuil belonged to the Premonstratensians.[49] The Montreuil attached to his name is probably the Montreuil which lies near the road from Troyes to Bar-sur-Aube.

It must be admitted that the name *Perceval* had a special meaning which was appropriate to one who had seen the Grail Procession at the Castle.[50] How can one argue differently? The name appears earlier in another work of Chrétien—in the *Erec et Enide*, the romance into which he introduced most of the proper names that he drew upon at later dates. When Enide

---

44. MGH SS, XII, 530.
45. *Ibid.*, XII, 312, and VI, 398.
46. *Collection des Chroniques belges inédites*, XXVI, I, 95 and 69.
47. *Ibid.*, XII, II, 540.
48. *Ibid.*, "Tables chronologiques," III, 147.
49. John Mahoney of Duquesne University has assisted me greatly in this and other matters. It is probable that he will soon have something further to report on this background of the Grail.
50. *Conte del Graal*, vv. 3573-7. See note 18 above and the text.

and Erec are returning from the beauty tourney (we can hardly call it a contest) at Lalut, a group of sensation seekers at Caradigan perch themselves so as to watch them come in:

> Queen Guenevere runs there, and the King himself came there, and Keus and Percevaus li Galois, and my lord Gawain afterwards, and Torz li fiz au roi Arés....[51]

"Torz li fiz au roi Arés" never appears again. Guenevere, Keu, and Gawain were principal characters drawn from Wace or Geoffrey. Whence did Chrétien acquire the name *Perceval?* If he invented it at this time or if he had happened to remember it as an existing baptismal name, he could not have missed the association with *percevoir* "to perceive." It is true that this character Perceval was one of the curious onlookers. This might well have been the only occurrence, as was so often the case with Chrétien's names; but in the *Cligés* the poet selects three champions to be worsted by the hero. Cligés, dressed in red, overcomes Perceval "Sanz grant bataille et sanz grant plet."[52] Hardly an invincible hero at this time in Chrétien's mind! Perceval does not occur again until identified with this name in the Grail passage just quoted. In my judgment, Chrétien selected from the list of knights already introduced into his "Comédie arthurienne" a name that suited well the idea that he now sought to convey. Perceval was a knight who had "pierced the veil" of the great mystery. At first of little consequence, the name, perhaps through chance homonymity, now assumes significance, suggesting a mystical experience within the Temple.

51. *Erec et Enide*, vv. 1695-9: "La reine Guenievre i cort, Et s'i vint meïsmes li rois, Keus et Percevaus li Galois Et mes sire Gauvains aprés, Et Torz, li fiz au roi Arés...." This is actually the earliest occurrence I have of the name *Perceval*. A distinguished expert on genealogy of the Société des Normannistes has searched the records and he assures me that Perceval is not a Norman-French name. He advises me that it might be Flemish.

52. *Cligés*, v. 4849.

CHAPTER FIVE

Summary

BEFORE OUR READERS begin the second part of this book, it would be well to review as briefly as possible some of the major claims which have been presented thus far concerning Chrétien and the Grail.

Chrétien was not merely a light-hearted entertainer. While serving contemporary taste for the marvellous, for strange adventure, and for love dialogue, he displays in all his romances some concern for the social problems of the second half of the twelfth century. He reflects also the immediate environment in which he was writing. It is quite possible that after some apprenticeship in adaptations from Ovid he journeyed to England and there was soon attracted by the welter of popular tales which professed to tell of the beginnings of Britain. (William of Malmesbury was attracted by these just as much, but with different emphasis.) Such tales were everywhere, particularly among the Celtic peoples: in Wales, Cornwall, and in the northern districts which had once been Cumbria and Strathclyde. There were many Continental Bretons holding lands and employment in Britain, some of them dating from the Conquest. The *Erec et Enide* was perhaps composed away from the Troyes area, hence the signature *Crestiens de Troyes*. *Chrétien* was far from being a frequent baptismal name in the twelfth century. It was so rare that we have identified Chrétien the poet, provisionally, with a certain chaplain, Chrétien de Saint-Maclou, which was a collegiate church established by Count Henry I of Champagne and his wife Marie. This chaplain had a son, Walter, who was later a chancellor of the Countess. Such positions of favor could pass from father to son.

It is reasonable to assume that Chrétien the poet was too busy for romances in his middle life, but that after 1185, when events were shaping for the Third Crusade, he was persuaded by Count Philip of Flanders (a frequent visitor at Troyes) to write a more serious romance, a more glorious one, after the "quest type" which he had foreshadowed in his earlier *Lancelot*. In the *Lancelot* it had been a quest by a perfect lover, who freed his lady (Guenevere) and many other people who owed allegiance to Arthur from the land of Pride and Vanity. This new romance would be concerned with one of the most serious of all problems. It would be a quest to win over the non-believers of the "Isles" to the kingdom of Arthur (who was a new Messiah). There were non-believers (shall we say, non-cooperators?) of various kinds; but prominent among these were the Jews who in many respects were blood brothers and extremely close neighbors. Such people could, as St. Bernard had said, be won by Grace and by the Mercy of God—by Charity. We think that Chrétien, with this hope in mind, began the story of the nameless young man from the Isles (the non-Arthurian, non-Christian land) who, aided only by Grace, sought to accomplish the Quest. Within the Temple of Solomon, the abode of the Old Law, the poet wished to propose a mass conversion to the New. Undoubtedly the name *Perceval* had special meaning related to the Quest. This no one can deny, for Chrétien tells it to us in so many words. As a foil to his high purpose, Chrétien placed beside it the adventures of another kind of knight—one who was charitable and virtuous in every worldly way but was not the recipient of Divine Grace. This was Gawain, the perfect worldly knight, who could bring about reforms through his own goodness and charity, but who could not effect the conversion of the Bleeding Lance of Synagogue by the Church Triumphant.

Between the *Conte del Graal* of Chrétien de Troyes and the *Queste del Saint Graal* of an unknown Cistercian monk, some twenty-five years intervened, a period during which details as given by Chrétien were obscured or at least transformed by the narratives of Robert de Boron and by the prose *Lancelot*. Yet the unknown Cistercian was much concerned with Lancelot, Gawain, and Perceval, so that in a way he seems to revivify their characters as first suggested by his great predecessor Chrétien. Lancelot is a splendid man but encumbered by his carnal love, the only sin by which the devil could tempt him—the sin that had seduced Adam, the first man, Solomon, the wisest of men, Samson, the strongest, and Absalom, the handsomest. It was done through Guenevere.[1] But Lancelot had not gone far into sin; he could be redeemed by penitence. His carnal love is almost sanctioned in the fact that he is the father of Galaad, the perfect one, by a union with the daughter of the Fisher King. Contrast all this with the Lancelot of Chrétien's romance by that name.

In the *Queste* as in the *Conte del Graal* Gawain is depicted as courageous, charitable, and beloved by all; but he is worldly. He refuses to be ascetic, and he does not repent. When, unknowingly, he has given Yvain a mortal wound, the dying knight remarks: "I do not mind since I am killed by the hand of a man as fine as you."[2] And yet Nasciens the hermit assures Gawain that he is in mortal sin and that the Grail cannot appear to him. The author of the *Queste del Saint Graal* placed Perceval among the elect, and the treatment given him was something very special.

In the *Queste* Perceval stops at the dwelling of a recluse, who is his aunt. She tells of his mother's death and then speaks of the three Tables: the Table of Jesus Christ, the Table of the Holy Grail, and the Round Table. Christ was master of the first, Joseph of Arimathea of the second, and the lord of the third will be the hero who can sit in the Perilous Seat, above the rest of Arthur's knights. This will be the knight who appeared to them first dressed in red (the color which denotes the Heavenly Fire of Pentecost). Perceval is following after this Red Knight (Galaad). He continues on his way and visits King Mordrain, the rescuer of Joseph of Arimathea from prison, who is kept alive miraculously, feeding only upon the Eucharist. Perceval loses his horse in a fight with twenty armed men, where he is

---

1. *La queste del saint Graal*, ed. Albert Pauphilet (Paris, 1923), p. 125.
2. *Ibid.*, pp. 153-4: "Dont ne me chaut, fet il, se je sui ocis par la main de si preudome com vos estes."

aided by the Red Knight. Without a horse he can go no farther, but the devil appears in the shape of a horse and carries him to a mountainous isle. There Perceval rescues a lion cub from a serpent, killing the latter. Then in a dream he sees an older woman riding upon such a serpent and a younger lady riding on a lion. (These are Synagoga and the New Law.[3]) Synagoga upbraids him for slaying the first serpent and demands that he renew allegiance to her. She adds:

> You were mine previously, before you received the oath of homage from your present lord. And because you were mine before any one else's, I will not renounce my claim to you.[4]

When he wakes, Perceval sees a ship which brings to him a venerable kingly priest, who identifies for him the two women in the dream. He says that Perceval belonged to Synagoga before his baptism, but it is not specified whether this was infant or adult baptism. The ship departs and Perceval is tempted again, by a lady who is the devil. When the priest returns he explains this also. Perceval exclaims, "... I should have been overcome if it were not for the Grace of the Holy Spirit which did not let me perish, thanks be to God."[5]

Here, as in the *Conte del Graal* of Chrétien, it is the Grace of God which guides the simple Perceval in his major dilemmas and brings him to success. Why did the author of the *Queste del Saint Graal* make use of this episode of the Old and the New Laws? The kingly priest explains further that the serpent on which Synagoga rides is the Scripture evilly taught and badly understood, meaning the Law as it was expounded by the Jewish

---

3. *Ibid.*, p. 103: "Cele dame a qui tu veis le serpent chevauchier, ce est la Synagogue, la premiere Loi, qui fu ariere mise, si tost come Jhesucrist ot aporté avant la Novele Loi"; p. 101: "Cele qui sor le lyon estoit montee senefie la Novele Loi. . . . et cele dame si est Foi et Esperance et creance et baptesmes."

4. *Ibid.*, p. 98: "Je voil, fet ele, que en amende de mon serpent deviegniez mes hons." Et il respont que ce ne feroit il pas.—"Non? fet ele. Ja le fustes vos ja; ançois que vos receussiez l'omage de vostre seignor estiez vos a moi. Et por ce que vos fustes ainz miens que autrui ne vos claim je pas quite; ainz vos aseur que en quelque leu que je vos truisse sanz garde, que je vos prendrai come celui qui jadis fu miens."

5. *Ibid.*, p. 114: ". . . j'eusse esté vaincu se ne fust la grace dou Saint Esperit qui ne me lessa perir, soe merci."

scholars—in Troyes? Perceval had taken from Synagoga her force and power, and this was the direct cause of her grievance against him.⁶

It is almost impossible to believe that this Cistercian did not have in mind the interpretation of both Perceval and Gawain and their struggle as we have presented it to our readers. His own life span was so close to that of Chrétien that he could easily have known some of those intimately associated with Chrétien and his original plan for the *Conte del Graal*. In the following chapters the importance of this motif of the Church Triumphant in the Champagne area, together with the concept of Arthur as leader of Christianity and the reflection of the Church's doctrines in Chrétien's story, will be completely unfolded.

6. *Ibid.*, p. 103: "Et li serpenz qui la porte, ce est l'Escriture mauvesement entendue et mauvesement esponse, ce est hypocrisie et heresie et iniquitez et pechié mortel, ce est li anemis meismes. . . . Et einsi l'oceis tu et destruisis et li tolis pooir et force de sa baillie et se son conduit, et si te quitoit il bien avoir gaangnié: et de ce est li grans duelx que ele [Synagoga] a a toi."

PART TWO

CHAPTER SIX

The Prologue of Chrétien's *Perceval*

THE FOLLOWING chapters are an attempt to re-evaluate Chrétien de Troyes and his *Perceval* through a detailed analysis of the poet's words, particularly in his prologue, and a further study of the inter-relation of the history, the art, and the literature of his day. For Chrétien, like any normal man, must have been influenced by contemporaneous events taking place about him. As a Christian poet, he could not have remained unaffected by the literary and artistic achievements of the times. After all, twelfth-century France was profoundly interested in the spreading of Christ's kingdom on earth. This is seen in the three great channels in which the Church spent her energies: the Crusades, the conversion of the Jews, and the didactic literature and art of the period, both of which were permeated with the rich symbolism of the liturgy as popularized by the Abbot Suger of Saint-Denis, a symbolism stemming from the writings of St. Paul.

A thoughtful consideration of Chrétien's prologue should throw light upon the poet's intent in writing his *Perceval*. Is it not the function of a prologue to attract attention and gain sympathy for what is to follow? And does not every prologue worthy of the name bear a close connection with that which it seeks to introduce? In the course of the sixty-eight verses which comprise his prologue, Chrétien mentions the romance he is about to begin, Philip of Flanders at whose command the poem is being written, and Philip's practice of Charity according to St. Paul. Nine-tenths of the prologue is given over to paraphrasing the Scriptures and to lauding a patron's many Christian virtues, particularly that of Christian charity.

Does it make sense, then, to suppose that Chrétien wrote such a prologue to introduce an Arthurian romance, made up of numerous meaningless and loosely connected incidents, intended to be interpreted only on a literal level? Or is it more reasonable to suppose that such a prologue was destined to introduce an allegorical tale with a serious moral, filled with the popular liturgical symbolism of the day and calculated thereby to please Philip of Flanders who "chérit sainte Eglise . . . hait toute vilenie . . . qui n'écoute nulle laide plaisanterie, nulle parole sotte"?[1]

In order that the prologue may be properly understood, we give it in entirety (from the Foulet translation) along with sources where these are traceable; the italics are the author's.

Chrétien	Sources
Qui sème peu récolte peu, et qui veut recueillir fera bien de choisir un terrain qui lui rende au centuple ce qu'il y aura mis.	*He who soweth sparingly, shall also reap sparingly;* and he who soweth in blessing shall also reap of blessings [St. Paul, II Cor. 9:6].
En terre qui rien ne vaut, la graine sèche et meurt.	*And other some fell upon stony ground,* where they had not much earth: and they sprung up immediately, because they had no deepness of earth; And when the sun was up, *they were scorched:* and because they had not root, *they withered away* [Parable of the Sower, Matt. 13:5-6].
Chrétien veut sémer le roman qu'il commence en si *bon lieu qu'il ne puisse manquer d'en tirer une riche moisson;* car il le fait pour le plus preux qui soit en tout l'empire de Rome: c'est le comte Philippe de Flandre, qui vaut mieux que ne fit Alexandre en son temps. On loue beaucoup Alexandre, mais il est clair qu'il n'approche pas du comte, car il avait en lui toutes les	And others fell upon *good ground: and they brought forth fruit,* some an hundred-fold, some sixty-fold, and some thirty-fold [Matt. 13:8]. But *he that received the seed upon good ground, this is he that heareth the word, and understandeth, and beareth fruit,* and yieldeth the one an hundred-fold, and another sixty, and another thirty [Matt. 13:23].

1. Chrétien de Troyes, *Perceval le Gallois,* français moderne par Lucien Foulet, introd. par Mario Roques (Paris, 1947), p. 3.

faiblesses et tous les vices dont le comte est exempt et net. Le comte est tel qu'il n'écoute nulle laide plaisanterie, nulle parole sotte. S'il entend dire du mal d'autrui, il en est peiné. Le comte aime droiture, *justice*, loyauté, il chérit sainte église, et il hait toute vilenie. Il est plus sage qu'on ne sait, car, sans hypocrisie et sans arrière-pensée il donne selon l'Evangile qui dit que *"ta main gauche doit ignorer le bien que fait ta main droite."* Que soient seuls à le savoir celui qui le reçoit, et *Dieu qui voit tous les secrets* et lit toutes les pensées qui se cachent dans les coeurs et les entrailles! Pourquoi l'Evangile dit-il: "Cache tes bienfaits à ta main gauche"? C'est que *la main gauche signifie la vaine gloire qui vient de l'hypocrisie trompeuse.* Et la droite? Elle représente la charité, qui *ne se vante pas de ses bonnes oeuvres,* mais les cèle si bien que nul ne s'en doute, sinon celui qui a nom Dieu et charité. *Dieu est charité, et quiconque vit en charité,* saint Paul le dit et je l'ai lu, *il demeure en Dieu et Dieu en lui.*

And God is able to make all grace abound in you: that ye always having all sufficiency in all things may abound to every good work. As it is written: He hath dispersed abroad, he hath given to the poor: his *justice* remaineth forever [II Cor. 9:8-9].

But when thou dost alms, *let not thy left hand know what thy right hand doth:* That thy alms may be in secret, and *thy Father who seeth in secret* will repay thee [Matt. 6:3-4].

Therefore when thou dost an alms-deed, *sound not a trumpet before thee, as the hypocrites do in the synagogues and in the streets, that they may be honored by men:* Amen I say to you, they have received their reward [Matt. 6:2].

God is charity: and he that abideth in charity, abideth in God, and God in him [I John 4:16].

Or, sachez que les dons du bon comte Philippe sont des dons de charité; il n'en dit mot à personne, sauf à *son franc et généreux coeur* qui lui conseille de faire le bien.

Every one as he hath determined in *his heart*, not with sadness or of necessity: for God loveth a *cheerful giver* [II Cor. 9:7].

Ne vaut-il mieux que ne valut Alexandre, qui jamais ne se soucia de charité ni de nul bien? Oui, certes, et Chrétien ne risque pas de perdre sa peine, quand, par le commandement du comte Philippe, il rime la meilleure histoire qui soit en cour royale. C'est *Le Conte du Graal*, dont son Seigneur lui donna le livre. Vous saurez bientôt comment Chrétien s'est acquitté de sa tâche.

Thus, in language that is not too difficult to follow, Chrétien tells us that he is about to sow the seed—"the word of God"—in good ground; and the good ground is "he that heareth the word, and understandeth, and beareth fruit." Chrétien has taken the pains to define *charité* in the words of St. Paul and equates it with God in the words of St. John. He has quoted St. Paul verbatim in his opening lines, and he has paraphrased at length the words of Christ as recounted by St. Matthew. In view of the portrait Chrétien has drawn of his patron, it is only fair to assume that Chrétien was thinking in terms of that patron's liberality to the Church and to the Crusades in which he was to lay down his life within a few years.[2] Nor can anyone rightly deny that Chrétien's very first words, translated directly from the Apostle to the Gentiles, have importance for poet and reader alike. It would be nonsense to argue as if the prologue does not set the tone for the poem which it introduces; it is even greater nonsense to suppose that a story is non-spiritual because "specifically doctrinal matter" fills up space in the amount of only 3.73%.[3]

The Church, in Chrétien's day, had taken over the Arthurian

---

2. Cf. Steven Runciman, *A History of the Crusades* (Cambridge, Eng., 1951-55), II, 415: "At last he [Philip of Flanders] revealed that his only object in coming to Palestine had been to marry off his two cousins... to the two young sons of his favorite vassal, Robert de Béthune. This was more than the barons of Jerusalem could bear." This appraisal of Philip does not disqualify Chrétien's view of him in the prologue. The Crusaders in Palestine did not discover Philip's reason for joining them until after his arrival, so Chrétien may not even have suspected anything wrong at the time he so warmly identified the Count with Charity.

3. See R. S. Loomis, "The Grail Story of Chrétien de Troyes as Ritual and Symbolism," *PMLA*, LXXI (1956), 844. Stefan Hofer, *Chrétien de Troyes— Leben und Werk* (Köln, 1954), criticizes interpretations of the *Perceval* as presented by Professor Loomis and other Celticist scholars. Who in twelfth-century France, asks the author, would have been interested in these imaginary Celtic tales of the god Bran? There was no common bond between these strange Celtic heroes and twelfth-century Frenchmen. (See pp. 196 ff.) Hofer analyzes the spiritual ascent of the young hero, an ascent culminating in the love of God— Charity—which the poet had praised in his prologue. According to Hofer, Chrétien's genius consisted in his ability to blend the worldly Arthurian romance of adventure, courtesy, and courtly love with the deeply religious theme of the Grail which gradually gains dominance—the theme of the Passion relics which becomes a sort of leit-motif for the rest of the tale.

theme for its own purposes, both in art and in literature. For example, the Arthurian motif on the Modena portal (Fig. 9) shows that even by the twelfth century the legend of King Arthur had been Christianized and that its liturgical symbolism was understandable to the people of that day. For twelfth-century cathedrals were Bibles in stone and, as such, were meant to be read and studied by those who entered.[4] Then, too, Gautier de Châtillon in the third quarter of the twelfth century had compared, in his *Tractatus contra Judaeos*,[5] the plight of the Synagogue awaiting its Messiah to that of the Britons awaiting the second coming of Arthur. The tract is a dialogue on the theme of converting the Jews to Christianity. Why not believe that Chrétien, in his turn, was working for the Church in like fashion in his *Perceval* and with much the same material?

It is not difficult to understand why Chrétien and his contemporaries were deeply interested in the Synagogue-Church motif popularized by Suger and utilized by Chrétien in his Procession of the Holy Grail.[6] The requisite conciliatory attitude toward

4. "Le moyen âge a conçu l'art comme un enseignement. [A ce temps-là] tout ce qu'il était utile à l'homme de connaître: l'histoire du monde depuis sa création, les dogmes de la religion, les exemples des saints, la hiérarchie des vertus, . . . lui était enseigné par les vitraux de l'église ou par les statues du porche. La cathédrale eût mérité d'être appelée de ce nom touchant, qui fut donné par les imprimeurs du XVe siècle à un de leurs premiers livres: 'la Bible des pauvres. . . .' Tous ceux qu'on appelait 'la sainte plèbe de Dieu' apprenaient par les yeux presque tout ce qu'ils savaient de leur foi.... Grâce à l'art, les plus hautes conceptions de la théologie...arrivaient confusément jusqu'aux intelligences les plus humbles. Mais . . . des générations nouvelles, qui portaient en elles une autre conception du monde, ne les comprirent plus. Dès la seconde moitié du XVIe siècle, l'art du moyen âge devint une énigme. Le symbolisme, qui fut l'âme de notre art religieux, acheva alors de mourir" (Emile Mâle, *L'Art religieux du XIIIe siècle en France* [Paris, 1948], p. vii). "The instant and irresistible success of the new style in France [the Gothic] was owing to its power as a symbol. In a language too lucid and too moving to be misunderstood, [it] evoked an ideological message that was of passionate concern to every educated Frenchman" (Otto von Simson, pp. 135 and 114-5). Beautiful reproductions of the Modena archivolt in question are to be found in R. S. Loomis and Laura H. Loomis, *Arthurian Legends in Medieval Art* (London and New York, 1938), Figures 4-8. The portal is discussed by Emile Mâle, *L'Art religieux du XIIe siècle*, pp. 266-70. See also Fig. 9.

5. See Migne, *P.L.*, vol. CCIX, cols. 423-58.

6. See chap. 7. Our interpretation of Chrétien's symbols has found support in Mario Roques' "Le Graal de Chrétien et la demoiselle au Graal," *Société de publications romanes et françaises*, L (1955). The Grail is a chalice (probably

Judaism had been presented to the faithful in many writings of the Fathers of the Church: St. Gregory the Great, Isidore of Seville, Leo VII, and Alexander II. In the eleventh and twelfth centuries, St. Ives of Chartres and St. Bernard of Clairvaux continued to write along the same lines. Early in the twelfth century, these attitudes were codified in a *Constitutio pro Judeis* which was reaffirmed five times during the century. Besides the *Constitutio* and the papal decrees intended to save Jews from persecution and forcible conversion, there were many popular writings—tracts, handbooks, dialogues or *disputoisons*—composed to guide Christians in religious arguments with the Jews.[7] The Victoria and Albert Museum in London has on display a small Champlevé enamel produced at Winchester about 1160 (under Bishop Henry of Blois—one of Chrétien's patrons?). It shows St. Paul disputing with the Jews. In fact, by 1182 things had come to such a pass in France that Philip Augustus banished all Jews from the country and confiscated their property.[8] In 1187-88, feeling ran high against the Jews in England. The following year, on the day of Richard's coronation (September 3), a notable massacre was inflicted upon the Jews of Lincoln. It is our belief that the movement to convert the Jews and save them from further persecution

---

the one used by Christ at the Last Supper); the beautiful damsel carrying the Grail is Ecclesia; the *tailleor* is a paten (probably the plate used by Christ at the breaking of the Bread); the Bleeding Lance is the Lance of the Passion; the bearer of the Lance is Longinus. For discussions of the Church-Synagogue symbolism see such works as Marcel Aubert, *Suger* (Paris, 1950), *passim*; Emile Mâle, *L'Art religieux du XIIe siècle*, pp. 151-85; von Simson, *passim*. "The iconographic programme was complex: one window would represent episodes of the first crusade, another, the legend of Charlemagne. But Suger's richest innovation was the revival of the traditional reciprocity between Old and New Testament (iconographically known as 'typologic') so that each incident in the life of Christ is shown with its Old Testament counterpart. Moreover, he gave their iconography a new form, synthetic and symbolic" (*The Stained Glass of French Churches*, with an essay by Louis Grodecki [London and Paris, 1948], p. 14). The Synagogue-Church motif symbolized by Chrétien in his Procession of the Holy Grail by the Bleeding Lance and the Chalice can be seen to this day in fine examples of twelfth-century art. See chap. 7 and Figs. 3-5.

7. See Margaret Schlauch, "The Allegory of Church and Synagogue," *Speculum*, XIV (1939), 448-64.

8. See Joseph McSorley, *An Outline History of the Church* (St. Louis and London, 1943), pp. 362-3: "In northern France many of the nobles expelled the Jews and appropriated their belongings; in 1171 the charge of murder caused the death of a number of Jews in Blois; and finally, in 1182, Philip Augustus banished them, recalling them to become royal serfs in 1198."

gained momentum in the hope that these Jewish converts could be used as powerful allies in saving Jerusalem from falling into the hands of Saladin (1187). Is it not significant that the first words in Chrétien's prologue are taken from St. Paul, II Cor., in which the Apostle begs for generous contributions to relieve the poor of Jerusalem? It is historical fact that in Chrétien's town of Troyes the two synagogues were converted into churches: Saint-Frobert and Saint-Pantaléon. Boutiot[9] dates the "conversion" of the former not earlier than circa 1183 and the "conversion" of the latter not later than 1216. Chrétien's own concern in the Synagogue-Church question has been expressed in so many words (Foulet, p. 148; Hilka, vv. 6254-57).

The great sanctuaries of twelfth-century France were sanctuaries in a two-fold sense: they invoked patriotic as well as religious sentiments. We find this two-fold theme also in the great epic poems of the day, particularly in the *Chanson de Roland*. For this was an age, as Otto von Simson has observed, "whose favorite saints were knights, an age apt to look upon the Christian knight defending his Church as a saint."[10] It is in such a light that the choice of subject in Chrétien's *Perceval* becomes intelligible for us, especially when we bear in mind that it was written for Philip of Flanders, who was a Crusader and whom the poet has described (for better or for worse) in his prologue as one who "chérit sainte Eglise."

Twelfth-century Frenchmen, and Chrétien de Troyes was one of them, had a tendency to interpret past history in the light of the present. Surely Charles Martel at Poitiers and Charlemagne

---

9. *Histoire*, I, 262.
10. Otto von Simson, p. 80, note 9. And see, for example, the fresco in the apse of the crypt of Saint-Etienne at Auxerre depicting Christ le Cavalier. In the Chapel of the Templiers at Cressac (Charente) there is a twelfth-century fresco showing a returning Crusader crushing Heresy underfoot; he is being greeted by Ecclesia. In August, 1957, we drove to Cressac hoping to be able to photograph this fresco. However, the doors were locked and there was a notice to the effect that all visits were suspended until the work on the chapel was completed. We were pleased, therefore, to discover that in Paris there is a full-size reproduction of this fresco in the Palais de Chaillot. See Fig. 7.

In the late thirteenth century, Nicholas Bozon tells us in his *Life of Mary Magdalene* (vv. 17-8) that Magadalene's brother, Lazarus, "ne entendi a autre rien Fors chivalerie garder bien."

and Roland in Spain had been Crusaders in every sense of the word. Suger, as von Simson notes,

> had a keen eye for great personalities and great historical **moments**; he had an equal ability to bring them back to life. It is in this vein that he reinvokes the conflict among the major powers of his day, which he had witnessed and in which he had taken so decisive a part. It is a drama played on two levels, the political and the theological, the human and the divine, and Suger is continually trying to render visible the ties that connect the two spheres.[11]

Are we to suppose that Chrétien, as an educated French churchman, was indifferent to all these things and indifferent to the canonization of Charlemagne in 1165 just a few years before the composition of the *Perceval?* And since Chrétien followed Suger in the tropologic symbolism he employed, is there any good reason for believing that Chrétien, in his *Perceval*, was not impressed also by Suger's patriotic and religious bent?[12] In the *Pèlerinage de Charlemagne* (v. 177), the relics which Charlemagne received from the Emperor of Constantinople include the Chalice of the Last Supper. Suger did not permit that legend to die. His window at Saint-Denis representing Charlemagne returning from Constantinople with his relics was based on the *Pèlerinage* (see von Simson, p. 90). Suger's window, anterior to 1145, was imitated some seventy years later in the lower portion of the celebrated Roland window at Chartres.[13] Are we not to suppose then that Chrétien would have thought of the *saint graal*, containing a consecrated host, only in terms of this Chalice of the Last Supper?[14]

To the nascent order of Knights Templar, Baldwin II, king of Jerusalem, handed over a part of his royal palace lying next to the former mosque of al-Aksam, the so-called "Temple of Solomon," on the site of the old Temple of Solomon whence these monks took their name, "Poor knights of Christ and of the Temple of Solomon." Is it not significant, then, that Chrétien should have recalled the Temple of Solomon in his description of the

---

11. Von Simson, p. 73.   12. Aubert, p. 6.
13. Emile Mâle, *L'Art religieux du XIIe siècle*, p. 305.
14. René Nelli, "Le Graal dans l'ethnographie," *Lumière du Graal* (Paris, 1951), p. 31: "Le graal de Chrétien de Troyes (1180-90) est un calice, contenant une hostie, c'est-à-dire le Christ incarné."

Grail Castle, where Perceval is initiated into things of the spirit?[15] For it is here that he beholds the mystic Procession of the Holy Grail and the Bleeding Lance. It is here that he receives his mystic sword from the hands of the Fisher King. The "good ground" upon which Chrétien sowed his seed ("he that heareth the word, and understandeth, and beareth fruit") knew that the sword was one of the distinguishing symbols of St. Paul.[16] And this symbol suggests that, for Chrétien, Perceval was symbolical of St. Paul. This all makes very good sense inasmuch as the *Perceval* is a tale of Christian knighthood, as nobody can deny, and St. Paul was patron saint of mediaeval knights.[17] St. Paul was also the first great convert from Judaism and, as such, would make an appropriate hero in a tale with the Synagogue-Church symbolism used by Chrétien during the Procession of the Holy Grail. Von Simson (p. 121) traces this symbolism straight to St. Paul.

John Mabillon (*Life and Works of Saint Bernard*, I, 145) gives the oath taken by the Templars at their profession. It is interesting enough to be cited here:

I swear that I will defend by my word, by my sword, by all means in my power, and even with my life, the mysteries of the faith, the seven sacraments, the fourteen articles of the faith, the Apostles' creed, and

15. Urban T. Holmes, Jr., "A New Interpretation of Chrétien's *Conte del Graal*," *University of North Carolina Studies in the Romance Languages and Literatures*, p. 13. This is a somewhat revised version of Holmes's article of the same title in *Studies in Philology*, XLIV (1947), 453-76. See also Otto von Simson, p. 95: "Aside from this church [Hagia Sophia at Constantinople], Suger admits to only one other source of inspiration: the Solomonic Temple.... Cosmological as well as mystical speculations prompted many a mediaeval builder to consider Solomon's Temple as a kind of prototype for his own work."

16. Arthur de Bles, *How to Distinguish Saints in Art* (New York, 1925), p. 63: "St. Paul, as a militant proselytiser to Christianity, bears a sword in striking position, and the Gospel. His sword, in such pictures, is symbolic of his earnest fight for the doctrine of his Master." When St. Paul's sword is shown turned downward, it represents the weapon of his martyrdom.

17. Mrs. Arthur Bell, *The Saints of Christian Art* (London, 1901), p. 105: "In the Middle Ages it became customary to explain its [the sword's] constant association with St. Paul by his having been a Roman soldier, a conclusion for which there is no foundation whatever. The belief, however, became so persistent that the Apostle was chosen as their patron saint by mediaeval knights—who, it is said, were in the habit of rising in church when the Epistle was read if it happened to be taken from the writings of St. Paul.... In the Middle Ages, there was a popular saying: 'Mucro furor Sauli, liber est conversio Pauli,' translated roughly 'The sword is the madness of Saul; the book is the conversion of Paul.' "

the creed of St. Athanasius, the Old and New Testaments, with the explanations of the Holy Fathers received by the Church, the unity of the Divine nature, and the trinity of the persons in God, the virginity of the Virgin Mary before and after the birth of her Son.

Furthermore, I promise obedience and submission to the Grand Master of the Order according to the statutes of our blessed Father Bernard. I will go fight beyond the seas as often as there shall be necessity. I will never fly before three infidels, even though I be alone. I will observe chastity. I will aid by my words, my arms, and my deeds, all religious persons, and especially the abbots and religious of the Cistercian Order, as our brethren and particular friends, with whom we are especially united. In witness whereof, I willingly swear that I will keep these engagements. So help me God, and His Holy Gospels.

The careful reader of the *Perceval* cannot but be struck by the many points of this oath which have been put into practice by Chrétien and his young hero. Stefan Hofer (p. 214) has commented on the parallel which Chrétien drew between the worldly knight Gornemanz and the spiritual knighthood of the Crusaders. It is therefore worthy of note that the Templars also took an oath to guard the public roads and to forsake worldly chivalry, of which human favor and not Jesus Christ was the cause (see "Templars," *Encyclopedia Britannica*). It was in 1128 at the Council of Troyes, at which St. Bernard was the leading spirit, that the Templars adopted the Rule of St. Benedict as recently reformed by the Cistercians. Hugo of Champagne went on Crusade three different times and became a Templar just before his death; St. Bernard wrote several letters to him, one in 1125. (See Mabillon, p. 200.) Count Henry II of Champagne went twice to the Holy Land. Philip of Flanders, for whom the *Conte* was written, died in Palestine in 1191.

Chrétien's tale, as his prologue gives one every right to believe, is a deeply mystical narrative in which Celtic details are used for literary adornment.[18] Just as the prologue is written with didactic intent, so is the poem. It must be interpreted on the multiple-sense levels so much in vogue in the Middle Ages: the

---

18. René Nelli, p. 35: "Mais tout ce qui était assimilable du génie celtique et d'un certain Esprit méditerranéen était déjà passé, me semble-t-il, dans Chrétien de Troyes."

literal level (romance of chivalry); the allegorical level (vices versus virtues and Synagoga versus Ecclesia); the moral level (Christian knighthood opposed to the worldly knighthood of Gornemanz); the anagogical level (Perceval's spiritual ascent through prayer and sacramental grace).

It is beyond the scope of this chapter to go into the identifications of the various characters in the *Perceval* and to explain the greater part of the symbolism. That I have attempted to do subsequently. But this much can be said here: Perceval on the Old Testament level can be Saul and on the New Testament level, St. Paul. He would represent the Virtue of Fortitude and the ideal Christian knight. In comparing Chrétien's text with the biography of St. Paul, some impressive analogies reveal themselves.

On the Old Testament level, the Hermit Priest can be Abraham and on the New Testament level, St. John the Evangelist, Disciple of the Eucharist. He would symbolize the Virtue of Temperance. The combination of Saul-Abraham and Paul-St. John for a twelfth-century Frenchman was readily understandable. St. Paul has said: "I say then: Hath God cast away His people? God forbid. For I also am an Israelite of the seed of Abraham, of the tribe of Benjamin" (Rom. 11:1); "They are Hebrews, so am I. They are Israelites, so am I. They are the seed of Abraham, so am I" (II Cor. 11:22). In the Martyrology for October 9, Abraham is referred to as "St. Abraham, Patriarch and Father of all believers." An apt choice for one destined to bring Perceval, the unbeliever, back to God and to lead him to the heights of sanctity. And St. Paul, Gal. 2:9, in opposing his enemies in Galatia, names John explicitly along with Peter and James the Less as a "pillar of the Church"; he refers to the recognition which his Apostolic preaching of a Gospel free from the Old Law received from these three, the most prominent men of the old Mother-Church in Jerusalem. While he was with his mother, Perceval had been much more interested in food for the body than in any spiritual advice coming from her. The Hermit Priest teaches Perceval the lesson of abstinence and instills in him a thirst for the Living Waters, a hunger for the Bread of Life.

In this connection, the Mass for the Saturday of Advent Ember Week is of interest. In the prophecy of Micheas which is read, mention is made of Abraham and Jacob and of the casting out of sin (which recalls Perceval's absolution after his contrite confession to the Hermit Priest). There follows a prayer for grace to abstain from sin as well as from bodily food. The Epistle for the Mass is taken from St. Paul (Heb. 9) describing the Temple of Solomon: the candelabra, the table with its loaves of proposition, the veil, the Holy of Holies, the golden altar, the Ark of the Covenant, the golden urn with the manna, the rod of Aaron which had blossomed, the tables of the Law, and the cherubim. Then St. Paul goes on to say why the sacrifices of the Old Law were inferior to the sacrifice of the New. The Gospel of the Mass is taken from Luke 13 and tells of Christ healing "the daughter of Abraham whom Satan hath bound, lo, these eighteen years." The Communion Prayer reverts to the Feast of Tabernacles (which Chrétien may well have symbolized in his description of the magnificent tent topped by an eagle and surrounded by arbors fashioned from boughs),[19] celebrated in memory of God's leading the children of Israel out of the land of Egypt.

Thus once again the liturgy supplies strong support and provides the probable key in identifying Chrétien's allegorical figures —this time the characters of Perceval and the Hermit Priest. Our identifications are still further strengthened and supported by the fact that the poem was written for a man vitally interested in the Crusades, by the fact that Troyes was the cradle of the Templars whose patron saint was St. Paul, and possibly by the fact that for the benefit of pilgrims on their way to the Holy Land, the Hospice of Saint-Abraham had recently been founded at Troyes.[20] Was it not a group of pilgrims who introduced Perceval to the Hermit Priest?

As for the lame Fisher King, either Chrétien took over an already Christianized lame Fisher King or else he had to go through the Christianizing process himself. What other lame

---

19. See F. R. Webber, *Church Symbolism* (Cleveland, 1938), p. 33.
20. This hospice had been founded in 1179 by Henry the Liberal and was bestowed upon the Bishop of Hebron, in the Holy Land, whose cathedral was called Saint-Abraham. See Boutiot, *Histoire*, I, 226.

character of Biblical times would fit the bill better than Jacob? The Judaeo-Christian interpretation of the poem is the only one which satisfactorily explains the need for healing the lame Fisher King (Jacob), who symbolizes the Jewish people awaiting the coming of the Messiah. Furthermore, even at the literal level, the parallel between Jacob and the Fisher King is remarkably close: Jacob wrestles with an angel and becomes lame with a withering of sinew in one thigh; in the poem, the Fisher King in an unidentified battle is wounded *parmi les hanches* (or *jambes*) and becomes lame (vv. 436-54, 3509-15; Foulet, pp. 13, 82). Then too, Chrétien must have been familiar with Jer. 30 which says that God will deliver His people from their captivity, Christ shall be their king, and His Church shall be glorious forever:

Therefore, fear thou not, my servant *Jacob*, saith the Lord. . . . but I will chastise thee in judgment, that thou mayst not seem to thyself innocent. For thus saith the Lord: *Thy bruise is incurable, thy wound is very grievous.* There is none to judge thy judgment to bind it up, thou hast no healing medicines. All thy lovers have forgotten thee; and will not seek after thee; *for I have wounded thee with the wound of an enemy, with a cruel chastisement: by reason of the multitude of thy iniquities, thy sins are hardened. Why criest thou for thy affliction? thy sorrow is incurable:* for the multitude of thy iniquity, and for thy hardened sins I have done these things to thee. . . . For *I* will close up thy fear, and *will heal thee of thy wounds* (10-17, author's italics).

At the beginning of the poem, when Perceval is conversing with Arthur's knights who have suddenly ridden across his path, he is made to say: "Dan chevalier, Dieu préserve les biches et les cerfs de pareille vêture [un haubert]! Je n'en pourrais plus tuer un seul: inutile alors de courir après" (Foulet, p. 10). In Church symbolism, the running hind represents Naphtali, and a hunted stag stands for the persecution of the early Christians.[21] On the Old Testament level, therefore, Perceval's mother would be Rachel, who symbolizes the Ancestresses of Israel.[22] Chrétien makes much of her lamentations when Perceval departs from her. Compare "A voice in Rama was heard, lamentation and great mourning; Rachel bewailing her children, and would not be

---

21. Webber, pp. 38, 371, 382.
22. See "Rachel," *Catholic Encyclopedia*.

comforted because they are not."[23] These words from Jeremias are incorporated in the Mass of the Holy Innocents. On the New Testament level, Perceval's mother would be the Virtue of Religion.

This interpretation is the only one to date which has even begun to make sense out of Perceval's mortal sin.[24] Perceval, who deliberately leaves his mother (Religion), is truly guilty of mortal sin as Chrétien declares. And again Chrétien is inspired by the teaching of St. Paul: "But if anyone does not take care of his own relatives, and especially of his immediate family, he has denied the faith and is worse than an unbeliever" (I Tim. 5:8). Thus at the very outset of the story, Chrétien has in effect equated Perceval "who has denied the faith and is worse than an unbeliever" with St. Paul or rather with Saul: "Still I obtained the mercy of God because I acted ignorantly in unbelief" (I Tim. 1:13).

Perceval's father, whose malady strangely resembles that of the Fisher King, would be Jacob on the Old Testament level. As described by Perceval's mother, the father recalls the Lord God of Hosts, the Sun of Justice: "The Lord is as a man of war: Almighty is his name.... Who is like to thee among the strong, O Lord? who is like to thee, glorious in holiness, terrible and praiseworthy, doing wonders" (Exod. 15:3, 11). He would symbolize the Virtue of Justice, most important of the cardinal virtues.[25]

That Perceval's parents should recall Christ and the Church,

---

23. Perceval's two elder brothers had been dubbed knights. On the way home after the ceremony, intending to give joy to their parents, they had been fallen upon and killed. Crows and ravens had pecked out the eyes of the elder. In the Mass for certain martyrs (i.e., that of Sts. Gervase and Protase, June 19), the Communion Prayer reads: "They have given the dead bodies of thy servants to be meat for the fowls of the air; the flesh of thy saints for the beasts of the earth" (Ps. 78:2). This psalm is one which describes the Church in time of persecution (see the commentary in *The Holy Bible*, Douay-Rheims Version [Benziger, 1941]). The preceding psalm is concerned with enumerating God's great benefits to the people of Israel notwithstanding their ingratitude and unbelief. The rain of manna is mentioned in particular, and Jacob is here named no less than three separate times. Psalm lxxix ends with the words: "O Lord god of hosts, convert us, and shew thy face: and we shall be saved."

24. See my article, "The Spiritual Ascent of Perceval," *Studies in Philology*, LIII (1956), 8 ff.

25. See *ibid.*, p. 10. We are reminded again of the twelfth-century fresco *Christ le Cavalier* at Saint-Etienne, Auxerre.

often referred to as the Bride of Christ, is again in keeping with St. Paul. The Apostle tells us that the union between Christ and His Church is the archetype of which human marriage is an earthly representation. Thus he bids wives be subject to their husbands, as the Church is subject to Christ (Eph. 5:22). He bids husbands love their wives "as Christ also loved the Church and delivered Himself up for it" (Eph. 5:25). The Church is so truly one with Christ that "we [Perceval-Paul included] are members of his body, of his flesh, and of his bones" (Eph. 5:30 ff.; Gen. 2:24).

Chrétien's symbol of the hunted stag (persecution of the early Christians) prepared his readers for the episode of the sleeping damsel which Loomis[26] describes as "boisterous ... a bit of a farce, from which Perceval emerges without learning any lesson, without any improvement in character." However, the "good ground" in which Chrétien sowed his seed—"he that heareth the word, and understandeth, and beareth fruit"—knew well that the scene of the sleeping damsel should mean one thing: Saul's persecution of the early Christians in which he acted "ignorantly in unbelief"— persecution of the early Church, which Mary symbolizes in liturgical language.[27] Incidentally, the very fact that stag hunts are routine material in mediaeval romance gives to this symbolism an added dosage of familiarity.

It may be argued that such-and-such hypothesis in this chapter depends on coincidence; but so many hypotheses fit together (even if only by coincidence) that the sheer weight of collectiveness reduces mere coincidence and guess to a minimum of importance. On the other hand, the interpretation which Celticist scholars offer makes little sense on the literal level; it takes no account of contemporaneous history or art nor of the temperament of the patron for whom the poem was written. To argue that the *Perceval* is not allegorical because it incorporates certain Arthurian trappings which were stock elements is somewhat illogical. Can it be con-

26. *PMLA*, LXXI (1956), 843.
27. In cathedral art, as in the two tympana of the south portals at Strasbourg, the Blessed Virgin is sometimes used to symbolize the Church. See "La Cathédrale de Strasbourg," *Encyclopédie Alpina Illustrée* (Paris, 1939), p. 2. See also Mâle, *L'Art religieux du XIIIe siècle*, p. 194.

vincingly argued that the *Hound of Heaven* is not allegorical because there have been thousands of other descriptions of hunting hounds which were not allegorical? Or that the *Roman de la Rose* is not an allegory because there are many other poems which speak of roses and which are not allegorical? We who have proposed a Judaeo-Christian interpretation of Chrétien's *Perceval* do not claim infallibility, but we maintain that criticism of our interpretation should be objective and well-documented.[28] As scholars, we are concerned with only one thing: an endeavor to arrive at the truth.

In conclusion and by way of summation, let it be repeated again: Chrétien's tale is in perfect harmony with the history, the literature, and the religious art of the times. It is bound up with the conversion of the Jews, with the suppression of the superstitious belief that Arthur would come again, and with the Crusades. In other words, Chrétien adapted the Arthurian material for a religious purpose—a didactic end—as had been done by the sculptor of the Modena archivolt and by Gautier de Châtillon in his *Tractatus contra Judaeos*. In keeping with the tone of the prologue, his tale, written for a supposedly devout patron who became a Crusader, has didactic implications from start to finish. It fits in with the teachings of St. Paul, whom the poet has quoted verbatim in his opening line. That these words of St. Paul are taken from an epistle in which the Apostle is seeking aid for the Christians of Jerusalem might indicate that Philip of Flanders and Chrétien undertook the writing of the *Perceval*, in part at least, to foster a new Crusade which would go to the aid of beleaguered Jerusalem.[29] In 1150, just before his death, Suger

28. Cf. articles by R. S. Loomis and by Raphael Levy, *PMLA*, LXXI (1956), 840-62. See also *infra*, "Partial List of Scholars," pp. 185 ff. For comments on this contribution by Loomis, see Mario Roques (*Romania*, LXXVIII [1957], 139) and Pierre Cézard (*ibid.*, pp. 274-5).

29. In connection with this hypothesis, one should remember Chrétien's symbolism of the hunted stag (see p. 103), the lamentation of Perceval's mother *(ibid.)*, and the symbolic crows and ravens which pecked out the eyes of the elder brother of Perceval (*supra*, note 23). In this light it is possible that Chrétien's Procession of the Holy Grail represents the Church Pre-Triumphant rather than the Church Triumphant, i. e., the Church Suffering. It will be remembered that Chrétien's *demoiselle au graal* does not carry the processional cross usually associated with the figure of Ecclesia, as in the famous statue counterbalancing that of Synagoga at Strasbourg (frontispiece) and in twelfth-century works of art men-

(whose tropologic symbolism Chrétien followed) was busy organizing such a Crusade. In literature, Chrétien was merely doing what Suger had previously done in art: for didactic purposes he employed typologic iconography which was well understood by twelfth-century Frenchmen who thought in terms of the poetic language of Scripture as kept alive by the Liturgy. In perfect harmony with our theory are two illustrations in R. S. and L. H. Loomis's *Arthurian Legends in Medieval Art*, Fig. 328 *(Perceval's Vision of the New Law and the Old Law)* and Fig. 343 (*The Marriage of Arthur*, where Arthur and his Queen are being united in matrimony directly in front of a statue of Moses holding the Tablets of the Law).

---

tioned *supra*, note 6. Nor does she carry the banner as in the window of Châlons-sur-Marne. The processional cross and the banner are symbols of Christ's triumph over sin and death (see Webber, gloss, pp. 359, 364).

CHAPTER SEVEN

Chrétien de Troyes and the Abbot Suger

TWELFTH-CENTURY ART and literature which have survived in France amply testify to the fact that twelfth-century Frenchmen dreamed and talked in terms of symbolism. In this respect, Chrétien de Troyes was a typical man of his day.

In the preceding chapter (p. 103) we have called attention to a passage occurring early in the poem (vv. 273-6) in which Perceval hopes that God will protect the hinds and the stags from all hauberks, for otherwise he could not kill any of them and would therefore never run after them. The passage is significant, for it gives a clue to much of the rich symbolism which follows. By means of these verses, Chrétien may be implying the Jewish origin of his hero (especially if inspired by the life of St. Paul) and his concern for the persecution of the early Christians, inasmuch as in Church iconography the running hind represents Naphtali and the hunted stag symbolizes the persecution of the first Christians.[1] To appreciate the poet's symbolism, one should refer to Matt. 4:13-16, where Naphtali is specifically mentioned:

And leaving the city of Nazareth, he [Christ] came and dwelt in Capharnaum, in the sea coast, in the borders of Zabulon and of Naphtali;
That it might be fulfilled which was said by Isaias the prophet: Land of Zabulon and land of Naphtali, the way of the sea beyond the Jordan, Galilee of the Gentiles:
The people that sat in darkness hath seen a great light: and to them that sat in the region of the shadow of death, light is sprung up.

1. Webber, pp. 371 and 382.

St. Paul (whom the poet admits having read and whom he has quoted verbatim in his opening line) is, of course, the Apostle of the Gentiles. One will recall the emphasis Chrétien places upon the bright light radiating from the Grail as it passes before Perceval in the Grail Castle. It will also be remembered that Perceval had been reared in the Waste Forest by a mother who "sat in the region of the shadow of death," the young hero's father had died of wounds received in battle, and the elder brothers had been killed as they journeyed homeward after being dubbed knights.

The Chalice and the Bleeding Lance of the Passion which figure so prominently in Chrétien's mystic Procession of the Grail should be the main symbols of the Church Triumphant and the Synagogue. We have referred elsewhere to this motif of the Synagogue-versus-Church which played such an important role in the illuminations, stained glass, and statuary of the Middle Ages as well as in mediaeval literature and to the two celebrated statues of the Strasbourg cathedral which depicted the motif.[2] Of course, these two statues post-date Chrétien's *Perceval*. However, as Charles Morey states,[3] "the introduction of Church and Synagogue into the scene is a French motif dating back to the [tenth-century] ivories of Metz." Among the best examples of this theme in the twelfth century are the portable altar of Stavelot,[4] a North German reliquary in the form of a portable altar now exhibited at the Victoria and Albert Museum in London,[5] Suger's window at Saint-Denis,[6] and the splendid window from Châlons-sur-Marne near the poet's Troyes (Fig. 3). There is a black and white reproduction of the Châlons window in Charles J. Connick's "Windows of Old France," p. 189.

2. "Chrétien's Symbolism and Cathedral Art," pp. 226 ff., 235-236; "The Spiritual Ascent of Perceval," p. 7; see frontispiece and Figs. 3-5.
3. *Mediaeval Art* (New York, 1942), p. 220.
4. See Fig. 4.
5. This reliquary is exhibited in the Central Court and bears the number 4524-1858. It is described by the museum as a "Reliquary in the form of a portable altar. Champlevé enamel on gilt copper; on a foundation of oak. On the top, the Crucifixion, with figures representing the Church and the Synagogue. Round the side, the Twelve Apostles. North German, late 12th century." See Fig. 5.
6. Mâle, *L'Art religieux du XIIe siècle*, p. 166, Fig. 130.

There is no mistaking the identity of either Church Triumphant or Synagogue in these twelfth-century representations, because of the fact that the mediaeval craftsmen have labelled the figures at Stavelot and at Saint-Denis. In each of the four cases—the two reliquaries and the two windows—the Synagogue is blindfolded and is shown with the great Lance of the Passion used by Longinus. Mario Roques, in his "Le Graal de Chrétien et la demoiselle au graal" (Plate III), has given a reproduction of the famous Synagogue-Church theme as it appeared in a twelfth-century illumination, the *Hortus Deliciarum* of Herrade de Landsberg, probably compiled between 1175 and 1195. In this case, as with Chrétien, the lance is in the hands of Longinus. Once again, there can be no doubt as to the identity of the figures, since Ecclesia, Longinus, and Synagoga have been painstakingly labelled by the illuminator. Ecclesia is crowned and she holds aloft a chalice in which she gathers the Precious Blood streaming from the side of the Crucified. Roques has explained the important contribution made by the sacred lance in the triumph of Ecclesia and has offered the interpretation that the continuation of the sins of mankind is the cause of the perpetual wounding of the side of Christ, which effects the continual bleeding of the lance (p. 18). Moreover, Roques shows that for Chrétien the word *graal* meant "un vase d'orfèvrerie monté sur pied" (p. 6). By considering the use to which Chrétien puts the vessel and the manner in which it is carried by the *demoiselle au graal*, Roques demonstrates that Chrétien's *graal* must have been a chalice (pp. 6-7).[7]

---

[7]. Nitze and Dargan, *History of French Literature* (New York, 1938), p. 47, point out that "to Crestien the word [*graal*] was still a common noun." And through the years the argument has been used that in the earliest text, that of Chrestien de Troyes, the grail is referred to as *un* graal and not simply *le* graal. We fail to understand how this argument can prove that for Chrétien his *graal* was not the Chalice of the Last Supper. Is it not true that *the* Chalice of the Last Supper (*the* Grail) was *a* chalice (*un* graal)? Only on one occasion, v. 3220, does the poet use the indefinite article in speaking of the grail. This verse occurs when the poet describes the passing of the grail before the uncomprehending Perceval, and Chrétien thereby achieves an effective air of mystery which would have been lost otherwise. To offset this single instance of the use *un graal*, Chrétien speaks of *le graal* at least fifteen times: vv. 66 (in which he calls his tale *li contes del graal*), 3223, 3232, 3235, 3239, 3245, 3256, 3561, 3565, 6379, 6401, 6413, 6419, 6425, 6428, 6431. See also R. S. and L. H. Loomis, *Arthurian Legends in Medieval Art*, Fig. 204 (Fr. 12576, f. 2617) from the *Conte del Graal*, c. 1250.

Among famous thirteenth-century examples of the Synagogue-Church theme, we might mention in addition to the Strasbourg statues, the central medallion of the Passion window at Bourges (see Roques, Plate I). Professor F. A. G. Cowper has called my attention to another example in the *Breviary of St. Etienne* of Châlons-sur-Marne (about 1297), Bibliothèque de l'Arsenal, 595, fol. 244, and reproduced in Henry Martin, *La Miniature française*. A curious fourteenth-century example is on display at the Yale Art Gallery: *Christ and the Virgin Enthroned* by Giovanni del Biondo of the Florentine School. The painting is described by Oswald Siren, *A Descriptive Catalogue of the Pictures in the Jarves Collection belonging to Yale University*, p. 47:

This is the central portion of a large altarpiece with rich and sumptuous colors. . . . In the pediment above the Gothic arch, which encloses the main composition, are represented the Christian Church and the Synagogue in the shape of allegorical figures. The first is standing at the side of a baptismal font with a chalice in her hand while the Synagogue is represented as a blindfolded woman with a child in her arms. The two large altar wings are in the Vatican Gallery; the whole was painted about 1370.

Over and above this description, we might add that in the upper right-hand corner the blindfolded Synagogue is holding the instruments of the Passion, the Lance and the sponge affixed to a long shaft. She is leading away a child from the bloody sacrifices of the Old Law. In the left-hand corner is another figure of Synagoga being baptized, by immersion, by Ecclesia, who holds in her left hand a chalice surmounted by a paten and a host. The host and the paten *(tailleor)* figure in Chrétien's Grail Procession, too, as Mario Roques notes (p. 21).

But let us revert now to the Châlons window, Figure 3. Connick (p. 190) describes it as follows:

A spirited example of figures on a white ground, unusual in the Twelfth Century, is a fragment from the ancient cathedral in Châlons. In characteristic symbolism it represents the Church and the Synagogue. The church is triumphant with the cross, banner, and chalice, while the synagogue, with eyes bound, holds the symbols of the Passion [the Lance and the sponge affixed to the long shaft used in offering vinegar to the Crucified]. The decorative drawing and the clever use of spaces, with the appreciation of the silhouette, gives this small piece great distinction.

A magnificent reproduction in color of this same window may be seen in *The Stained Glass of French Churches* with an essay by Louis Grodecki, Plate 8. Grodecki (p. 18) dates the glass between 1160-1180. The Musée des Arts Décoratifs, p. 43, adds the following useful information:

Crucifixion, entourée de figures symboliques et de scènes de l'Ancien Testament. Vers 1155.

Ces panneaux, provenant de la cathédrale romane de Châlons, consacrée en 1147 et brûlée en 1230, ont été remployés, mutilés et découpés pour s'adapter aux nouvelles armatures, dans des fenêtres de l'église gothique. Retirés de l'église en 1872, ils ont été exposés à Paris au Musée du Vitrail (1884-1898), à l'Exposition Universelle de 1900 et au Musée de la Sculpture Comparée (1910-1934). Après leur restauration par J.-J. Gruber, ils seront restitués à la cathédrale de Châlons.[8]

Technique. Les parties anciennes ont été complétées par des verres modernes sans peinture, afin de restituer la forme primitive des panneaux; elles ont gardé, par endroits, leurs plombs d'origine, travaillés au rabot, à ailes étroites et âme épaisse. L'assemblage des panneaux se faisait à l'aide d'une armature forgée curvilinéaire; c'est le plus ancien exemple connu de cette technique. Les couleurs sont nombreuses et variées: deux bleus, deux verts, deux jaunes, etc.; le blanc joue un rôle important dans la gamme qui reste claire. La peinture des pièces est très chargée, posée en épaisseur, presque en relief, en plusieurs couches de grisaille.

Style. La composition, en quadrilobe, est semblable à celle des oeuvres

---

8. In July, 1957, these panels were set into openings especially made for them in the walls of the Romanesque north tower of the cathedral. I visited Châlons in August; I am very much indebted to M. le Curé who graciously unlocked the tower so that I might enjoy the treasures collected there. (The tower is to be kept locked until minor restorations on the windows are completed.) Most ingeniously, openings have been made in two of the walls of the tower, high and wide enough to allow the glass panels to be inserted. These openings were not cut through the ancient walls for fear of weakening them and causing them to collapse; but the openings are deep enough to form a hollow niche behind the glass panels. In this hollow niche electrical illumination has been installed. The final effect is one of exquisite beauty and splendor.

d'orfèvrerie émaillée de la Meuse; le découpage concentrique des fonds confirme ce rapprochement. Le style de l'ornementation (les bordures) et des figures est sans rapport avec l'art de l'Ouest et avec celui de Saint-Denis; il est à peu près identique à celui d'un orfèvre mosan, autrefois identifié avec Godefroi de Huy, auteur de *l'autel portatif de Stavelot*, au Musée de Bruxelles, œuvre voisine de 1155. C'est à cette même date qu'il faut placer le vitrail de Châlons.

The volume just cited carries an excellent black and white reproduction of the *Synagogue and Church Triumphant* which complemented the Crucifixion window (see No. 7, Planches 4 and 5, "Eglise et Synagogue, vers 1155").

A close comparison of the pictures of our two stained glass figures as reproduced (a) by Connick, (b) by Grodecki, and (c) by the Musée des Arts Décoratifs offers some intriguing discoveries. In 1923 (a) shows a very much blurred first word in the inscription of the circular frame above Synagoga. One is tempted to read: "SALOM OR · SIC (T?) · FER CU." And one wonders if the first word is not a case of a badly restored SALOMON. Then, in 1948 (b) shows a very clear lettering of SALOM (in blue) followed by ON · SIC (in gold) and FER CU (in green). The lettering starts directly over the cross held in the right hand of the Church Triumphant. By 1953 (c) shows lettering which is clear and readable for SALOMON; but the whole inscription has been moved further down to the left so that the wording now starts on a level with the lower edge of the banner suspended from the cross carried by the Church Triumphant. Evidently, the most recent restorers thought more space should be left for the words that were missing in the inscription. But for us an important discovery was that one figure in (c) is referred to as that of "l'Eglise comparée au Trône de Salomon." The other figure is described as "La Synagogue, comparée à l'autel d'infamie (Fiat Mensa Eorum in Laqueum—Psaumes, xxviii, 63 [68:22-23: And they gave me gall for my food: and in my thirst they gave me vinegar to drink. Let their table become as a snare before them, and a recompense, and a stumbling block])." Let us note, then, that in this window of Châlons we have two of Chrétien's most prominent symbols of the Procession of the Holy Grail: the Lance of Longinus (used as a symbol of the Synagogue) and the Grail or chalice in the hands of Ecclesia or the Church Triumphant. And since in the Châlons window the Church is compared to the Throne of Solomon, perhaps one will not go too far wrong in interpreting the Grail Castle as Holmes has done,[9] as an allegorical representation of the Temple of Solomon.[10]

Grodecki (p. 14) says of Suger's windows at Saint-Denis:

The iconographic programme was complex: one window would represent episodes of the first Crusade, another, the legend of Charlemagne. But Suger's richest innovation was the revival of the traditional Christian reciprocity between the Old and New Testament (iconographically known as "typologic") so that each incident in the life of Christ is shown with its Old Testament counterpart. Moreover, he gave their iconography a new form, synthetic and symbolic. . . . With five or six exceptions, the medallions that have been preserved are very much restored. But what remains of the originals allows us to perceive the extraordinary skill of the glass-painters. Colours are pure—limpid and transparent blues, "flashed" and pot-metal reds, clear and sustained greens. Flesh is rendered by pale rose, and modelled in bistre with astonishing precision. Here was an erudite and harmonious craft, undoubtedly the fruit of long experience and perfect balance.

In his chapter on Abbot Suger, Emile Mâle[11] writes:

Je suis convaincu que l'iconographie du moyen âge lui doit autant que l'architecture, la sculpture, et la peinture sur verre. L'Abbé Suger fut, dans le domaine du symbolisme, un créateur; il proposa aux artistes des types nouveaux, des combinaisons nouvelles que le siècle suivant adopta. . . . Un médaillon résume toute sa pensée: Jésus-Christ couronne d'une main la Loi Nouvelle, et de l'autre enlève le voile qui cache le visage de l'Ancien Loi; au-dessous, on lit le vers: Quod Moyses velat Christi doctrina revelat. Qu'un tel homme ait remis en honneur le symbolisme dans l'art, et que de Saint-Denis le symbolisme ait, comme nous allons le voir, rayonné sur toute l'Europe, c'est ce dont on ne doit pas songer à s'étonner.

9. See chap. 4. See also Mâle, *L'Art religieux du XIIIe siècle*, p. 158 and note 6.

10. Cf. Otto von Simson, p. 11: "The Temple of Solomon . . . evoked in the dedication rite [of a chapel or church] and the Temple of Ezekiel were . . . also understood as images of heaven. They, no less than the Heavenly City, were looked upon as archetypes of the Christian sanctuary."

11. *L'Art religieux du XIIe siècle*, pp. 151-85.

Thus Suger's symbolism travelled from Saint-Denis to Stavelot, to Châlons, and to Troyes. And Chrétien seems to have bathed in its mystic waters. It seems most probable to us that Gamaliel inspired Chrétien's portrait of Gornemanz.[12] Is it merely coincidence that one of the Châlons windows, representing the story of Saint Etienne, shows Gamaliel, the celebrated Hebrew teacher, appearing to the priest Lucius (see Musée des Arts Décoratifs, No. 9, Planche 6)? As already shown, in Chrétien's day the Cité of Troyes, as opposed to the Portus or merchant quarter of the town, was confined between two canals (construction began in 1072) which were built around the old Gallo-Roman Oppidum. About all there was to be found inside the Cité was the Cathedral of Saint-Pierre, the collegiate church which was really the chapel of the Count's palace, the Palais, the Broce as Juis with its synagogue, the castellum novum or feudal donjon, and the great Abbey of Saint-Loup. Of course there were the *estuves* or baths managed by the collegiate Church of Saint-Etienne. Plate I in Grodecki shows a fine design of the Ark of the Covenant in a Saint-Denis window. It is our belief that Chrétien symbolized this idea in his Inner Room of the Grail Castle.[13]

12. Gamaliel was a learned doctor of the law of the sect of the Pharisees, preceptor of St. Paul, and adviser of the council of Sanhedrin in regard to their treatment of the Apostles. Ecclesiastical tradition makes Gamaliel become a Christian and relates that he was baptized by Saints Peter and Paul, but the story does not seem to be supported by any evidence. The *Catholic Encyclopedia* adds that in the Talmud, this Gamaliel bears, like his father Hillel, the surname of *the Elder*, and is the first to whom the title *Rabban*, "our master," was given. Jewish accounts make him die a Pharisee and state that "when he died, the honor of the Torah [the law] ceased, and purity and piety became extinct." Chrétien apparently had good reason for clothing Gornemanz in ermine. This small animal, because of the whiteness of its fur and the legend that it preferred death to impurity, is used to symbolize purity. See George Ferguson, *Signs and Symbols in Christian Art* (New York, 1954), p. 14. It will be recalled that when Perceval takes leave of Gornemanz, the latter makes the sign of the cross over him and begs God's blessing on his journey. (See vv. 1351-2, 1694-8; Foulet, pp. 36 and 44.)

13. See chap. 1; see also *supra*, note 10. When he sets out on his final Grail quest, Perceval makes an oath (vv. 4727 ff.) never to sleep more than a single night under any one roof until he accomplishes his mission. This language is reminiscent of Ps. 131:1-5: "O Lord, remember David and all his meekness; How he took an oath to the Lord and vowed to the God of Jacob saying: 'I will not enter the tent of my house, I will not go up to the bed of my couch, I will not give sleep to mine eyes, nor slumber to mine eyelids, Until I have found an abode for the Lord, a dwelling for the God of Jacob.'" In the first part of this psalm,

Marcel Aubert, p. 70, gives a full-page illustration of the "Vase du Trésor," a magnificent eagle that Suger had designed. One wonders if this eagle also influenced Chrétien's description of the blazing eagle atop the tent of the sleeping damsel whom Perceval encounters in his first adventure. But Suger's influence over Chrétien seems quite certain in other respects:

Suger fit aussi exécuter une grande croix, qui avec son piédestal, mesurait plus de six mètres de haut. Elle était de cuivre revêtu d'or et enrichie de rubis, de saphirs, d'améthystes, de topazes, de grenats et de perles. . . . La croix était montée sur un pilier de cuivre doré orné, sur chaque face, de dix-sept émaux historiés, séparés par des plaques de cuivre doré enrichies de pierres précieuses et de perles. Ces soixante-huit petites scènes émaillées représentaient l'ensemble le plus complet que l'on ait encore imaginé de cette concordance de l'Ancien et du Nouveau Testament si chère au cœur de Suger et des hommes de cette époque: c'est ce même thème qu'il avait fait figurer sur la table du maître-autel et sur plusieurs verrières des chapelles autour du choeur.

That Chrétien in his *Perceval* is concerned with this theme of the Old Law giving way to the New is borne out not only by his symbolism of the Synagogue-versus-Church theme (the Bleeding Lance and the Chalice), but also by the words of the pilgrim whom the hero meets on his way to the hermitage on Good Friday:

. . . "Biaus sire chiers,	. . . "Beau sire,
Don ne creez vos Jesucrist,	Ne croyez-vous donc pas en Jésus-Christ
Qui la novele loi escrist,	Qui apporta la nouvelle loi
Si la dona as crestiiens?"	Et la donna aux chrétiens?"[14]

David promises, under oath, that he will build a fitting abode for the Ark in Jerusalem (vv. 1-5). These promises will be fulfilled when the Ark has been enshrined in the Temple (vv. 6-10). (See James A. Kleist, S. J., and Thomas J. Lynam, S. J., *The Psalms in Rhythmic Prose* [Milwaukee, 1954].) This psalm was probably composed and chanted at the dedication of Solomon's Temple. It was one of the Gradual Psalms sung by the pilgrims going up to Jerusalem. (See Charles J. Callan, *The Psalms* [New York & London, 1944], p. 163.) How appropriate, therefore, is Perceval's language as he sets out to discover the truths concerning the mysteries of the Grail and the Bleeding Lance which he beheld at the Grail Castle—an allegorical representation of the Temple of Solomon.

14. Hilka, vv. 6254-7; Foulet, p. 148.

The history of mediaeval glass can be traced in literary accounts from the end of the tenth century, but documented with existing works only from the twelfth, when the art took on a sudden popularity and expansion that seem, like the rapid rise of Gothic architecture, to be in no small measure due to the Abbot Suger of Saint-Denis.

This churchman of humble origin rose to be not only abbot of the great royal [Benedictine] monastery near Paris, but prime minister of the kingdom, which he managed so well while Louis VII pursued the second Crusade as to be titled *pater patriae* by his royal master on his return. Suger's importance for mediaeval art is enormously enhanced by the account he has left us, in his *De rebus in sua administratione gestis*, of his activities as abbot and especially of his reconstruction of Saint-Denis, whose west façade he dedicated in 1140, and choir in 1144. Suger's contribution to Gothic lay in the assembly by his invitation of craftsmen "from all lands" (meaning probably from all parts of France rather than from foreign countries), at a time when the Romanesque was fully developed and ready for new ways; the motley atelier of Saint-Denis was thus a natural crucible for innovations. For the windows of his abbey church, the artists used cartoons of his devising, and though most of his glass is gone, the few fragments that remain are sufficient to show by comparison that the influence of his atelier spread far and wide.[15]

A superb example of the tropologic iconography which Suger made fashionable in his day and which our poet imitated in his symbolism is the portable altar from Stavelot now on exhibit at the Brussels Museum, Parc du Cinquantenaire, 10. At the four corners of the little altar are gilded statuettes of the four Evangelists seated. Around the four sides are twelve small Champlevé enamel panels depicting the martyrdom of the twelve Apostles. The top, or table, of the altar is one of the best examples of twelfth-century art of the Old Law giving way to the New (Fig. 4). At the very center are the words *Sanctus, sanctus, sanctus*, taken from the solemn part of the Mass. Ecclesia at the top of this inset is counterbalanced by Synagoga below it. To the left and right are Old Testament figures celebrated for their faith: Abraham and Isaac, Moses with the brazen serpent, Samson, Jonas,

---

15. Charles Morey, p. 266.

Melchizedek with his Old Testament grail, and Abel. At the upper and lower edges are two series of pictures which complement each other: scenes depicting the Last Supper, Pilate declaring himself innocent of the blood of his prisoner, the scourging at the pillar, the carrying of the Cross, the Crucifixion, and the Resurrection. The pictures are laid out in such a way as to create much food for thought: the sacrifices of Isaac and Abraham, Abel, and Melchizedek offset the Sacrifice of Calvary. Melchizedek with his Old Testament grail is immediately over Christ with His *saint graal* of the Last Supper. (We have elsewhere suggested that the Being of Chrétien's Inner Room is Melchizedek.) Jonas—who was in the belly of the whale for three days and three nights—is immediately below the panel of the Resurrection which he typified (see Matt. 12:40).

Otto von Simson (p. 121) makes the following interesting comments on the windows at Saint-Denis:

> ... In Suger's windows the exposition of Dionysian theology is singularly impressive. These translucent panels, "vested," as he puts it, with sacred symbols, are to him like veils at once shrouding and revealing the ineffable. What they meant to him, what they were to mean to others, is best shown in Suger's selection of the scene of Moses appearing veiled before the Israelites. St. Paul had used the image to elucidate the distinction between the "veiled" truth of the Old Testament and the "unveiled" truth of the New. . . . Suger (*De admin.* xxxiv, 205) obviously leans on St. Paul (*II Cor.* iii, 12-18), who interprets the Moses episode as follows: "Seeing that we have such hope, we use great plainness of speech: And not as Moses, which put a veil over his face. . . ." The frequent mediaeval references to the "blindness" of the Jews—and the iconography of the blindfolded Synagogue—are based on this passage; see St. Bernard, *P.L.*, CLXXXII, 570; also Valois, *Guillaume d'Auvergne*, p. 131. Nevertheless, when it shall turn to the Lord, the veil shall be taken away. For St. Paul, as for Suger, the veil of Moses denotes the dullness of the senses of those not yet illumined by grace; and the "denuding" of Moses, far from being an offense, signifies that the "veiled" truth of the Old Testament has been replaced by the revelation of the New. . . .

In this connection see Chapter 4 and Holmes, "A New Interpretation" (p. 26): "It is evident that Chrétien attached special

Fig. 7 (top). Ecclesia greets a returning Crusader crushing Heresy underfoot, twelfth-century fresco in the Chapel of the Templars at Cressac (Charente), as reproduced in the Palais de Chaillot, Paris (Archives Photographiques, Paris). Fig. 8 (bottom). Two Combats. Jacob wrestles with the Angel; Truth tears out the tongue of Fraud. Twelfth-century bas-relief near the Porta dei Principi, Cathedral of Modena (From R. Salvini, *Wiligelmo e le Origini della Scultura Romanica*, Milan: Martello, 1956).

FIG. 9 (top). The architrave and Arthurian archivolt of the Porta della Pescheria, Cathedral of Modena, twelfth century (Phot. A. K. Porter).
FIG. 10 (bottom). Three Apostles spreading the Truths of the Gospel. Tympanum of western façade, Cathedral of Angoulême, twelfth century.

significance to the name [Perceval]. Perceval 'devines' his name because of the *sens* which it implies. Perceval suggests *perce voile*. . . ." That "Suger leans on St. Paul" as von Simson puts it is seen again in the portable altar from Stavelot: once more we have the blindfolded Synagogue. But we also have a series of Old Testament figures, all of whom are mentioned specifically or by implication in St. Paul, Heb. 11: Abraham and Isaac (11:17-19), Moses (11:23-29), Samson (11:32), Jonas (11:32), Melchizedek (5-7), Abel (11:4). In Heb. 11, St. Paul is explaining the doctrine of Faith. Just as the artist who created the Stavelot altar and the craftsmen who made the stained glass at Saint-Denis used St. Paul for didactic purposes, so did Chrétien.

We are not the first to see a likeness between the manner in which Chrétien and the artisans of the great cathedrals handled their themes based on the rich liturgical heritage of the Church. In *Mont-Saint-Michel and Chartres* (pp. 214-5) Henry Adams compares the Mystery of *Perceval* to "that of the Gothic... rivers of colour." It is extremely difficult to believe that Chrétien in choosing his symbolism would not have been affected by the glaziers who made the Saint-Denis and the Châlons windows under the direction of the Abbot Suger himself. This theory becomes all the more plausible when it is recalled that Marie de Champagne (wife of the Count of Champagne) was a daughter of Louis VII and Eleanor of Aquitaine and that Henry I (Count of Champagne) was one of Chrétien's patrons. As Henry Adams reminds us (p. 214):

The court poet was Chrétien de Troyes, whose poems were new when churches of Noyon and Senlis and Saint Leu d'Esserent, and the flèche of Chartres, and the Leaning Tower of Pisa, were building, at the same time with the Abbey of Vézelay, and before the church at Mantes. . . . While the "Lancelot" gave the twelfth-century idea of courteous love, the "Perceval" gave the twelfth-century idea of religious mystery. Mary certainly was concerned with both.

Since Suger was important enough to be styled *pater patriae* by Louis VII on his return from the Second Crusade, perhaps it is not pushing things too far to suggest that Suger may have influenced not only the artistry and symbolism of Chrétien, but also his political beliefs. Suger had been one of the few persons of any consequence in Europe who had opposed the Second Crusade. In 1148 Suger wrote to the king "again and again to beg him to come back to France" (see Runciman, II, 252, 285). It is even possible that it is Suger's opposition to this Crusade which is symbolized by Chrétien when Perceval's mother (whom we have identified as Religion, the Virtue of Piety)[16] weeps inconsolably as her youngest son, Perceval, departs to become a knight at King Arthur's Court. Perceval's father and two elder brothers had already died as knights.[17] There was scarcely a family in Europe which did not lose father, brother, or son in this costly Second Crusade. And it was this expedition which terminated in Germany with a lamentable persecution of the Jews (see *infra*). The First Crusade, as we have seen (*supra*, p. 114), had been pictured in Suger's window at Saint-Denis.

In view of what we have already said concerning the windows at Châlons, it should be noted that Suger, like St. Bernard,[18] had visited that town: "Quelques jours plus tard (3-10 mai, 1107), Suger, accompagnant son abbé Adam, assistait à Châlons-sur-Marne, à l'entrevue du pape et des ambassadeurs de l'empereur."[19] And, although heartily opposed to the Second Crusade, he was actually preaching a new Crusade at the time of his death in 1151.

Comme on ne pouvait compter sur saint Bernard à cause de la faiblesse de sa santé, il [Suger] serait le chef de la [troisième] croisade. Il réunit les fonds nécessaires, et les fit porter à Jérusalem par les Templiers.... Lorsque, à l'automne de cette même année 1150, la fièvre le prit, légère d'abord, mais qui devint plus forte, il comprit que, vu son âge et son état de santé, il ne pouvait plus espérer conduire lui-même la croisade, "Puisqu'il devait gagner la Jérusalem céleste." Il envoya à Jérusalem un guerrier expérimenté, de sang noble, qu'il avait pourvu d'une grosse somme d'argent, pour étudier les derniers préparatifs. Nous ne savons rien de la personnalité en question, ni du résultat de son voyage.[20]

16. "The Spiritual Ascent of Perceval," p. 8.
17. See chap. 6, note 23.
18. Among the treasures I was privileged to see in the north tower of the Châlons cathedral is the mat on which St. Bernard is said to have died.
19. Aubert, p. 6.
20. *Ibid.*, p. 59.

At the Abbot Suger's funeral which followed shortly after, the Grand Master of the Templars was present.[21]

The four twelfth-century representations of the Synagogue-Church motif which we mentioned above (the Stavelot altar, the reliquary from North Germany, and the windows from Saint-Denis and Châlons near Troyes) all bear a striking resemblance in symbolism. However, in the Châlons glass and on the Stavelot portable altar, the Synagogue is associated with the words of the Jews recorded in Matt. 27:25: "Sanguinis eius super nos et super filios nostros." Chrétien probably thought of those words when he had his pilgrim refer to "the felonious Jews whom one should kill like dogs" (vv. 6292-3). It may well have been events in his own day and in his own Order which inspired Suger to work for the conversion of the Jews by peaceful methods rather than by the sword.

It was at Easter, 1146, that Louis VII took the cross, and the crusading spirit quickly crossed the Rhine. But in Germany, St. Bernard's emissary—Rudolf, a monk from Clairvaux—damaged the cause by raising the cry against the Jews instead of against the Turkish infidel. Persecution of the unhappy Israelites was the first sign of crusading ardor among the German people, and St. Bernard himself had to hurry into their country to counteract the misplaced zeal of his fellow-worker.[22]

In Chrétien's time in France there does, indeed, seem to have been a concerted effort on the part of the Church to convert the Jews.[23] This is evident not only from the *Constitutio pro Judeis*,

21. *Ibid.*, p. 63.
22. See Runciman, II, 254. Also, the enthusiasm of the English for the Third Crusade manifested itself at first by a violent persecution of the Jews, great numbers of whom were massacred in the cities of London and York. These horrible scenes were renewed every Crusade. When money was required for the expedition, it was perceived that the Jews were the depositaries of the general wealth, and the knowledge of the treasures accumulated in their hands seemed to lead the people to remember that it was the Jews who had crucified God.
23. In fact one wonders if this movement is not one of the many things parodied in the *Pèlerinage de Charlemagne*. See Ronald N. Walpole, "The *Pèlerinage de Charlemagne*: Poem, Legend, and Problem," *Romance Philology*, VIII (1955), 173-86, especially p. 176. The Synagoga-Ecclesia theme which was everywhere treated by church artisans in the twelfth century could not have made the Jews very happy. Even on the façade of Notre-Dame de Paris, there were formerly two huge statues of Synagoga and Ecclesia which have since been replaced by nineteenth-century replicas (see Mâle, *L'Art religieux du XIIIe siècle*, p. 195).

to which we referred in Chapter 6 (p. 96), reaffirmed five times during the century, in the papal decrees intended to save the Jews from persecution and forcible conversion, and in the tracts, handbooks, and dialogues composed to guide Christians in their religious arguments with the Jews; it is also evident from the *Tractatus contra Judaeos* by Gautier de Châtillon (and based on the Arthurian theme); it is evident from the universal interest in St. Paul, Apostle of the Gentiles. See for instance the Winchester enamel plaque at the Victoria and Albert Museum (chap. 6, p. 96) depicting St. Paul disputing with the Jews. And see Suger's symbolism, stemming from the teaching of St. Paul, and the Synagoga-Church theme in the *Hortus Deliciarum*, the Stavelot altar, the North-German reliquary, Suger's window at Saint-Denis, and the Crucifixion window at Châlons. Then there was the actual conversion of the two synagogues in Chrétien's town of Troyes, Saint-Frobert and Saint-Pantaléon. We believe it extremely probable that the Church hoped to use such converts as valuable allies in preventing Jerusalem from falling into the hands of Saladin, a catastrophe which took place in 1187. Chrétien's *Perceval* seems to have been part of the movement—its opening words are merely a translation from St. Paul begging for help for the Christians of Jerusalem. Of one thing we may be sure: no literate man of 1180 in Troyes could possibly have failed to know of Suger. What more reasonable than that one of Chrétien's interests and his literary bent should have been profoundly absorbed with Suger's rôle in art, with his influence in religion and politics?

CHAPTER EIGHT

Chrétien de Troyes, the Modena Archivolt, and the Otranto Mosaic

THE CELEBRATED Porta della Pescheria of the Modena Cathedral, depicting King Arthur and his knights (Fig. 9), has been the object of countless discussions. R. S. and L. H. Loomis have treated it in *Arthurian Legends in Medieval Art*[1] and elsewhere. R. S. Loomis follows G. L. Kittredge[2] in believing that Artusius is a form of *Arthur* (p. 32). However, U. T. Holmes states,[3] "Pio Rajna discovered in the Italian archives some Arthurian names and among them was *Artusius (Rom.* XVII, 161 ff., 355 ff.). Faral[4] is not wrong in arguing that this *Artusius* is not the same as *Arturus* or even *Artorius*. It should be noted that *Arturus* is the Latin form of the king's name in the proved references. The other names found by Rajna apparently are later in date than Geoffrey of Monmouth's chronicle." In attempting to prove that the sculpture of the archivolt dates to the first decade of the twelfth century, Loomis leans heavily on A. K. Porter,[5] who has been criticized by such distinguished scholars as René Jullian (see *infra*). Loomis's proof is of a five-fold nature:

(1) Documentary evidence, assembled by Porter and others, testifies to the existence at Modena of astonishingly fine sculptures before 1106.

(2) An examination of the shields, helmets, hauberks, and riding equipment of the Modena figures shows that the archivolt was designed

1. Pp. 32-8.
2. *Study of Gawain and the Green Knight* (Cambridge, Mass., 1916), p. 96.
3. *History of Old French Literature*, p. 160.
4. *La Légende arthurienne* (3 vols.; Paris, 1929).
5. *Lombard Architecture* (New Haven, 1917).

at a time not incompatible with a date in the first decade of the century.

(3) Two of the name-forms *(Galvaginus* and *Isdernus)* on the relief are more archaic and closer to the Welsh than those of Geoffrey of Monmouth's *Historia* of 1136-38, "though of course they appear in forms modified by Bretons speaking French."

(4) Loomis relies heavily on Porter's discovery of Modena's borrowing from San Niccola at Bari.

(5) The name *Winlogee* on the Modena archivolt is clearly derived from the Breton *Winlowen,* and points directly to a Breton *conteur* as the source of the tale.... The Breton contingent to the First Crusade under their duke spent four months of the winter of 1096-97 at Bari.

Loomis admits (p. 33) that "the first three considerations do not, of course, demonstrate conclusively that the carving was made in the first decade of the century. They merely render it highly probable. The remaining considerations are more cogent."

One of the best contemporary authorities on the romanesque sculpture of northern Italy is René Jullian, Directeur of the Musée de Lyon. He has discussed the Modena Cathedral at considerable length in his monumental thesis.[6] Emile Mâle and Paul Deschamps had accepted the second third of the twelfth century as the date for the completion of the façade and its sculpture; A. K. Porter believes they were finished in 1106; Jullian dates the sculpture between 1106 and 1120. He rejects a Provençal influence for Guglielmo (p. 44), who worked at Modena, and sees certain resemblances between Saint-Martin-d'Ainay at Lyon and Modena (pp. 45-6). In his discussion of the Porta della Pescheria (pp. 150 ff.) Jullian examines closely and rejects Loomis's arguments for the dating of its sculpture. According to Jullian, the jambs of the portal can be dated at about 1120, the architrave at about 1130, and the archivolt—which is in question here—in the fourth decade of the twelfth century (p. 153). "Il semble qu'en la [la date] fixant à la quatrième décade du XIIe siècle on ait chance de satisfaire à peu près aux exigences de l'épigraphie comme à celles de l'iconographie vestimentaire." Jullian has remarked correctly that there is little in the costuming of the

---

6. *L'Eveil de la sculpture italienne* (Paris, 1945).

knights which permits one to attribute them to any particular date. There are no mailed chausses, there is an absence of cotte over hauberk, and the shape of the helmet is slightly distinctive.

Loomis[7] declares: "There is, however, one point which may properly provoke startled inquiry: how did a subject utterly without religious significance find a place in the decoration of the house of God? If excuse there was, we do not know and in all probability never will know what it was. But was an excuse necessary?" Loomis then gives several instances where unedifying subjects had crept within sacred precincts: monastic cloisters, capitals of church pillars, tiles of monastic chapels. However, we do not find examples of subjects "utterly without religious significance" carved over cathedral portals in mediaeval Europe. That the Arthurian legend worked itself into the archivolt of the Porta della Pescheria at Modena is proof in itself that by the twelfth century the Arthurian theme had a symbolism which twelfth-century Christians understood. It will be remembered that the Church had taken over this Arthurian theme also in Gautier de Châtillon's *Tractatus contra Judaeos*, where the plight of the Britons waiting for the second coming of Arthur was compared to that of the Jews awaiting the coming of the Messiah. In our "Alphabetical Key to the Symbolism of Chrétien's *Perceval*" we have sought to identify Arthur as Charity, a symbol of Christ. Winlogée, imprisoned in the Tower on Mont Douloureux, we would identify with Truth; her captors Burmaltus, Caradoc, and Mardoc we would identify with Falsehood (Satan), Hypocrisy and Deceit (Judas), and Injustice (Jezebel). This explanation would account for the fact that Winlogée is to be found at Modena in the place frequently reserved in Cathedral tympana for the Crucified of Calvary. We have also identified the lame Fisher King with Jacob, who was lame after having wrestled with the Angel of the Lord. In view of these identifications suggested by internal evidence in Chrétien's *Conte*, the following from Jullian (pp. 46-7) is very pertinent:

La présence d'un artiste étranger auprès de Guglielmo est un fait certain pour le Languedoc. Dans le mur méridional de la Cathédrale de Modène, se trouve maintenant encastré un relief étonnant qui repré-

---
7. *Arthurian Legends*, p. 35.

sente le *Combat de la Vérité contre la Fraude* et, dans un format plus réduit, la *Lutte de Jacob avec l'Ange*. Cette œuvre n'est pas seulement isolée matériellement dans l'ensemble du monument, elle l'est encore par son style. On l'a prétendue parfois d'inspiration bourguignonne et, récemment encore, M. de Francovich, la rattachant, assez arbitrairement à mon sens, à l'activité des successeurs de Guglielmo qui ont travaillé aux sculptures du flanc méridional de la Cathédrale, y voyait le témoin le plus significatif d'un courant d'influence bourguignonne parvenu en Émilie dans le second quart du XIIe siècle; il y a effectivement quelques affinités entre cette œuvre et la sculpture bourguignonne, mais elles ne sont pas aussi étroites qu'on veut bien le dire et ne permettent guère de rapprochement précis. On peut signaler cependant une ressemblance, qui n'a pas été indiquée, entre la tête de la Vérité et celle de saint Paul sur le chapiteau du Moulin mystique à Vézelay.[8] Les ressemblances avec la sculpture languedocienne apparaissent bien plus fortes: c'est parmi les sculptures de Souillac ou du porche de *Moissac* [italics mine] qu'on trouve les meilleurs termes de comparaison.

Loomis (*Arthurian Legends*, pp. 32-3), in describing the tower in which Winlogée is imprisoned, speaks of the moat surrounding it and mentions "the double-ax pattern to depict water." In this connection, cf. Mâle:

Un chapiteau de *Moissac* [italics mine here and after] nous montre dans la scène du sacrifice d'Abraham une particularité singulière: Isaac est monté sur un tertre qui semble fait de petites vagues recourbées. Cette étrange façon de dessiner les montagnes avait été adoptée par les miniaturistes du Midi; elle se rencontre dans l'*Apocalypse* de Saint-Sever aussi bien que dans le beau Lectionnaire de l'école de Limoges [B. N. latin 9438, f° 20 v°]. Les sculpteurs ont parfois imité le procédé des miniaturistes. En Espagne, un bas-relief du cloître de Silos, étroitement apparenté à notre art méridional, représente la Descente de Croix; on y remarque que *le rocher du Golgatha* [Chrétien's Mont Douloureux?] *est fait d'une superposition de petites vagues:* l'imitation n'est pas ici moins évidente qu'à Moissac.[9]

Speaking of the Modena reliefs on the southern façade of the Cathedral, Jullian continues (p. 47):

---

8. See also Mâle, *L'Art religieux du XIIe siècle*, pp. 166-7 and Fig. 132.
9. *Ibid.*, p. 20.

L'auteur du relief des Combats est un Aquitain qui... fait jaillir de son ciseau impétueux, habitué à sculpter dans la lumière ardente du ciel toulousain, deux groupes où la passion s'exprime en blanc et en noir. (Pietro Toesca l'a bien vu, tandis que Porter se trompe manifestement en attribuant l'œuvre à Guglielmo lui-même).... Il nous est d'ailleurs difficile de connaître l'importance exacte de son œuvre. Le relief a été utilisé pour la construction même du mur à une place quelconque, au point même qu'un des piliers sur lesquels s'appuie la Porte des Princes interrompt le corps de Jacob et l'inscription qui explique la scène. Cette sculpture était de toute évidence vouée primitivement à un autre rôle. Faisait-elle partie d'une Psychomachie à laquelle auraient travaillé un ou plusieurs artistes languedociens fixés à Modène et que l'on aurait destinée à la décoration d'une partie importante de la façade? Etait-elle l'unique témoignage laissé par un sculpteur nomade ayant séjourné quelque temps dans l'atelier de Guglielmo avant de poursuivre sa route vers des pays plus lointains? Il est impossible de le dire, mais peu importe, car le fait intéressant et qui demeure, c'est la présence d'un sculpteur languedocien sur les chantiers de Modène au début du XIIe siècle.

If our interpretation of the Arthurian archivolt is correct, there is, of course, a close connection between the archivolt and the bas-reliefs of the two *Combats* (Fig. 8). Was Chrétien familiar with the carvings on the Cathedral? It would be interesting to know; but in any event, it is surely curious that, in speaking of the assault of the tower on Mont Douloureux into which Gawain has penetrated, Chrétien should write:

Lors veïssiez vilains angrés,	Alors il aurait fallu voir des vilains
Qui pranent *haches* et jusarmes;	en fureur prendre *haches* et guis-
Cil prant *un escu sanz anarmes*,	armes, d'autres *un écu veuf de sa*
Et cil *un huis* et cil un van.	*guiche*, d'autres encore un van ou
Li crïere crie le ban,	un battant de porte. Le crieur
Et trestoz li pueples aüne.	crie le ban et tout le peuple s'as-
Sone li sainz de la comune	semble; les cloches de la commune
Por ce que nus n'an i remaingne;	sonnent, il ne faut pas qu'un seul
N'i a si mauvés qui ne praingne	manque à l'appel. Il n'y a si
Forche ou flael ou pic ou *mace:*	pauvre hère qui ne saisisse fourche
Ainz por assaillir la limace	ou fléau ou *massue* ou pique. Ja-
N'ot an *Lombardie* tel noise;	mais encore pour assaillir la limace

N'i a si petit qui n'i voise Et qui aucune arme n'i port. (Hilka, vv. 5936-49; my italics)	il n'y eut en *Lombardie* un tel tohu-bohu. *Il n'est si petit qui n'accoure,* et aucun qui vienne les mains vides. (Foulet, p. 139; my italics)

Given that we have here a direct allusion to the Latin poem *De Lombardo et lumaca*[10] it is probably only coincidence that Chrétien should have mentioned Lombardy in describing the scene so vividly depicted on the celebrated Lombard Cathedral. Yet it is very possible that the sculptors of the Modena archivolt and Chrétien were familiar with a common source from which the thirteenth-century *Roman de Lancelot* also stemmed. Emile Mâle[11] suggests as a possible source some version of the *Chevalier aux deux épées*. Many of the Modena figures are not named in the *Perceval,* but we do find there Arthur of Britain, Gawain with his two shields, and Keu. And in vv. 4724 ff. Chrétien writes:

"Et je sor le Mont Dolereus, Fet Kahedins, monter irai Ne jusque la ne finerai."	"Et moi, dit Kahedin, je monterai sur le Mont Douloureux, et je ne m'arrêterai pas avant." (Foulet, p. 112)

Loomis[12] points out that the Duke of Brittany was associated with Robert Curthose, Duke of Normandy, destined to achieve glory at the siege of Antioch, and that William of Malmesbury mentions Robert's showering of wealth into the laps of mimes and worthless fellows. Loomis conjectures that one of the *mimi* whom the Duke rewarded so lavishly was responsible for having provided the theme of the Modena archivolt. This is, indeed, possible; it is certainly very probable that the tale of Arthur had been popularized in Italy by the Crusaders. And Loomis well notes William of Malmesbury's reference to "that Arthur concerning whom the trivial tales of the Bretons rave wildly even today," a point which "illustrates the hostility between the secular story-tellers and the monks." But what possible explanation is there for the Arthurian tale appearing in the Modena Cathedral

---

10. Cf. Hilka's edition of *Perceval,* p. 731.
11. *L'Art religieux du XIIe siècle,* p. 269.
12. *Arthurian Legends,* p. 34.

archivolt unless we are willing to believe that this legend had been thoroughly Christianized by the twelfth century, that the archivolt represented the liberation and diffusion of Truth, which was the ostensible aim of every Crusader? Incidentally, San Geminiano, in whose honor the Cathedral was built, was renowned primarily because of his tireless efforts to spread truth and crush heresy.

Mâle describes (p. 402) the tympanum over a portal of one of the transepts in the Angoulême Cathedral (Fig. 10):

On voit dans chaque tympan trois apôtres, qui semblent marcher d'un pas rapide, un livre à la main, et, parmi eux, saint Pierre se reconnaît à ses clefs (fig. 230). Ils s'en vont, maintenant que leur maître a disparu, porter sa parole jusqu'aux extrémités du monde. C'est la diffusion de l'Evangile sur la terre. La nécessité d'enfermer douze apôtres dans quatre tympans a obligé l'artiste à les grouper trois par trois. Ces mêmes apôtres, groupés de la même manière, se retrouvent pareils à Saint-Amand-de-Boixe, dans la Charente; ils sont l'œuvre du même atelier.

This is all that Mâle says of the tympanum at this point. One wonders how he interprets the strange beast in the beautiful design of the archivolt above the tympanum, and the warriors on horseback on the architrave. For the more one studies mediaeval cathedral tympana, the more one is struck by the unity of theme which usually pervades each of them. Then (pp. 310-11) Mâle raises the thought-provoking questions:

Que signifie, au portail de l'Abbaye aux Dames de Saintes, cette scène romanesque qui décore un chapiteau du portail de gauche: deux chevaliers s'élançant l'un contre l'autre, pendant que des femmes se désolent ou essaient de les retenir? Quel poème a inspiré l'artiste? quelle chanson chantée par les jongleurs pour les pèlerins de Saint-Jacques qui s'arrêtaient à Saintes? Nous ne le saurons peut-être jamais. Quels sont, à la cathédrale d'Angoulême, ces cavaliers qui attaquent un château, et qui font penser aux chevaliers de la Table Ronde de Modène? Quel est ce Sarrasin qu'on voit jouer aux échecs avec un roi chrétien dans un fresque de Notre-Dame du Puy? Nous sentons que tous ces sujets sont empruntés à l'épopée, mais nous ne pouvons en expliquer aucun avec certitude.

That these carvings are related seems most likely. And, starting with the Angoulême tympanum, perhaps we can offer a possible solution. Angoulême and Saintes are both very close to the twelfth-century chapel at Cressac, which has a charming fresco employing some of Chrétien's symbolism. It has been reproduced in Larousse[13]; the caption reads: "Un prince victorieux, au retour des Croisades, après avoir foulé l'Hérésie, est accueilli par l'Eglise." The Pope had selected Adhemar, bishop of Le Puy, as leader of the First Crusade. In him was vested the central authority; he was the moral head of the whole Crusade, representing the Pope, who had created the movement. Does it not seem plausible, therefore, that these three churches—Saintes, Angoulême, and Notre-Dame du Puy—all depict scenes of the First Crusade? For the zealous Crusaders, this was God's war; the idol-worshipers of Satan had troubled Him—the beast Leviathan was rising from the sea. The hordes of Anti-Christ had pitched their tents opposite the holy city of Jerusalem. The heavenly city was calling. And so the stone carvers depicted the Crusaders going to free Jerusalem, God's city.

If interpreted in this light, the Angoulême portal has exquisite unity. In the archivolt is shown the beast Leviathan, with Bohemoth at the very center top. Then there are the three Apostles hurrying to spread the Gospel to the utmost bounds of the earth: Peter with his keys (as Mâle has observed), Paul almost always associated with him in the Liturgy (and also patron saint of mediaeval knights), and Andrew with his nets. It was the last who had revealed to the weary Crusaders the whereabouts of the sacred Lance which had led them to such glorious victory at Antioch.[14] Then, on the architrave below are the mediaeval Crusaders who, in their turn, are rushing to spread the Gospel by freeing Jerusalem from the Moslems. In the center is a standard which to twelfth-century Frenchmen must have symbolized the sacred Lance. If one looks closely, one can find the circular shields and short swords of the Moslems. This was, indeed, an age "whose favorite saints were knights, an age apt to look upon the Christian

---

13. *Histoire de France* (2 vols.; Paris, 1954), I, 232.
14. See Runciman, I, 241-7, 253-4, 273-4 etc.

knight defending his Church as a saint."[15] In trying to understand the Arthurian archivolt at Modena, let us recall Loomis's theory that the theme may have been suggested by members of the First Crusade and Jullian's conclusion that artisans from Languedoc had worked on it. Then let it be remembered that Adhemar, leader of that Crusade, had been bishop of Le Puy.

Mâle has compared the Modena sculpture not only with that of Angoulême but also with that of San-Niccolà at Bari on the route to Jerusalem. He remarks (p. 266) that if it cannot be proved that Roland figured in the Vercelli mosaics, yet it is certain that he is portrayed in the portal of the Verona Cathedral, where on the sword of the hero is engraved *Durindarda* (Durandal), and the author notes that it was at Vercelli that the route of St. Bernard met that of Mont-Cenis and that Verona is on the Venice route—many of the Crusaders preferring to sail from Venice rather than from Bari or Brindisi. For, after all, Venice had the body of the Evangelist Mark, and was therefore, after Rome and Gargano, the most celebrated pilgrim shrine in Italy. He adds (p. 268):

Le pavé de la cathédrale d'Otrante, exécuté, nous dit une inscription entre 1163 et 1166, nous montre à côté des scènes de la Génèse et du Jugement dernier, le roi Artus monté sur un animal fabuleux. On lit son nom près de lui: Rex Arturus. On se souvient qu'Otrante était avec Brindisi, le port où les pèlerins s'embarquaient pour la Terre Sainte.

This series of cathedrals along the old pilgrim routes of the Crusaders seems to testify to the fact that in the minds of twelfth-century Christians there was a close connection between the Apostles spreading the Gospel, the Crusaders fighting under the standard of the Holy Lance to free Jerusalem, and the knights of King Arthur in search of the Holy Grail and the Bleeding Lance— both relics of the sacred Passion. It is not surprising, therefore, as Stefan Hofer, Mario Roques, and Mme Lot-Borodine have remarked, that Chrétien should have employed the two symbols in such close proximity in his mystical Procession at the Grail Castle. We have seen (in chap. 7) the pains Suger had taken to

---

15. Von Simson, p. 80.

memorialize in stained glass at Saint-Denis the legend that Charlemagne had brought back to France from his Crusade the Chalice of the Last Supper along with other priceless relics. We saw how the legend was again immortalized in the celebrated Roland window at Chartres. It is not strange then that King Arthur, whose knights were pledged to seek the Bleeding Lance and the Holy Grail, should often find his place in mediaeval art side by side with the French Charlemagne. See, for instance, their representations in the Hansasaal of the Rathaus at Cologne, in the MS Bib. Nat. Fr. 12559, f. 125, and in a mural of La Manta.[16] By the twelfth century, the Arthurian legend had already taken on profoundly mystical implications. (The Biblical scenes surrounding Arthur in the Otranto mosaic attest this fact.) These mystical implications may already have been incorporated in the *livre* to which Chrétien refers (vv. 67, 2723, 2807, 4617, 6217) and may well have provided the theme for some of these twelfth-century cathedrals where Arthurian scenes are depicted. Chrétien's names *Montesclaire* (4706) and *Mont Douloureux* (4724) must have had religious connotation for Chrétien's contemporaries. Surely the poet was not merely writing so many words when he said:

Mes qui voldroit le pris avoir De tot le mont, je cuit savoir Le leu et la piece de terre Ou l'an le porroit miauz conquerre, Se il estoit qui l'osast feire: *Au pui qui est soz Montescleire* A une dameisele assise. Mout grant enor avroit conquise Qui le siege an porroit oster Et la pucele delivrer, Si avroit totes les loanges, *Et l'Espee as Estranges Ranges Porroit çaindre tot a seür* Cui Deus donroit si buen eür. (Hilka, vv. 4701-14; author's italics)	Mais qui voudrait avoir le prix par dessus tous les chevaliers du monde, je crois connaître la pièce de terre où on pourrait plus sûrement le conquérir, si on avait la hardiesse. C'est sur *une colline que domine Montesclaire.* Là une demoiselle est assiégée: qui pourrait lever le siège et délivrer la pucelle, il y acquerrait un suprême honneur. Mieux encore, *il pourrait, celui à qui Dieu donnerait cette victoire, ceindre sans crainte l'épée aux étranges attaches.* (Foulet, p. 111; author's italics)

---

16. Loomis, *Arthurian Legends*, Plates 11, 13, 14.

In the Modena archivolt, the tower is on the very top of the "Ascent" and replaces the Cross of Calvary which so frequently figures in cathedral tympana. We have noted *supra* (p. 126) that Golgotha had elsewhere been represented by a superposition of little waves as here at Modena. For the Crusader, was it not true that "the kingdom of heaven suffereth violence and the violent bear it away" (Matt. 11:12)? Is not this the interpretation that fits equally well the Charlemagne-Roland windows at Saint-Denis and at Chartres, the Crusade windows in the same two places, the fresco at Cressac of the returning Crusader, the Angoulême tympanum, and the Arthurian motifs at Otranto and at Modena? It should be noted that this verse of St. Matthew is taken from a chapter in which Christ upbraids the Jews for their incredulity. Does this not all readily fit Chrétien's words just cited, where we are told that he to whom God would grant the victory of liberating Winlogée (Truth) could, without fear, gird the sword ("not of man" [Faith])?[17]

As for the architrave below the Arthurian theme at Modena, is it not very possible that the mythical monster at the left, ridden by an ugly misshapen man, may symbolize Leviathan as at Angoulême?[18] Whether the immediate inspiration of the two medallions at Modena, showing cocks with the fox, is the *Renart* is difficult to say. (The same motif is to be seen in the mosaic of the floor near the north portal in the Cathedral of San Marco, Venice.) But from the earliest times, the fox and the wolf have stood for craftiness, deceit, sin, and the devil, in the iconography of the Church. Birds represented human souls.[19] In a vine, birds represented souls abiding in Christ. The last medallion of the architrave shows the fox together with birds and the vine.

Satan, in Church iconography, is also represented frequently by a serpent and by the ostrich. The serpent is plainly discernible in the second medallion from the right in the Modena architrave. It is extremely possible that the conventionalized birds in this medallion are ostriches. In Isa. 43, which Isaias begins, "And now

17. See Isa. 27:1, 31:8, and "Alphabetical Key" under Sword.
18. The *New Catholic Dictionary* (Vatican Edition, 1929) defines Leviathan as "an enormous beast. . . . It may have had the indefinite signification of a monster. . . ." See Fig. 9.
19. Webber, p. 259.

thus saith the Lord that created thee, O Jacob, and formed thee, O Israel: Fear not for I have redeemed thee, and called thee by the name: thou art mine," and where he expostulates with the Jews for their ingratitude, he continues (verse 20): "The beast of the field shall glorify me, the dragons and the ostriches...."

It is more than possible that the architrave of the Porta della Pescheria was inspired by this passage. As a matter of fact, Isaias is one of the Prophets prominently portrayed in a jamb of the great central portal of the western façade.[20] In view of his countless references to Jacob, it is not strange that we find near the Portal of the Princes the bas-relief of Jacob wrestling with the Angel. And if one takes into account the main carvings of the Cathedral, one is impressed by the theme which is common to most of them: man's struggle with Satan. Thus, at Modena the sculptors have treated the story of Adam and Eve and of Cain and Abel, counterbalancing that of Noah. Then there are the two *Combats* (Fig. 8) mentioned *supra*, p. 126: Truth wrestling with Fraud and Jacob wrestling with the Angel. Finally, there is the architrave of the Porta della Pescheria with its many symbols of Satan and Sin, effectively counterbalanced by the motif of the archivolt, the liberation of Truth on Calvary's hill. If one is familiar with the Scriptures, it is impossible to hold with A. K. Porter that the sculpture of the Modena Cathedral is bereft of iconography.

One must not underestimate the importance of Biblical knowledge in the lives of mediaeval men. We have seen *supra* (chap. 6, pp. 99 ff.) that at their profession, the Templars took an oath to defend by word, by sword, by all means in their power, even with life, the sacred mysteries of the Faith, the Seven Sacraments, the fourteen Articles of the Faith, the Apostles' creed and the creed of St. Athanasius, the *Old* and the *New Testament*, with the explanations of the Holy Fathers of the Church. It is inconceivable that the sculptors at Modena were not inspired by their knowledge of the Scripture in general. The *Benedicite* (Canticle of the Three Youths, Dan. 3:26 ff.) and the *Laudate* (Ps. 148) which follows it in the *Little Office* have much in common and

---

20. See Jullian, Plate XVI, 2.

FIG. 11. The King Arthur Tapestry (part of the Nine Heroes Tapestries), about 1385, as it appears today (Courtesy of The Metropolitan Museum of Art, The Cloisters Collection, Munsey Fund, 1939, and Purchase, 1947).

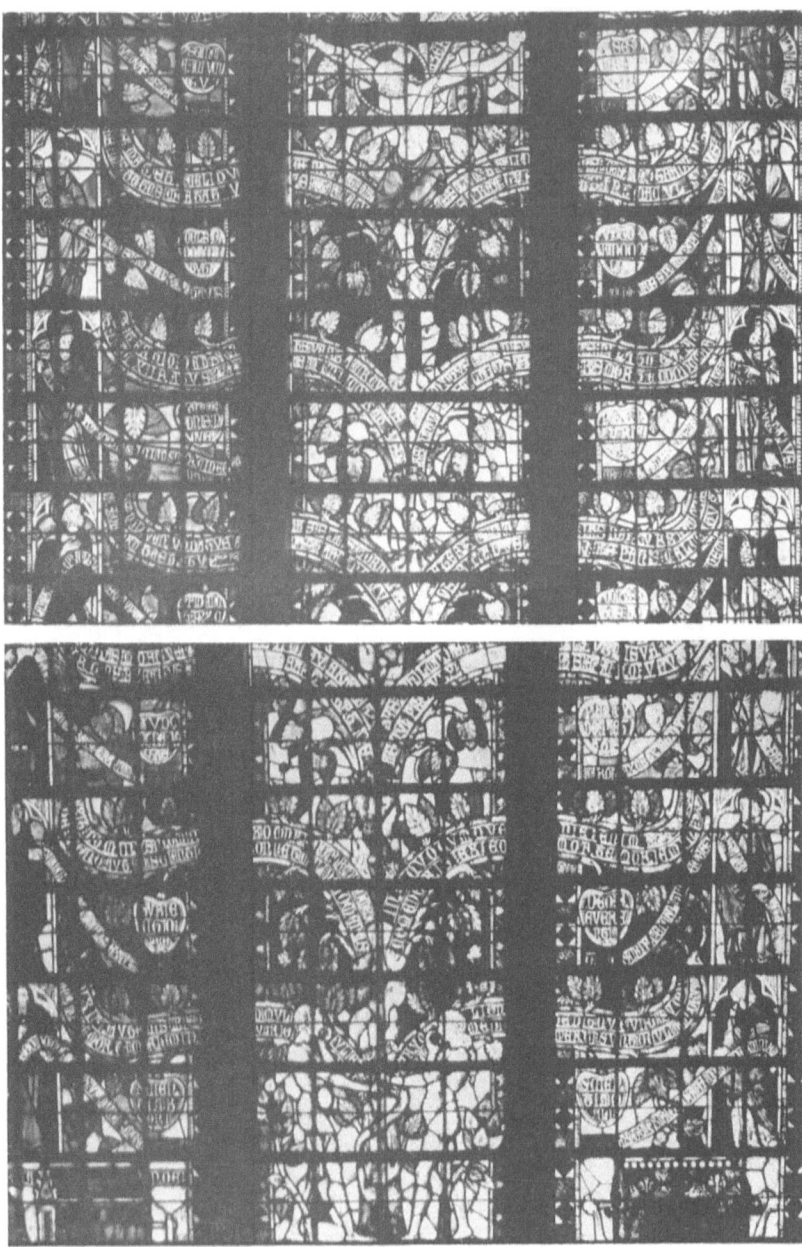

Fig. 12. The Tree of Life, twelfth-century window in the Church of Saint-Nazaire, Carcassonne. At the top, the Crucified Christ; at the bottom, Adam and Eve between Noah's Ark and the Ark of the Covenant (Archives Photographiques, Paris).

Chrétien, Modena, and Otranto 135

may well have had a part in inspiring those who designed the Porta della Pescheria, particularly the architrave.

The Benedicite	*The Laudate* (vv. 7 ff.)
Ye mountains and hills, bless the Lord: *all ye things that spring up on earth*, bless the Lord. [See second medallion] Ye fountains, bless the Lord: ye seas and rivers, bless the Lord. Ye *whales* and all that move in the waters, bless the Lord: all *ye fowls of the air*, bless the Lord. All *ye beasts* and cattle, bless the Lord: ye sons of men, bless the Lord. Let Israel bless the Lord: let them praise and exalt Him forever.	Praise the Lord from the earth, *ye dragons* and all ye deeps: Mountains and all hills, fruitful trees and all cedars: *Beasts* and all cattle; *serpents* and *winged fowls:* Kings of *the earth* and all peoples; princes and all judges of the earth. Young men and maidens, let the old with the younger praise the name of the Lord, for the name of Him alone is exalted. . . . A hymn for all His saints, for the children of Israel, a people approaching Him. (author's italics)

As for the fox which appears in the Modena architrave, in the mosaic of the floor at San Marco (Venice), and again in the Otranto mosaic below Abel with his sacrificial lamb (see Fig. 6), is it not plausible that the artisans should have had in mind Ps. 62:9, recited daily in Lauds of the *Little Office*:

But they have sought my soul in vain; they shall go into the lower parts of the earth; they shall be delivered into the hands of the sword: they shall be the portion of foxes.

This verse leads us to believe that in the Otranto mosaic, the figure being consumed by a fox, below Abel, may well be Cain, "the portion of foxes." And in regard to the foxes of the Modena architrave, cf. also:

Catch us the little foxes that destroy the vines: for our vineyard hath flourished. (Cant. 2:15)

Incidentally, in the Middle Ages, Abel killed by Cain was a symbol of Christ killed by the Jews.[21] In the Otranto mosaic the murder of Abel is worked out in three insets. As for the large

---

21. Mâle, *L'Art religieux du XIIIe siècle*, p. 146.

birds which are seen with the fox in the last medallion of the Modena architrave, cf. Ezech. 17 (the parable of the two eagles and the vine). Before leaving the Modena portal, perhaps it should be noted in passing that in the center of the architrave, below the Arthurian archivolt, there is a beautiful little medallion of purely Celtic origin, an "entrelacs." Is this the sculptor's way of saying that the Church had Christianized those Celtic legends of "that Arthur concerning whom the trivial tales of the Britons rave wildly even today"? Perhaps.

It seems evident that twelfth-century Frenchmen looked upon King Arthur as a sort of *Christus Domini*.[22] Chrétien gives us a hint of this at the beginning of his *Conte*. When Perceval is about to enter the court of Arthur for the first time, he meets and kills the Red Knight who had just stolen the King's golden cup, dons the red armor of his vanquished foe, and returns the cup to the King. Surely this golden cup has special significance for Chrétien, and it must have something to do with Arthur's identity. Henry Adams offers what may prove to be an important clue: "In the central circle [of Pierre de Dreux's rose window], Christ as King is seated on a royal throne, both arms raised, one holding the golden cup of eternal priesthood, the other, blessing the world" (p. 187). We would identify Arthur with King David on the Old Testament level, with Christ on the New Testament level (see "Alphabetical Key"). Does the following from Ps. 22 (Heb. 23) which is a psalm for David, have more than mere coincidence?

Thou hast prepared a table before me, against them that trouble me [Arthur was profoundly troubled and still at table when Perceval first saw him, because the Red Knight—his worst enemy—had just stolen his golden cup]. Thou hast anointed my head with oil: and my cup which cheereth me, how goodly it is!
And Thy mercy shall follow me all the days of my life:
That so I may dwell in the house of the Lord unto length of days. (vv. 5-6)

Psalm 109 is also a psalm for David—in which it is a question of

---

22. See my two articles, "Some Mediaeval Concepts of King Arthur," *Kentucky Foreign Language Quarterly*, to be published, and "The *Christus Domini* Concept in Mediaeval Art and Literature," to appear in *Studies in Philology*, LVI (1959).

"Christ's exaltation and everlasting priesthood" (see commentators)—and opens Vespers of the *Little Office*:

The Lord hath sworn, and He will not repent: Thou art a priest forever according to the order of Melchizedek. (v. 5)

Chrétien tells us that Arthur's court was at Dinasdaron (vv. 2732, 2753). *Dinas* in Welsh means "castle"; therefore, for Chrétien, *Dinasdaron* could mean the "castle of Aaron."[23] All scholars, however, admit that in Aaron's High Priesthood, the sacred writer intended to describe a model, the prototype, so to say, of the Jewish High Priest. He alone was allowed to enter the Holy of Holies, there to offer incense once a year on the great day of atonement.[24]

We have said before that the meaning of the Angoulême and Modena tympana seems to reflect Christ's words, "The kingdom of heaven suffereth violence and the violent bear it away." The Knights Templar were surely familiar with the celebrated words of their patron saint, "Let us therefore cast off darkness and put on the armour of light" (Rom. 13:12). This whole chapter of St. Paul is devoted to lessons in obedience and charity which were the underlying spirit of the oath taken by the Templars. Obedience and charity are also the characteristic traits of Arthur's knights, with the one exception of Keu, who is everlastingly being rebuked by Arthur for his lack of charity. See vv. 1008, 1240-1300, 2878-81, 4078-81.[25] Is it not, therefore, very likely that the Templars saw in Arthur and his knights a symbol of the Church Militant led by the King of Kings—Christ, Eternal Priest? For the leit-motif of Arthur's appearances is Charity.

If we accept this interpretation, that for the Crusaders Arthur was a type of the Eternal High Priest, it becomes understandable why Chrétien should have incorporated St. John's "Dieu est Charité" into his prologue (v. 47), throughout which the accent is on Charity à la Saint Paul. It now becomes clear why, at the outset of the story, the poet introduced the golden cup of eternal priesthood. This interpretation would explain why, on the Mo-

---

23. Cf. Nitze and Williams, pp. 271-2.
24. Cf. Lev. 23:27; Heb. 5:4-5 and 7:11-12.
25. Foulet, pp. 28, 33-4, 68, 94-5.

dena archivolt, the *Tour Douloureuse* replaces the Cross of Calvary. This would explain why, from the very beginning, Chrétien underscores so heavily the virture of charity in a poem whose hero becomes a vassal of King Arthur. It should not be forgotten that, although Arthur rebukes Keu time and time again for his sharp tongue, he loves him with deep affection (vv. 4338-9). God loves the sinner but hates the sin.

Arthur rules with firmness and gentleness combined. All his knights love, honor, and obey him. His worst enemy is the Red Knight, whom Perceval overcomes. Clamadeus, when sent to Arthur's court after being conquered by Perceval, says on his arrival, "Deus saut et beneïe Le meillor roi qui soit en vie, Le plus franc et le plus jantil" ("Dieu sauve et bénisse le meilleur roi qui soit en vie, le plus noble et le plus généreux!").[26] It is when Arthur is regarded as typifying Christ that one understands why he is so grieved when he fears that Perceval is lost to the court, because of Keu's stupidity and rashness:

"Ha! Keus, con m'avez hui fet mal!	"—Ah! Keu, dit le roi au sénéchal, quel mal vous m'avez fait aujourd'hui. Pourquoi votre langue, votre méchante langue ne peut-elle se tenir de dire des folies? Elle m'aura perdu un chevalier qui en ce jour m'a rendu un bien grand service. . . . Ah! Keu . . . comme vous m'avez courroucé aujourd'hui! Qui eût pris le valet en main et l'eût instruit à l'emploi de la lance, de l'écu et de l'armure, quel bon chevalier il eût fait! Mais il ignore tout des armes, sans parler du reste, et ne saurait même en un besoin tirer l'épée. Or le voici maintenant sur son cheval; vienne à passer un gaillard en quête d'aventure, pour gagner le cheval ne va-t-il pas se jeter sur le maître et l'occire ou l'estropier, car le
Par vostre langue l'envieuse,	
Qui avra dite mainte oiseuse,	
M'avez tel chevalier tolu	
Qui hui cest jor m'a mout valu."	
. . . . "Haï! haï!	
Keus, con m'avez correcié!	
Qui assené et adrecié	
Le vaslet des armes eüst,	
Tant qu'un po eidier s'an seüst,	
Et de l'escu et de la lance,	
Bons chevaliers fust sanz dotance;	
Mes il ne set ne po ne bien	
D'armes ne de nule autre rien,	
Que neïs treire ne savroit	
L'espee, se besoing avoit.	
Or siet armez sor son cheval,	
S'ancontrera aucun vassal	
Qui por son cheval gaeignier	
Nel dotera a maheignier:	

26. *Ibid.*, p. 67.

Chrétien, Modena, and Otranto

Tost mort ou maheignié l'avra;
Que desfandre ne se savra,
Tant est nices et bestïaus,
Tost avra fez ses anvïaus."
  (Hilka, vv. 1240-1300)

jeune homme ne saura se défendre, tant il est simple et de pauvre entendement? L'autre lui règlera son compte en un tournemain." (Foulet, pp. 33-4)

Then, too, there is Arthur's long speech, which in its conclusion recalls the Hound of Heaven:

"Puis m'a si bien a gré servi
Que par mon seignor saint Davi,
Que l'an aore et prie an Gales,
Ja mes an chanbres ne an sales
Deus nuiz pres a pres ne girrai
Jusqu'atant que je le verrai,
S'il est vis, an mer ou an terre,
Einz movrai ja por l'aler querre."

"Puis . . . il m'en servit si bien et si à mon gré que, par monseigneur David que l'on honore et prie en Galles, jamais je ne reposerai en chambre ni en salle deux nuits de suite, tant que je ne l'aurai pas vu, s'il est vivant, en mer ou sur terre. Et je n'attendrai pas plus longtemps pour partir à sa recherche." (Foulet, pp. 95-6)

The primitive rule of the Templars seems to have enjoined them especially to seek out excommunicated knights and to admit them, after absolution by the bishop, to their order; they thus served the useful purpose of both disciplining and converting the unruly rabble of "rogues and impious men, robbers and committers of sacrilege, murderers, perjurers, and adulterers" who streamed to the Holy Land in hope of plunder and salvation. Would this not help to explain why Perceval sends his vanquished foes, one by one, to the court of Arthur, where they must make public confession of their crimes? And would this not help to underscore the priestly nature of King Arthur?

In tracing the identity of Burmaltus[27] we have had recourse to Isaias. He is depicted, as we have stated *supra*, on the left jamb of the main portal of the western façade. Contrary to the opinion commonly held about the Porta della Pescheria, there is splendid unity between the architrave and the archivolt, despite the fact that they may have been put into place at slightly different dates. And how beautifully this portal relates to the Combat of Truth and Fraud near the Portal of the Princes and also to the

---

27. See "Alphabetical Key" under Guinloie.

Combat of Jacob and the Angel. We have already quoted the words of Isaias spoken about Jacob (*supra*, p. 133). But it was Jeremias who prophesied concerning the cure of the "wound of an enemy" inflicted upon Jacob (the lame Fisher King), and his affliction (the mournfulness of the Fisher King). See Jer. 30:10-17, and Chapter 6, p. 103. Is it mere coincidence that on the left jamb of the main portal at Modena, Jeremias takes his place directly below Isaias?[28]

Professor Loomis[29] discusses the representation of King Arthur in the mosaic of the Otranto Cathedral, both before and after restoration (p. 36):

Apparently the Arthurian interest in Italy displayed by the names at Padua and Modena [i.e., *Artusius* and *Galvaginus*] and the Modena relief continued to be felt throughout the century. At Otranto, not far from Bari, the nave of the cathedral is covered by a large mosaic of marble and colored stone. It possesses little of the brilliant color and delicate design of contemporary mosaics in Sicily, but it is a strange conglomerate of beasts and men, delineated with some animation but little beauty, and though it has escaped the destructive mania of the nineteenth century, has suffered considerably from earthquakes and restorers. Inscriptions tell us that it was precisely in the year 1165 that archbishop Jonathan commissioned the work to be carried out by the priest of Pantaleone. *Near the sanctuary* [italics mine] is a curious group (Fig. 9): a man labeled "Rex Arturus," equipped with crown and sceptre, rides a beast identified clearly (by his horns, short tail, and cloven hoofs) as a goat. In front there leaps up a black panther-like creature. Since the figure of the king has been crudely restored, we reproduce, in addition to a photograph, a drawing by Millin now in the Cabinet des Estampes, Bibliothèque Nationale. (Fig. 9a)

One thinks at first of Arthur's combat with the giant cat of Lausanne, the Capalus; and this must be an ancient tradition, despite its localization in the Alps, for Graindor de Brie incorporated it in the *Bataille Loquifer* about 1175 [the date is vague, but it can be only a few years before 1200 at the very earliest], and the Welsh original of Capalus, the Cath Palug, is mentioned in the *Black Book of Carmarthen*, transcribed about the same time, but containing of course much older material. But the panther may be merely one of the

---

28. See Jullian, Plate XVI, 2.
29. *Arthurian Legends*, p. 36. See also Fig. 6.

Chrétien, Modena, and Otranto

multitude of beasts which sprawl rather carelessly around the mosaic; and it is hard to believe that Arthur would enter a conflict with a monster so formidable armed only with a sceptre and riding on a goat!

Is there any explanation for the goat? Only one, and that purely conjectural, has suggested itself. There is ample testimony that Arthur was supposed to be living on in two supernatural forms,—one as leader of the Wild Hunt, the other as the Maimed King, a sort of year-spirit whose wounds annually reopened. The latter tradition was preserved with peculiar force in Sicily where it is localized by Gervase of Tilbury. *It is therefore possible that other traditions of a supernatural Arthur may have persisted in Apulia* [italics mine]. Now the Welsh held one strange conception of a supernatural king which is attested by Walter Map. One of the most ancient of British kings, Herla, it is said, was on a time interviewed by another king who was a pigmy in respect of his low stature, not above that of a monkey. The little creature was mounted on a large goat. The dwarf king resembles the conception of *the immortal Arthur* [italics mine] in being possessed of infinite riches and dwelling in a mysterious palace entered through a cave. It is possible therefore that Arthur, in assuming the traits of various Otherworld kings, acquired the uncouth mount of the pigmy potentate. It is also easy to see why the grotesque image of Arthur bestriding a goat, the beast associated in the medieval mind, as in Spencer's allegorical pageant, with the sin of lechery, should have been rapidly suppressed, and have left no trace save in the Otranto mosaic. Perhaps a more satisfactory interpretation may be offered, but at least this is a plausible guess.

A close look at the section of this mosaic which Loomis has reproduced in his volume will reveal several important things: (1) there is no panther, (2) Abel—plainly labeled—with his sacrificial lamb appears at the right of the picture, below the sun and the outstretched hand of God ready to accept the sacrifice, (3) Adam and Eve are at the left under the tree of Paradise, (4) below Adam and Eve, in front of Arthur's mount, is a gate, and (5) a decorative vine plays a prominent part in the mosaic.

Webber (gloss) states that the sun represents God the Father, as does a hand issuing from clouds; a gate symbolizes Paradise. A closed gate—the one in the mosaic is closed—signifies Ezechiel, one of the four major Prophets. A cursory look at the chapter headings in Ezechiel will clarify a large part of the mosaic. We need not have recourse to any Welsh legends. Ezechiel prophesies concerning the judgments of God upon the Jews because of their idolatry and their false prophets whose lies had deceived the people (5-13). He foretells the annihilation of the city of Jerusalem and of the temple (15, 21, 22). Christ the true pastor shall come (34). The temple shall be rebuilt (40). For our purposes, the following passages are especially revealing:

Thy mother is like a vine in thy blood planted by the water: her fruit and her branches have grown out of many waters.
And she had strong rods to make sceptres for them that bear rule, and her stature was exalted among the branches: and she saw her height in the multitude of her branches. (19:10-11)
And say to them: Thus saith the Lord God: In the day when I chose Israel, and lifted up my hand for the race of the house of Jacob, and appeared to them in the land of Egypt, and lifted up my hand for them saying: I am the Lord your God.
In that day I lifted up my hand from them to bring them out of the land of Egypt, into a land which I had provided for them, flowing with milk and honey: which excelleth amongst all lands. (20:5-6)
In my holy mountain in the high mountain of Israel, saith the Lord God, there shall all the house of Israel serve me; all of them, I say in the land, in which they shall please me, and there will I require your first fruits, and the chief of your tithes with all your sanctifications. And you shall know that I am the Lord, when I shall have brought you into the land of Israel, into the land, for which I lifted up my hand to give it to your fathers. (20: 40, 42)

In chapter 34, Ezechiel prophesies that the Lord will cause the evil shepherds to perish; He will gather in, guide, and feed the sheep by means of the second David, the Messias:

Behold I myself will seek my sheep, and will visit them. . . .
I will feed them in the mountains of Israel, by the rivers, and in all the habitations of the land.
And as for you, O my flocks, thus saith the Lord God: Behold I judge between cattle and cattle, of rams and of he-goats.
And I will set up one shepherd over them, and he shall feed them, even my servant David: he shall feed them and he shall be their shepherd. And I the Lord will be their God: and my servant David, the prince in the midst of them.

And the tree of the field shall yield its fruit, and the earth shall yield her increase, and they shall be in their land without fear: and they shall know that I am the Lord, when I shall have broken the bonds of their yoke, and shall have delivered them out of the hand of those that rule over them.
And they shall be no more for a spoil to the nations, neither shall the beasts of the earth devour them. . . .
And you my flocks, the flocks of my pasture are men: and I am the Lord your God, saith the Lord God. (34:11-5, 17, 23-4, 27-8, 31)

And again:

But as for you, O mountains of Israel, shoot ye forth your branches, and yield your fruit to my people of Israel: for they are at hand to come. (36:8)

In 37, Ezechiel prophesies that Ephraim and Juda shall, under the second David (The Messias), be united into one kingdom, and the Lord shall dwell in their midst. In the last prophetic vision, God shows the new temple (40-42), the new worship (43-46), the return to their own land, and the new division thereof among the twelve tribes (47-48), as a figure of His foundation of a kingdom where He shall dwell among His people and where He shall be served in His tabernacle according to strict rules, by priests of His choice, and by the prince of the house of David.

Turning to Ferguson[30] we find that the ram is used as a symbol of Christ. In the same way that the ram fights with the wolf and vanquishes him, so Christ battles with Satan and is victorious. The ram, placed in a thorny bush so that Abraham might sacrifice it in place of his son Isaac, "represents Christ crowned with thorns and sacrificed for mankind. In a general sense, the ram is used as a symbol of strength." Now, in an effort to find the Biblical source for Arthur bestriding a goat, let us turn to Dan. 8:4-6:

I saw a ram pushing with his horns against the west, and against the north, and against the south, and no beasts could withstand him, nor be delivered out of his hand: and he did according to his own will, and became great,
And I understood: and behold a he-goat came from the west on the

---

30. P. 18.

face of the whole earth: and he touched not the ground: and the he-goat had a notable horn between his eyes.
And he went up to the ram that had the horns, which I had seen standing before the gate, and he ran towards him in the force of his strength.

Then there follows the account of the temporary victory of the he-goat over the ram. Ferguson (p. 16) reminds us that in early Christian art, the goat was taken as a symbol of the damned in the Last Judgment, the interpretation based upon a passage in the Bible (Matt. 25:31-46) which relates how Christ, upon His coming, shall separate the believing from the unbelieving, as the shepherd separates the sheep from the goats.

Dan. 8:12 continues:

And strength was given him [the he-goat] against the continual sacrifice because of sins [Mario Roques' explanation of the continuous bleeding of the Lance should be remembered here]: and truth shall be cast down on the ground [Modena's Combat between Truth and Fraud should be recalled, as well as the imprisonment of Winlogée on Mont Doulouroux depicted on the archivolt of the Porta della Pescheria], and he shall do and prosper.
And I heard one of the saints speaking: and one saint said to another, I know not to whom, that was speaking: How long shall be the vision concerning the continual sacrifice, and the sin of the desolation that is made: and how long shall the sanctuary, and the strength be trodden underfoot?
And he said to him: Unto evening and morning two thousand three hundred days: and the sanctuary shall be cleansed.

We ask again, is it mere coincidence that Daniel is carved on the right jamb of the main portal at Modena, directly opposite Isaias? In view of the fact that the mosaic at Otranto is near the sanctuary and that the sanctuary is mentioned many times by both Daniel and Ezechiel, does our explanation seem more satisfactory than Loomis' "guess"? And in connection with the he-goat, let it be remembered that in the *Hortus deliciarum* of the Abbess Herrade, "la Synagogue, sous les traits d'une femme, les yeux voilés... tient à la main une tablette sur laquelle sont écrits ces mots: '*Et ego nesciebam.*' Elle porte sur ses genoux le bouc d'iniquité. Elle est assise sur une ânesse...[qui] symbolise le peuple juif, et le bouc les sacrifices de l'ancienne loi."[31] Webber (gloss) also states that the he-goat symbolizes the Old Testament sacrifices. Therefore, Arthur crowned and with scepter in hand (David>Christ) seated on a he-goat is merely the artist's way of saying that the sacrifices of the Old Law have given way to the sacrifice of the New. It is the same message which Chrétien gives us in his celebrated Procession of the Holy Grail, based on St. Paul's Epistle to the Hebrews addressed to Christian Jews in danger of falling away from the Gospel.

It might be well to point out also that the ram is associated not only with Christ, but also with David, who sacrificed an ox and a ram when the Ark of the Covenant was brought to his city (II Kings 6:13). In the "Alphabetical Key," we have identified Arthur as typifying Christ the King, Lord God of Hosts. (In the Otranto mosaic Arthur is pictured with royal scepter and crown, attributes of both David and Christ.) On the Old Testament level, Arthur presumably was David, prototype of Christ. And in the mosaic, Arthur as Christ (the ram) is pictured as having finally triumphed over the he-goat by his resurrection from the dead. A parallel to this symbolism is to be found in Arthur's pennon of the Paris tapestry (see p. 155 and Fig. 11).

We have maintained consistently that Chrétien's *Perceval* is based on the teachings of St. Paul. Therefore it is cogent to point out that this saint figures prominently in the Modena sculpture, where the Arthurian theme has been treated. Describing the Portal of the Princes, Jullian writes (p. 156):

Sa donnée générale est conforme au modèle qu'offrait le portail principal: sous un porche supporté par des lions [Webber tells us that the lion symbolizes Our Lord, the Lion of the Tribe of Judah; also, David and Daniel] se développe la continuité des piédroits et de l'archivolte; la face antérieure est décorée de rinceaux entremêlés de figurines; d'autres rinceaux se déroulent sous la courbe de l'arc, tandis que sur la face intérieure des montants, des arcades superposées abritent la suite des douze apôtres, qui répondent aux prophètes du grand portail et qui se complètent, sous l'architrave, par la représentation de saint

---

31. Roques, "Le Graal de Chrétien et la demoiselle au Graal," pp. 14-15.

Jean-Baptiste, de saint Paul et de l'agneau mystique dans un médaillon soutenu par deux anges. . . .

Jullian tells us that it was Arthur Kingsley Porter—frequently cited by Loomis in *Arthurian Legends* where he speaks of the Modena archivolt—who identified[32] the statue of Saint Paul by means of the inscription he bears. This inscription is taken from St. Paul, Rom. 6:3, "Know you not that all we, who are baptized in Christ Jesus, are baptized in his death?" Is it caprice that makes the sculptors at Modena place St. John the Baptist opposite St. Paul preaching baptism in Christ Jesus? Is it coincidence that St. Paul is placed in the Portal of the Princes in a position similar to that of the Prophets who inspired so much of the sculpture that decorates the Cathedral, which parallels Chrétien's *Perceval* and the Otranto mosaic in the paving near the sanctuary where the sacrifice of Calvary is daily repeated in an unbloody manner?

As Emile Mâle has said:

Le symbolisme du culte familiarisait les fidèles avec le symbolisme de l'art. La Liturgie chrétienne est, comme l'art chrétien, une perpétuelle figure: le même génie s'y montre. . . . Le moyen âge eut la passion de l'ordre. Il organisa l'art comme il avait organisé le dogme, le savoir humain, la société. La représentation des sujets sacrés fut alors une science qui eut ses principes, et qui ne fut jamais abandonnée à la fantaisie individuelle. Nous ne pouvons douter que cette sorte de théologie de l'art n'ait été réduite, de bonne heure, en un corps de doctrine, car nous voyons les artistes s'y soumettre, d'un bout à l'autre de l'Europe, dès les temps les plus anciens.[33]

Much as we admire the brilliant scholarship of Professor William Roach and his magnificent contribution to Chrétien studies, we would disagree with him when he says,[34]

Chrétien's story certainly antedates Robert's more circumstantial account, possibly by as much as twenty years or more, but Chrétien's references to the Grail are veiled and ambiguous, and they leave the reader with no clear idea of what the Grail was or what purpose it served. This vagueness may be a quality which the author deliberately

---

32. *Lombard Architecture*, III, 39.
33. *L'Art religieux du XIIIe siècle*, pp. 16, 1.
34. In *Romance Philology*, IX (1956), 313.

sought to give his narrative: he may have been using the Grail as a mysterious, half-understood symbol that would evoke in his readers a feeling of awe, of reverence, of wonder, or merely bewilderment. Or he may, on the other hand, have had a fairly clear conception of the Grail, of its history, of its form and associations, and of the function that it would have fulfilled in his story if he had lived to finish it. Both of these views of Chrétien's notion of the Grail have been advanced with equal sincerity and have been attacked with equal ardor. All that can be said with certainty is that Chrétien's text does not provide clear and definite justification for either side of the debate.

But Gautier de Châtillon's *Tractatus contra Judaeos*, the Modena portal, and the Otranto mosaic rather conclusively support the possibility that, whatever the Grail may have meant in the *Perceval*, its symbolism was obvious to Chrétien's contemporaries. Even in the unfinished poem, Chrétien writes of the Grail as something well known and symbolically understood, as Mario Roques, Mme Lot-Borodine, and Stefan Hofer, among others, have perceived. Moreover, we cannot cite with certainty one single mediaeval text which was obscure to its mediaeval reading public.

Von Simson (p. 87) has remarked about the mediaeval inability to distinguish past and present, more exactly, about the tendency to see in the past the justification for the present. And so it was that the Crusaders identified themselves with Christ and the Apostles in their effort to overcome unbelief. The sculpture of the numerous cathedrals along the old pilgrim routes testifies to this fact. What was more natural, then, than that Winlogée (Truth) would be imprisoned on Mont Douloureux (Calvary) by Chrétien and the sculptors at Modena?

We have already spoken of the Prophets Isaias, Jeremias, Ezechiel, and Daniel and their influence at Modena and of the fact that these four major Prophets are depicted on the main portal of the western façade (see *supra*, pp. 133-34, 140, 141-44). Fine portraits of them appear also in the northern windows of the New Alliance at Chartres, where each Prophet bears one of the Evangelists on his shoulders.[35] But so far we have not mentioned Zacharias, shown below Daniel on the right jamb of the main

---

35. Henry Adams, *Mont-Saint-Michel and Chartres*, p. 186.

portal.[36] Surely he is there for some good reason. Turning to his prophecies, we can unravel a little more of the mystery which veils the Otranto mosaic and the Modena sculptures. In the course of his fourteen chapters, Zacharias makes mention of the Lord (God) of Hosts no less than fifty-one times. Jullian (p. 156) has called attention to the "rinceaux entremêlés de figurines" which decorate the main portal of the western façade and also the Portal of the Princes.

In that day saith the Lord God of hosts, every man shall call his friend under the vine and under the fig-tree. (Zach. 3:10)

Loomis (see *supra*, p. 140), in describing the Otranto mosaic, has called it "a strange conglomerate of beasts and men":

And he said to them: Run, speak to this young man, saying: Jerusalem shall be inhabited without walls, by reason of the multitude of men, and of beasts in the midst thereof.
And I will be to it, saith the Lord, a wall of fire round about: and I will be in glory in the midst thereof. (Zach. 2:4-5)

Is it not true that at Otranto Arthur (Christ) crowned and with scepter in hand is in glory in the midst of the city with its multitude of men and beasts? The following from Zach. 10:3 may also have some significance for the he-goat which Arthur rides at Otranto and the horse which Christ rides in the twelfth-century fresco (*Christ le Cavalier*) in the apse of the crypt of St.-Etienne at Auxerre:

My wrath is kindled against the shepherds, and I will visit upon the buck-goats: for the Lord of hosts hath visited his flock, the house of Juda, and hath made them as the horse of his glory in the battle.

To be convinced that in the Otranto mosaic King Arthur typifies Christ, one should have the opportunity to study the mosaic as a whole as I had the happy privilege of doing in the Cathedral itself. The mosaic extends from the sanctuary right down to the portals of the western façade. And as one enters the Cathedral and walks up the center of the nave toward the sanctuary, one follows a heavy black line which gradually tapers as one advances.

---

36. See Jullian, Plate XVI, 4.

Upon further examination, one realizes that this is the trunk of a huge Tree of Life. We have already mentioned Adam and Eve, Arthur, and Cain and Abel at the very top. Immediately below them are twelve huge circles arranged in three rows of four. They contain the signs of the zodiac and occupations of the months of the year so dear to the builders of the mediaeval cathedrals. (They appear, too, on the inner side of the jambs of the Porta della Pescheria with its Arthurian archivolt at Modena.) The two fish, which in Loomis's picture are shown below the feet of Arthur's goat, are the Pisces. Below them is the seated figure of a man removing a thorn from his heel.

Still further down the tree, below Adam and Eve, is depicted the building of the Tower of Babel. This is counterbalanced, on the right, by the building of Noah's Ark. What has a pagan Celtic legend or a Welsh goat of lechery to do with all this? Those who still need to be convinced of the identity of King Arthur at Otranto should visit, as I did, the beautiful old church (formerly the cathedral) of Saint-Nazaire at Carcassonne, within the Cité. One of the five windows of the apse—the one immediately to the right of the main altar—shows a Tree of Life (Fig. 12). Near the top of the tree, nailed to it, is a large crucifix which is the most beautiful ornament and the center of the whole composition, inasmuch as it is Christ who is the "bois de vie."[37] It should be noted that the crucified Christ at Carcassonne is in the same relative position in this Tree of Life as King Arthur is in the Otranto Tree of Life. Speaking of the Carcassonne window, Mot writes (pp. 52 ff.):

Sous une même division en triptyque que l'arbre de Jessé, c'est ici un autre arbre qui s'épanouit, non plus pour porter les Ancêtres du Fils mais pour donner la Vie, le Sauveur avec tous ses mystères joyeux, douloureux, glorieux, prédits et annoncés par les Prophètes qui portent le témoignage écrit de leur prophéties. Ce thème du bois de vie est celui même contenu dans l'opuscule de saint Bonaventure intitulé: "Lignum vitae". L'artiste a transposé une œuvre mystique en vitrail, traduit un traité en verre. . . . Le tronc central s'élève orné de feuilles,

---

[37] See G.-J. Mot, *Les Vitraux de Saint-Nazaire de Carcassonne* (Toulouse, 1954), p. 53. This is an extract from the *Mémoires de la Société Archéologique du Midi de la France*, Tome xxii.

d'oiseaux, de nids, d'insectes, lançant ses fortes branches en accolades où sont inscrites les têtes de chapitres du Traité, honorant la vie, la mort, la résurrection du Christ, et ces branches portent un fruit qui est une vertu. Vers le haut, cloué sur l'arbre, un grand crucifix figure le plus bel ornement et le centre de la composition, le sujet et la clé de la figure, est le Christ qui est le bois de vie. Pour terminer le fleuron extrême de l'arbre, l'Esprit-Saint énonce ses sept dons.

Then the author goes on to complain about the manner in which the window's lower portion was restored in the nineteenth century. With his complaint we do not wholly agree:

Malheureusement les panneaux du bas, qui manquaient lors de la restauration de 1853, ont été composés à contre-sens; ignorant l'idée et l'origine de la composition, l'atelier de Gérente, se basant sur des traces de flots subsistant encore, a cru qu'il s'agissait de la mer et a fait flotter l'arche de Noé; par symétrie, en face il a placé une autre arche, naturellement d'Alliance, et pour faire naître l'arbre il n'a pas cru trouver un meilleur terrain que le Paradis terrestre et de meilleurs jardiniers qu'Adam et Eve croquant la pomme sous les yeux du serpent; sans s'en douter certainement le maître-verrier du XIXe siècle transformait l'arbre de vie en arbre de mort. Très certainement ces flots, vus par Gérente, n'étaient que le vestige des quatre fleuves qui s'épandaient de la source de vie, fécondant la terre d'où jaillissait l'arbre de vie, dans l'enceinte de la Cité céleste, comme l'indique saint Bonaventure d'après la vision apocalyptique. Souhaitons que ces derniers panneaux disparaissent et soient remplacés par une composition en harmonie avec l'ensemble. Car véritablement cette verrière est très certainement la seule subsistante du XIVe siècle qui présente une page enluminée de théologie; ici ce sont les inscriptions qui forment le fonds de la décoration, et pour rompre la monotonie de l'écriture tous les agréments de la nature ont été mis à contribution, flore, faune, êtres humains, illustrent, éclairent et réjouissent un sujet austère et sévère. Sans doute l'idée première d'illustrer ainsi le bois de vie n'appartient pas au maître-verrier qui a pu s'inspirer de fresques et de miniatures répandues à profusion dès la parution de l'œuvre franciscaine, mais il est peut-être le premier, voire le dernier, qui en a réalisé une transposition si translucide et harmonieuse.

We do not gainsay the author's claim that there is a close affinity between the Carcassonne Tree of Life and St. Bonaventure's

"Lignum vitae." But because Adam and Eve and Noah's Ark appear in Otranto's Tree of Life, we maintain that St. Bonaventure and/or the designer of the Otranto mosaic and/or the glaziers of the original Carcassonne window may have been inspired by a still older source in which Noah's Ark and Adam and Eve appeared on the Tree of Life. It is even possible that the nineteenth-century restorers of the Carcassonne window were familiar with the Otranto mosaic and/or an older source in which Noah's Ark and Adam and Eve made their appearance. And we trust that the lower panels of the Carcassonne windows will not be removed too hastily. For in our opinion the presence of Adam and Eve does not make a Tree of Death out of the Tree of Life. If King Arthur at Otranto represents the Crucified Christ of Carcassonne as we maintain, then his presence at Otranto between Adam and Eve on the one hand, Cain and Abel on the other hand, makes extremely good sense. For Christ by His incarnation had taken upon Himself the sins of the world which He would redeem; He is therefore placed between those with whom we associate Original Sin and the classic hardened sinner, Cain. Then, too, it makes very good sense to associate the sacrifice of Abel with that of Christ even as the craftsman of the Stavelot altar has done. The building of the Tower of Babel and Noah's Ark are merely further reminders of the sins of mankind which Arthur (Christ) took upon Himself.[38]

As far as the archivolt of the Porta della Pescheria is concerned, the following from Zach. 8:3, 19, is perhaps the most telling:

Thus saith the Lord of hosts: I am returned to Sion, and I will dwell in the midst of Jerusalem: and Jerusalem shall be called the City of Truth, and the Mountain of the Lord of hosts, the sanctified Mountain. . . . Thus saith the Lord of hosts. . . . only love ye truth and peace.

We have already referred to "the double-ax pattern of the waves" at Modena, symbolizing a mountain (see *supra*, p. 126). It is a commonplace that a tower pierced by a door represented a city

---

38. Mâle, *L'Art religieux du XIIIe siècle*, pp. 138, 155-6, 194, offers several pertinent reminders regarding the symbolism which the Middle Ages attached to Adam and Eve, Cain and Abel, Noah and the Ark.

in mediaeval art.[39] And so, on the Modena archivolt we have Arthur (the Lord of Hosts) riding up to Jerusalem—the city of Truth, the sanctified Mountain—to liberate Winlogée (Truth). Burmaltus and his associates on the portal, the he-goat of the Otranto mosaic, and the Red Knight in Chrétien's *Perceval* are all parallels. They all represent the Jews who by their envy delivered Christ up to be crucified (see Matt. 27:18; Mark 15:10). Let us look again at Arthur's words to Perceval about the Red Knight (my italics):

". . . li pire anemis que j'aie,	"Le pire ennemi que j'aie, celui
Qui plus me het et plus m'esmaie,	de tous les hommes qui me hait et
M'a ci ma terre contredite,	me tourmente le plus, vient de me
Et tant est fos que tote quite	réclamer ouvertement ma terre, et
Dit qu'il l'avra, ou vuelle ou non.	il est assez fou pour dire qu'il l'aura
Li Vermauz Chevaliers a non	toute à lui, que je le vueille ou
De la forest de Quinqueroi."	non. C'est le Chevalier Vermeil
(Hilka, vv. 945 ff.)	de la forêt de Quinqueroi. . . ."
	(Foulet, p. 26)

And, through envy, did the Red Knight not steal the golden cup of Arthur's eternal priesthood—the cup which Perceval soon restored to him?

An animal which is prominent in the decorations of the main portal of the Modena cathedral is the griffin.[40] Of this fabulous animal, Ferguson says (p. 18):

Because it is a combination of the preying eagle and the fierceness of the lion, [it is used] to symbolize those who oppress and persecute the Christians.

Chrétien's hunted stag, the ravens and crows which pecked out the eyes of Perceval's elder brother, and Perceval's harsh treatment of the lady of the wondrous tent are all parallels and they all symbolize persecution of the early Church.

What are we to think of the pagan Celtic sources for the *Perceval*, sources which Loomis and other Celticist scholars have been defending for many years? What of the guess which Loomis makes about the "panther" and "Arthur bestriding a goat, the

---

39. See Mâle, *L'Art religieux du XIIIe siècle*, p. 2.
40. See Jullian, Plate XVI, 3.

beast associated in the medieval mind...with the sin of lechery"? What of the analogy Loomis sees between King Arthur and the Welsh King "who was a pigmy in respect of his low stature, not above that of a monkey...mounted on a large goat"? Loomis has written cogently about the Otranto mosaic that "it is hard to believe that Arthur would enter a conflict with a monster so formidable [as the panther] armed only with a sceptre and riding on a goat!" But what are we to think of Loomis's suggestion (p. 35) that the Modena archivolt depicted "a subject utterly without religious significance"?

The Arthurian archivolt at Modena, the Arthurian mosaic at Otranto, and Chrétien's *Perceval* are all deeply mystical, based in very great measure on the prophecies and the writings of St. Paul and St. John the Evangelist. This is particularly true of the Grail Procession. Cf. St. Paul, I Cor. 11:23 ff.:

For I have received of the Lord that which also I delivered unto you, that the Lord Jesus, the same night in which he was betrayed, took bread, and giving thanks, broke, and said: Take ye and eat: this is my body which shall be delivered for you: this do for the commemoration of me. In like manner also the chalice, after he had supped, saying: this chalice is the new testament in my blood; this do ye as often as you shall drink, for the commemoration of me.
For as often as you shall eat this bread, and drink the chalice: you shall shew the death of the Lord, until he come.
Therefore whosoever shall eat of this bread, or drink the chalice of the Lord unworthily: shall be guilty of the Body and of the Blood of the Lord.
But let a man prove himself: and so let him eat of that bread, and drink of the chalice.

Is this not precisely the lesson that Chrétien teaches in recounting Perceval's worthy communion received at the hermitage on Easter Sunday? And does it not make sense, as we have suggested, that the artisans at Reims should have chosen to "illustrate" this episode in the charming sculpture on the inside of the western façade, below the rose window, where a standing knight is to be seen receiving holy communion from a priest?

The article on "The Holy Grail," written in 1909 by Arthur Remy for the *Catholic Encyclopedia*, needs to be corrected. For it is scarcely accurate to maintain that in Chrétien's version the Grail has no pronounced religious character. Nor can we believe any longer that the Church took no notice of the Arthurian legends. For Chrétien, as at Modena and at Otranto, the Arthurian theme is bound up with a search for Truth, of conversion of the Jews by means of the Prophets and Saint Paul. And this, as we have remarked, was also the case in Gautier de Châtillon's *Tractatus contra Judaeos*. If the Arthurian story originally had some of its roots in Celtic pagan legends, as Celticists would quite reasonably have us believe, those roots had long since been regrafted by the Church. In the twelfth century, the Arthurian legend was a healthy Christian plant flourishing in mystical soil.

In its series of pictorial essays on the historical development of Western cultures, *Life* (April 7, 1947, pp. 80-81) reproduced in color the famous King Arthur Tapestry woven in Paris toward the end of the 14th century (Fig. 11), one of the earliest representations of the legendary British ruler. As even the *Life* author says below the picture,

Arthur became one of the towering figures in Middle Age art and story because the church surrounded him with a saintly aura and claimed him as the embodiment of the perfect Christian king. Wandering troubadours, in secular songs and ballads, also endowed King Arthur with supernatural majesty. In this tapestry he is depicted seated on a throne in a Gothic niche in a cathedral, surrounded by bishops and archbishops bearing crosses and crosiers. Figures at the far left are knights who figured conspicuously in Arthurian folklore.

It is amazing how close Loomis can come to the truth and yet miss it in describing the statue of King Arthur in the Hansasaal of the Rathaus in Cologne. He remarks (p. 38) that "Arthur's visage is rather world-weary than handsome, and he raises his hand to doff his helmet with a tired gesture." Is it not understandable that the Lord of Hosts should be weary of the sins of the world?

In describing the Paris tapestry, Loomis says (p. 38):

The figure of Arthur is not unlike the venerable bearded figures seated under a Gothic canopy, which preceded each of the seven great sequences of St. John's vision woven in tapestry for Louis of Anjou, and for the most part still preserved at Angers. . . . *The whole conception is significantly like that of God the Father in majesty* painted early in the fifteenth century in the *Missel de l'Eglise de Paris* and figured in Martin's *Miniature française*, fig. CVI. He is surrounded by *obsequious* clergy—two archbishops in the upper niches, two bishops in the lower. [In 1947, with funds given by John D. Rockefeller, Jr., three cardinals at the top of the tapestry were acquired. See Fig. 11.] . . . Arthur himself is easily identified by the *three gold crowns* repeated on his *blue* surcoat and *pennon*. With scowling brow and portentous and predatory nose, "lik a *grifphon* loketh he aboute." (Italics mine)

Loomis is surely aware of the fact that three signifies the Trinity; that gold and a crown each signify Our Lord's kingly office; that a pennon or banner signifies triumph, the resurrection, victory over sin and death; that the crown also symbolizes eternal life; and that blue signifies Heaven, truth, wisdom, and charity. The griffin was sometimes used to represent the Savior. Despite the connotation Loomis gives to *obsequious*, i. e., "compliant, devoted," much more frequently it means "servilely attentive, fawning." Is there any reason why the bishop, archbishops, and cardinals surrounding the King of Kings should not be devoted? Does not the enormous stature given to Arthur in comparison with the other figures underscore the artist's symbolism? Can it be possible, as Mme Lot-Borodine declares,[41] that for several generations Celticist scholars have "deliberately falsified" the true meaning of the Grail legend?

J. S. P. Tatlock states[42]: "I know of no evidence of any Breton tales of Arthur. . . . No more evidence is there for Breton origin of Arthurian matters in Chrétien de Troyes' romances (about 1160-80); almost all the localities for Arthur himself are insular, and scarcely any for anyone are Breton." Tatlock hopes "to reduce the presumption existing perhaps in some people's minds that anything in a legend which cannot be positively proved later than Geoffrey [of Monmouth] probably antedates him" (pp. 358-65). Tatlock makes an interesting assertion (p. 358):

Nearly all the evidence for the vogue of Arthur before Geoffrey relates

41. In *Romania*, LXXVII, 235.
42. "The Dates of the Arthurian Saints' Legends," *Speculum*, XIV (1939), 357.

merely to the Briton hope in Wales and Brittany for his messianic return; which no more proves an active cycle of stories about him than American popular observances about Santa Claus prove the familiarity of stories about him.

Miss Helaine Newstead[43] resumes one of the arguments Loomis had used in 1938[44] in trying to date the Modena archivolt. She says:

The name *Isdernus*, for instance, is closer to Welsh *Ederyn* son of Nudd than either Geoffrey's *Hider* filius Nucii or Chrétien's *Yder* fiz Nut, both of which have lost the final *n* of the Welsh name; and *Winlogée* is obviously an intermediate form between *Winlowen* and French *Guinloie*. . . . [These names] reveal affinities with earlier Welsh and Breton forms.

But Jullian says, "Une grande incertitude pèse sur l'origine et la propagation des légendes bretonnes" (p. 150). We have no way of knowing, for example, that the Breton forms of these names on the Modena archivolt were not taken from Breton legends which had already been thoroughly Christianized. Even if we accept Loomis's plausible theory that some Breton Crusader had passed on the name forms to Italian artisans, we do not know whether this was done before or after the First Crusade or in connection with some later Crusade. Nor do we know how much time elapsed between the transmittal of the *matière* and its adaptation at Modena. In other words, the name forms are of no help in dating with any certainty the archivolt in question.

We have noted above (p. 124) that there is little in the costuming of the Modena knights which permits one to attribute them to any particular date. These knights wear no mailed chausses and no cotte over hauberk; the shape of their helmet is slightly distinctive. This "isosceles-triangle" helmet appears early in the twelfth century, as Loomis states, for instance on the sculpture of the principal portal at Angoulême[45] and on a capital of Notre-Dame-du-Port in Clermont-Ferrand (Mâle, *L'Art religieux du XIIe siècle*, p. 23). Loomis (*Arthurian Legends*, p. 33) states that "the helmet with the profile of an isosceles triangle, worn by Carrado, Galvaginus, and Galvariun [at Modena] is very rare

---

43. In *Romance Philology*, X (1956), 58.
44. *Arthurian Legends*, p. 33.   45. See Fig. 10.

after that period [the first decade of the twelfth century]." However, in Mâle[46] there is an excellent reproduction of a thirteenth-century window of Laon's Cathedral showing Gideon thus attired. The choir of Laon Cathedral was not completed until 1180-1220.[47] Furthermore, this same helmet is also to be seen in Chartres windows dating 1194-1260. Such windows are reproduced in color in *Life* and *Time* magazines: for instance, the helmeted figure just below the celebrated panel of the angel with swinging censor (*Life*, April 7, 1947, p. 73—extreme right of page), and the soldier in the medallion of the Massacre of the Holy Innocents (*Time*, December 24, 1951, p. 36). Are we to suppose that these thirteenth-century figures were wearing helmets discarded by their early twelfth-century forbears?

We repeat: it seems impossible to date with any certainty the Modena archivolt. The reader is free to agree with Porter and Loomis, who attribute it to the first decade of the twelfth century, or with Jullian, who dates it as the work of the fourth decade of the century, or with Paul Deschamps and Emile Mâle, who believe that the sculpture is of the second third of the twelfth century. But one thing is certain: the Otranto mosaic was laid between 1163-1166 (see Mâle whom we cited *supra*, p. 131); Loomis states that the mosaic is of 1165 (see *supra*, p. 140). This proves beyond question that the Arthurian legend had been taken over by the Church before Chrétien penned his *Conte del Graal*. And Chrétien, in writing his poem, followed the mystical trail which had been blazed by Gautier de Châtillon and by the artisans at both Modena and Otranto—a trail which was still very much in vogue at the end of the fourteenth century when the Paris tapestry was woven and when Giovanni del Biondo painted his *Christ and Virgin Enthroned* where Synagoga is shown being baptized by Ecclesia, who is holding the chalice surmounted by the paten and host, after that same Synagoga had left the bloody sacrifices of the Old Law (see *supra*, chap. 7, p. 111).[48] There is no need to draw upon ancient Welsh legends to find out why a twelfth-century King Arthur is depicted riding a goat.

46. *L'Art religieux du XIIIe siècle*, p. 15.
47. See *Cathédrales de France*, Editions des Deux Mondes (Paris, 1950), p. 20.
48. See also the fifteenth-century woodcut where Arthur is referred to as *Künig Artūs ein Crist*, Loomis, *Arthurian Legends*, Fig. 393.

CHAPTER NINE

Summary

Too MUCH HEAT and unruly passion have already been generated in learned circles by confusion of the *Perceval's* source problems with its actual twelfth-century meaning. Therefore, let it be said once again that the authors of this book are not concerned with tracing ultimate sources nor in vanquishing theories of Celtic origin. The intent of these pages has been merely to present a twelfth-century poet of special talent, through his own words and in the light of twelfth-century history, art, and literature—all of which must have made an impact upon any well-educated man of the time.

We have insisted that Chrétien meant what he wrote, that the *Perceval* was penned to please one who "hait toute vilenie... qui n'écoute nulle laide plaisanterie, nulle parole sotte." The romance was a serious work dealing with spiritual ascent, with the popular themes of Virtues versus Vices and of Ecclesia versus Synagoga. It owed much to the teaching of St. Paul, whom the poet quotes in his prologue. And, since Paul was the patron saint of mediaeval knights, what was more natural than for Chrétien to use him as a model for a hero attaining Christian chivalric ideals?

It was in Troyes that the Templars gained their status through the Council of 1128, at which St. Bernard was the leading spirit. It was in Troyes that Henry the Liberal, in 1179, founded the Hospice of St. Abraham for the benefit of pilgrims on their way to the Holy Land. It was also in Troyes that two Jewish synagogues had been converted into Christian churches, thus indicating that the Ecclesia-Synagoga question was vital to the inhabitants of the town.

St. Paul had taken a burning interest in the conversion of the Jews: so did Chrétien. Twice in his poem he has recounted the Passion and the part in it played by the Jews. The tropologic iconography which Suger had popularized stemmed from St. Paul (II Cor. 3:12-8): "Seeing that we have such hope, we use great plainness of speech: And not as Moses, which put a veil over his face." The iconography of the blindfolded Synagoga is also traceable to this passage. It found its way not only into the art of the times but also into the literature: the *Hortus Deliciarum*, for example, and the *Tractatus contra Judaeos* by Gautier de Châtillon, in which the Britons waiting for the second coming of Arthur are likened to the Jews awaiting the coming of the Messias.

The allegorical figures of Ecclesia and Synagoga, usually portrayed with chalice and Bleeding Lance of the Passion, are everywhere depicted—in stained glass, statues, reliquaries, portable altars, and manuscript illuminations. They are to be found in the Châlons *Bréviaire de Saint-Etienne* in juxtaposition with the Canon of the Mass and the words "Adoramus te Christe et benedicimus tibi quoniam per sanctam crucem tuam redemisti mundum." The very proximity of these allegorical figures with the solemn words argues strongly that Chrétien, in his Procession of the Holy Grail, was indeed inspired by the Liturgy—although he was not necessarily representing any ceremonies of any particular rite. It was but natural that Chrétien should adopt the chalice and the Bleeding Lance for the purpose of explaining the necessity of the Old Law giving way to the New:

> ".... Biaus sire chiers,
> Don ne creez vos Jesucrist,
> Qui la novele loi escrist,
> Si la dona as Crestiiens?" (Hilka, vv. 6254-7)

William of Malmesbury (*De Gestis Regum*, I, xxviii) relates that because the sepulchre of Arthur was not to be found, ancient ballads had fabled that he was still to come. Then we have the "finding" of Arthur's tomb at Glastonbury between two pyramids. In other words, the Church, far from ignoring the Arthurian legends, deplored the superstition which it feared that they fostered and consequently strove to Christianize the old tales. Thus we have Arthur on the archivolt of the Porta della Pescheria, in the Cathedral of Modena; and as early as 1166 we find him again in the mosaic of the floor of the Cathedral at Otranto. Furthermore, as already noted, the Arthurian legends were put to good advantage in the *Tractatus contra Judaeos.*

At Otranto, King Arthur takes a place on the Tree of Life analogous to that of the Crucified Christ in a twelfth-century Tree of Life window in the Church of Saint-Nazaire at Carcassonne. Indeed, Arthur has become a type of Christ. This helps to explain why, at Modena, he appears about to help free Winlogée (Truth?) from her prison on Mont Douloureux. The diffusion of Truth was a passion for twelfth-century Christendom. We see this carved in the tympana of the Angoulême Cathedral and at Saint-Amand-de-Boixe where, in groups of three, the Apostles are hurrying to spread the Gospel to the ends of the earth. The same striving is reflected at Cressac, where the returning Crusader, crushing Heresy underfoot, is welcomed by Ecclesia. It is found again at Modena in the bas-relief near the Porta dei Principi of the Cathedral, where Truth tears out the tongue of Fraud. Incidentally, it should be noted again that the Modena Cathedral was built in honor of San Geminiano, fourth-century bishop of the city, who had spent the greater part of his life extirpating heresy and spreading the truths of the Gospel. Legend has it that he wielded extraordinary powers in repulsing the Evil Spirit. To this day, his remains, in a glass-covered tomb, are held in great veneration in the crypt of his cathedral.

Arthur was treated as a type of Christ not only at Modena and Otranto, but also in the Nine Heroes Tapestries emanating from Paris in the fourteenth century (now at The Cloisters, New York) and in a woodcut of the following century which is preserved at the Bürgerbibliothek in Bern, in which he is called "Kŭnig Artŭs, ein Crist" (*Rex Arturus, alter Christus*). Accordingly, Chrétien linked him intimately with the Charity so highly lauded in the prologue, where the poet echoes St. John's equating of God with Charity. It therefore seems inevitable that Chrétien introduces his audience to Arthur in terms of his golden cup, symbol of eternal priesthood. The concept of Gawain as Charity acting only within limits of worldly resources becomes all the more admirable a testimony to Chrétien's art. The waters which flowed under Noah's Ark at Otranto in close proximity to the figure of King Arthur spoke to the twelfth century of the necessity of baptism in a manner as forceful as that assumed by Gautier de Châtillon. We have seen that in the Otranto mosaic Arthur was surrounded by figures of Adam and Eve, Cain and Abel, Noah and his Ark, all symbolizing the Passion (see chap. 8, note 38). Furthermore, Arthur was also associated with the Passion by his very proximity to that sanctuary where the Passion of Christ was constantly re-enacted in the Sacrifice of the Mass. Nor must one forget that for twelfth-century Frenchmen, Arthur's Round Table spoke of the Table of the Last Supper, as Mrs. Laura Hibbard Loomis so ably demonstrated in her series of articles:

Inspired by the sight in some cases [where Crusaders and pilgrims had seen the *mensa rotunda coenae*], by the story of it in others, pious Bretons at the beginning of the twelfth century were unquestionably in a position to transfer to their hero Arthur the table that was associated with the holiest of human fellowships. In so doing they would simply be paralleling the tellers of the Carolingian story who gave the Twelve Peers to Charlemagne in memory of the twelve apostles. (*Modern Language Notes*, XLIV [1929], 515; see also Erich Köhler, *Ideal und Wirklichkeit in der höfischen Epik*. . ., pp. 18-9.)

Why, in the face of all this, should anyone be surprised if Chrétien de Troyes introduced into his Arthurian tale the themes of the conversion of the Temple and the Passion relics?

It is by reading the *Perceval* only on the multiple-sense levels, so much in vogue in Chrétien's day, that we shall ever understand why Perceval, by leaving his mother, committed a mortal sin, and why the Fisher King was lame, and how he could be cured according to sacred prophecy. Twelfth-century Frenchmen were used to thinking in terms of allegorical symbols. After all, the Champenois poet wrote for them and not for us. To be more specific, the *Perceval* was written for an audience which, like Philip of Flanders (as Chrétien says), "aime droiture, justice, loyauté, et chérit Sainte Eglise."

APPENDICES

BIBLIOGRAPHY

INDEX

Note on Reality versus Ideality in Chrétien

NATURALLY some revolt has arisen in recent years against the excessive search for motifs and the picture of Chrétien as only an elegant poet in a sophisticated society. This incessant search for the "flowers" on which Chrétien, like a busy bee, may have alighted does some violence to what must have been the realities of the second half of the twelfth century. Erich Köhler, in *Ideal und Wirklichkeit in der höfischen Epik*, apparently believes that he is the first to react against this discrepancy. He had said earlier that it is time "to return to the reality of the extant texts, and from within them to determine their substance and spirit by means of an interpretation not dependent upon mere motifs. In this way the personality of the poet behind them will emerge more clearly" (quoted from H. Tiemann in *Romanische Forschungen*, LXIII [1951], 321). Köhler begins with a statement made by Gröber, as early as 1902, that the courtly epic (meaning romance) is a reaction of the individual against the idea of nation and state. There is, Köhler says, a causal relationship between reality and ideal—between objective data and the kind of subjective meaning which wishes to prevail over reality. Exhaustive study of the historical problem-and-form relationships among Chrétien's works shows that the thought in his Arthurian romance is moving steadily upward. This thought, masked behind narrative tales, is close to universal history—it reflects the contradictions of the chivalric-courtly world. There, chivalry has contradictions within itself and wishes to head in a direction which is contradictory to the realities of history. These contradictions force the return to a non-compulsory ideality which is an end in itself and which is more aesthetic than moral. In the romances of Chrétien the interlocking of function and problem has a background of reality, while undergoing a poetically idealized transformation. In present-day research we must be content with nothing less than an effort to determine the character, value, and signification of his poetic achievement.

This is all very difficult for most of us to understand, and we ask pardon if we have misinterpreted it in any way. Beginning with vv. 27-39 of the *Cligés*, where Chrétien remarks that chevalerie and clergie reached their heights in Greece, before passing to Rome and France (where he hopes they will remain), Köhler maintains, therefore, that in Chrétien's thinking chevalerie and clergie were blending (*Doppelbestimmung*). (This seems to have been a poetic thought, far from the reality of the latter half of the twelfth century. The terms *chevalerie* and *clergie* had large gamuts of meaning to Chrétien and his contemporaries. In the passage in the *Cligés* they probably meant "practice of arms" and "practice of learning." There were four estates, not three, in the Middle Ages: chevalerie, clergie, marchandie, and vilenie. Chrétien merely says that the two noble ones shone in the Byzantine area—a proper preface to a partially Byzantine romance. The bankruptcy of knighthood in favor of petty clerks in administration and law courts was not visible enough in Chrétien's day for him to have developed a *Weltanschauung* with this as his principal theme.)

In elaborating upon these factors Köhler leaves aside many matters which are insistent in Chrétien (at least in the *Lancelot* and the *Conte del Graal*) but which do not fit into his pattern. There are the Isles of which the people are the true enemies of King Arthur and his court. The people of the Isles take prisoner Arthur's men and women; and they must be redeemed by such great knights as Lancelot and Gawain. The Hideous Damsel on the tawny mule is associated with the Isles. Why Köhler's interpretation of her as *Fortuna?* Much of Köhler's picture of the workings of Chrétien's mind is based on his attempted reinforcement of the idea that Robert de Borron preceded the *Conte del Graal*, and this is a theory which Bodo Mergell and others have not been able to establish. Köhler thinks that the Gawain section of the *Conte del Graal* demonstrates the inadequacy of courtly love as a code. He claims that the failure of Perceval at the Grail Castle is due to the failure of chivalry which seeks to fulfil its obligations only by its own code. Clergie in the *Conte del Graal* becomes a knowledge which certifies a holy mission involving the noble man's direct and mystical communion with God (pp. 64-5). This religio-chivalric idealism was aroused by Chrétien's awareness of the inadequacy of chivalry which was declining in his day, in Köhler's view.

To us Köhler's study seems a highly subjective synthesis based on philosophically tinged elaboration rather than on facts associated with the twelfth century (as the author claims). However, Köhler's work may doubtless serve as a point of departure for many studies yet to come.

Partial List of Scholars and Some of Their Views Regarding the *Perceval*

1894 Jessie L. Weston, commenting on Wolfram von Eschenbach's *Parzival*, IX, 465 ("And as fitted the Holy Season, the Altar was stripped and bare"), writes: "It is curious that *Chrétien, otherwise more ecclesiastical in his details than Wolfram* [italics mine], has missed the characteristic feature of the stripped altar; on the other hand, he notes that Perceval spends Easter with the Hermit and receives the Sacrament, while Wolfram passes Easter over without mention. (It is rather odd to find Chrétien's Hermit saying Mass on Good Friday!)" See *Wolfram von Eschenbach's "Parzival,"* trans. Jessie L. Weston (London), p. 326. [What Miss Weston says here is perfectly true, except that in regard to the Mass on Good Friday, it is Miss Weston who has slipped in the Liturgy, not Chrétien.] (See my "Liturgy and Allegory in Chrétien's *Perceval*," pp. 10 ff.)

1909 G. Roger Hudleston, "Glastonbury Abbey," *Catholic Encyclopedia:* "In the 'Gesta Regum' (I, xxviii) William of Malmesbury says expressly that the burial place of Arthur was unknown. However, in his 'De Antiquitate Glastoniensis ecclesiae' (Cap. De nobilibus Glastoniae sepultis), the text of which is in a very corrupt state, a passage asserts that Arthur was buried at Glastonbury *inter duas piramides*. Professor Freeman rejects this as an interpolation added after Geoffrey of Monmouth's time [after 1154], when the Arthurian legend had reached its final form through that writer's fabrications. [This may, indeed, be an interpolation after 1154, but it would seem to have been made before Chrétien's *Perceval*.] There is clear evidence that the two pyramids did actually exist, and in 1191, we are told, Abbot Henry de Soliaco made a search for Arthur's body between them. Giraldus Cambrensis, who writes apparently as an eyewitness of the scene, relates (*Speculum Ecclesiae,* dist. ii, cap. ix) that at a depth of seven feet a large flat stone was found, on the under side of which was fixed a leaden cross. This was removed from the stone and in rude characters facing the stone were the words *Hic jacet sepultus inclitus Rex Arturius in insula Avallonia.* Under this at a considerable depth was a huge coffin of hollowed oak containing the bones of the king and his Queen Guinevere in separate compartments. These were later removed to a shrine in the great church. [Visitors at Glastonbury even today can see the empty double-grave.] Leland (*Assertio Arthuri,* 43, 50, 51) records that he saw both the tomb and the leaden cross with the inscription, and Camden (Britannia, Somerset) states that the latter still existed in his day, though he does not say where it was when he saw it."

1909 Arthur F. J. Remy, "Grail, The Holy," *Catholic Encyclopedia:* "The name of a legendary sacred vessel, variously identified with the chalice of the Eucharist or the dish of the Paschal lamb, and the theme of a famous mediaeval cycle of romance. In the romances the conception of the Grail varies considerably; its nature is often but vaguely indicated, and, in the case of Chrestien's Perceval poem, it is left wholly unexplained. . . . It [*grail*] certainly means a dish. . . . When we come to examine the literary tradition concerning the Grail we notice at the outset that the Grail legend is closely connected with that of Perceval as well as with that of King Arthur. Yet all these legends were originally independent of each other. The Perceval story may have a mythical origin, or it may be regarded as the tale of a simpleton (Fr., *nicelot*) who, however, in the end achieves great things. . . . The poem of Chrestien, regarded by many as the oldest known Grail romance, tells of Perceval's visit to the Grail Castle. . . . Mindful of an injunction not to inquire too much, Perceval does not ask concerning the significance of what he sees, and thereby incurs guilt and reproach. Undoubtedly, Chrestien meant to relate the hero's second visit to the castle, when he would have put the question and received the desired information. But the poet did not live to finish his story, and whether the explanation of the Grail, offered by the continuators, is that which Chrestien had in mind, is doubtful. As it is, we are not informed by Chrestien what the grail signifies; in his version it has no pronounced religious character.... There are undoubtedly Celtic elements in the legend as we have it; the Perceval story is probably, and the Arthurian legend certainly, of Celtic origin."

1922 Gustave Lanson, *Histoire de la littérature française* (Paris), pp. 56 ff.: "Ce Champenois avisé et content de vivre était l'homme le moins fait pour comprendre ce qu'il contait. Jamais esprit ne fut moins lyrique et moins épique, n'eut moins le don de sympathie et l'amour de la nature: mais surtout jamais esprit n'eut moins le sens du mythe et du mystère. Rien ne l'embarrasse: il clarifie tout, ne comprend rien, et rend tout inintelligible. Son positivisme lucide vide les merveilleux symboles du génie celtique de leur contenu, de leur sens profond extra-rationnel, et les réduit à de sèches réalités d'un net et capricieux dessin. Si bien que du mystérieux il fait de l'extravagant, et que sous sa plume le merveilleux devient purement formel, insignifiant, partant absurde. Ne lui demandez pas ce que c'est que ces pays d'où l'on ne revient pas, ces ponts tranchants comme l'épée, ces chevaliers qui emmènent les femmes ou les filles, et retiennent tous ceux qui entrent en leurs châteaux, cette loi de ces étranges lieux, que si l'un une fois en sort, tout le monde sort; ce sont terres féodales et coutumes singulières; s'il ne croit pas à leur réalité—comme il se peut faire—ce sont fictions pures, dont il s'amuse et nous veut amuser. Il ne songe pas un moment que derrière l'extérieure bizarrerie des faits il y ait une pensée vraie, un sentiment sérieux.... Ce bourgeois de Troyes avait du talent: mais son talent était contraire à son sujet; il le dissolvait en le maniant.

Appendix

"Chrétien de Troyes avait commencé de raconter l'histoire de Perceval, qui est bien la plus étrange, invraisemblable, incohérente collection d'aventures qu'on puisse voir: tout y arrive sans raison ou contre raison.... Le bon Chrétien n'avait pas l'âme mystique, et n'était nullement symboliste."

1923 Edmond Faral's treatment of Chrétien and the *Perceval*, given in Bédier et Hazard, *Littérature Française* (Paris), I, 18 ff., 40 ff., we highly commend. Faral discerns that we cannot assume that Chrétien borrowed from pagan Celtic sources whose very existence has never been established. "Les littératures celtiques (galloise et irlandaise) ne fournissent aucun de ces prétendus modèles qui auraient servi aux romanciers français.... On peut donc imaginer à son aise l'existence de poèmes celtiques qui auraient été la source des romans français; mais le fait est que nous ne connaissons absolument rien de ces poèmes hypothétiques, que rien n'en subsiste et que nul auteur n'en a fait mention; en sorte qu'on se demande s'il en a jamais existé un seul." However, Faral (opposite p. 18) shows a picture of the Modena tympanum and he follows Emile Mâle in believing that the lintel is inspired by scenes of the *Roman de Renard*.

1927 R. S. Loomis, *Celtic Myth and Arthurian Romance* (New York). Loomis endeavors to explain the myths themselves among the Gaelic folk. He believes that these *fabulae* were of Irish origin, spreading from Ireland to Wales or Cornwall, thence to Brittany and France where Chrétien used them.

1930 W. A. Nitze and T. P. Cross, *Lancelot and Guinevere* (Chicago), identify the "fairy Winlogée" [whom we identify as the Virtue of Truth] with Guinevere.

1931 Mme Lot-Borodine (*Romania*, LVII, 196-8): "La mise en scène du conte de Chrétien de Troyes ne nous paraît relever d'aucun rite exotique.... Il est assez piquant de voir Chrétien de Troyes, traité d'habitude comme un aimable sceptique et un simple amuseur, promu subitement au rang d'écrivain quasi ecclésiastique.... Moraliste, il l'a toujours été, posant et s'efforçant à résoudre de délicats problèmes de psychologie sentimentale, dénouant adroitement les conflits entre amour et chevalerie. En un mot, un écrivain à thèse, capable, en plus, d'atteindre à une certaine spiritualité à mi-côté, à preuve son *Perceval* inachevé. Rien de moins, rien de plus." Mme Lot-Borodine also asserts (*ibid.*, pp. 186-9) that the chalice and the paten must be made of the same material. Because Chrétien's *graal* is of gold, and his *tailleor* (or paten) of silver, she concludes that the grail is not a chalice. She has misinterpreted her Latin citation, inasmuch as different metals are admissible together today just as in the twelfth century (see my "Liturgy and Allegory in Chrétien's *Perceval*," p. 13). At Toulouse, in the Cathedral of Saint-Etienne, there was represented the story of Saint Exupère, who in time of great stress had sold the ornaments of the church, even the chalice and the paten, to relieve the poor. Henceforth, he used a glass chalice and a paten made of reeds (Mâle, *L'Art religieux du XIIe siècle*, p. 190).

Incidentally, if for Chrétien the silver *tailleor* was also one of the vessels used by Christ at the Last Supper—similar to one of those supposedly brought back to France by Charlemagne in the *Pèlerinage*, v. 177—it is understandable that Chrétien's *graal* should have been of a different metal; the record does not show that the table-service of the Last Supper was either all of gold or all of silver. Moreover, Mme Lot-Borodine flatly denies contact of the consecrated host with the chalice and paten. "Où se trouve déjà une hostie consacrée, la patène n'a rien à faire; elle accompagne obligatoirement le calice, jamais le ciboire, *intra ou extra missam*" (*ibid.*). She overlooks the Liturgy for Holy Week when, during the Mass of Holy Thursday, the host is placed in a chalice covered with the paten, where it is reserved until the Mass of the Presanctified on Good Friday. During each Mass, there is contact between the consecrated host, the paten, and the chalice, in the Roman and the Dominican rites.

1932 Lanson and Tuffrau, *Manuel d'histoire de la littérature française* (Paris and Boston), pp. 28-30. "Chrétien de Troyes est un adroit faiseur de vers, sans conviction, sans gravité.... Il est entièrement dépourvu du sens du mystère. Il dessèche tout, il clarifie tout.... Les conventions de l'amour courtois se sont substituées à la passion celtique, trop profonde, trop orageuse pour notre superficiel Champenois et ses lecteurs.... Tous ces éléments [du *Conte du Graal*] semblent être des débris d'anciens mythes auxquels Chrétien, à son ordinaire, n'aura rien compris."

1938 Nitze and Dargan, *A History of French Literature* (New York), p. 47: "What the Grail originally was no one knows, although attempts to explain it are not lacking. To Crestien the word was still a common noun, *graal* meaning a dish or platter ordinarily used in the houses of the wealthy. Yet he himself speaks of it as *tant sainte chose* and gives it qualities which are marvelous and in part mystical. When the dish is carried in a procession, the 'gleam' of the Grail is beheld by hundreds of knights; and *a single wafer on it* [italics mine] sustains the life of a century-old king."

1947 Mario Roques, in his introduction to Foulet's translation of Chrétien's *Perceval le Gallois ou le Conte du Graal* (Paris), pp. xxi-xxiii, states that Chrétien's graal is a ciborium, but later modified his views in his "Le Graal de Chrétien et la demoiselle au Graal." Here he asserts, as we do, that the Grail is a chalice. See *infra*, 1955.

1947 Urban T. Holmes, Jr., "A New Interpretation of Chrétien's *Conte del Graal*," *Studies in Philology*, XLIV, 453-76.

1948 Helaine Newstead, "The Besieged Ladies in Arthurian Romance," *PMLA*, LXIII, 828, note 109: "It is difficult to understand how Blancheflor's conduct can be interpreted as chaste."

1948 Urban T. Holmes, Jr., "A New Interpretation of Chrétien's *Conte del Graal*," *University of North Carolina Studies in the Romance Languages and Literatures*, VIII. This is a somewhat revised version of Professor Holmes's article of the same title (see *supra*, 1947).

1949 R. S. Loomis, *Arthurian Tradition and Chrétien de Troyes* (New York), p. 172, maintains that Chrétien, in regard to the Grail, was "drawing upon a tradition concerned with a horn (nom. *corz* or *cors;* oblq. *cor*)." He contends that the immediate prototype of the Grail was a Welsh platter (*dysgl*) of plenty (p. 387). Loomis is convinced that in the *Conte del Graal* the flagrant violation of the most elementary proprieties of Christian ethics and ritual should be enough to condemn any theory of pious fabrication (pp. 372, 476). "Nor can I believe as some have maintained, that because Chrétien's last poem contains a short passage (some 300 out of 9,200 lines) relating the visit of Perceval to his Hermit Uncle, describing the graal as a receptacle for a magical mass wafer, and setting forth some rudimentary lessons in Christian faith, the poet turned over a new leaf in his old age and consecrated his declining years to a work of piety. The last 2,800 lines of the poem as well as the flagrantly unsanctified atmosphere of the Grail scene itself, should suffice to condemn such a theory. If, as I believe, Chrétien was a man of high intelligence, literary genius, and a more than elementary knowledge of religious matters, he could not have been satisfied with the inadequate motivation, the rambling plot, the strange moral emphasis, and the fantastically uncanonical representation of the Grail as a receptacle for the Host which we discover in his romance; far less could he have invented them. We know that the choice of a source was made for him; he seems to have followed it through thick and thin, happy when he dealt with the humorous escapades of his simpleton hero or with the romance of the Maid with the Little Sleeves, but somewhat embarrassed by the Blancheflor affair, puzzled by the procession of *graal* and lance, probably even more puzzled by the casual explanation of the Hermit, finally pursuing with resigned bewilderment the erratic itinerary of Gauvain and his capricious guide, Orguelleuse de Logres." Loomis continues: "Nowhere in all this can I discover any sign of marked independence, of addition or alteration. Just as in the *Charrete* Chrétien did just what he said he did, so we can believe him when he professed to do no more with Count Philip's book than to turn it into rime" (p. 466). See Stefan Hofer's comment on this (p. 219; *infra*, 1954) and also J. J. Parry, *Modern Language Quarterly*, XII (1952), 99.

1949 W. A. Nitze maintains that *Perceval* has an obvious pagan background and that the inexact reference to Saint Paul in the prologue is no more significant than the one in the *Cligés* 5324; that *Perceval* is a romance of adolescence compounded out of separate strains: the themes of the Tent-Lady and of the Hospitable Host are borrowed by Chrétien from his own *Erec* and *Yvain*, the golden cup and the vessel of plenty are derived from Celtic folklore, and the Bleeding Lance and the Procession before the Fisher King are taken from Byzantine sources; that this method of combining disparate elements is just what we would expect in the twelfth century and that it is not at all monstrous. ("Perceval and the Holy Grail," *University of California Publications in Modern Philology*, XXVIII, No. 5, 301, 324, 325.)

1950 Albert Pauphilet, *Le Legs du Moyen Age* (Melun), p. 180, finds that Perceval's silence at the Grail Castle accords well psychologically with the clumsy way he had previously conducted himself. However, Pauphilet censures Chrétien for having Perceval reproached three times by different characters, of whom two attribute his silence to the mortal sin he had contracted in causing his mother's death by departing against her wishes. Pauphilet considers the moral explanation of Chrétien at this point "artificiel et, au fond, assez absurde." And he believes that it was totally indifferent and without consequence to the continuation of the story whether Perceval's mother lived or died. (I have discussed these attitudes of Pauphilet in my article on "The Spiritual Ascent of Perceval," pp. 8-9.)

1950 Raphael Levy, "Quest for Biographical Evidence in *Perceval*," *Medievalia et Humanistica*, VI, 82 and note 29: "I did not deem it necessary to challenge his [Holmes's] interpretation of the *Perceval*, preferring to await the decision of others. H. Newstead [*supra*, 1948] wonders how Holmes could find a chaste motive in Blancheflor's nocturnal visit to Perceval." Moreover, in this article Levy has twisted Holmes's study into a syllogism which Holmes never formulated. Holmes set out to demonstrate three independent hypotheses: (a) that Chrétien may possibly have been a converted Jew, also known as *Crestiens li Gois;* (b) that the *Perceval* is an allegory in which the "Quest of the Holy Grail is the conversion of the Jewish Temple to Christianity"; (c) that the Fisher King is Jacob, who was lame as a result of his struggle with the Angel of the Lord and is also High Priest in the Grail Castle, a symbolic representation of the Temple of Solomon in Jerusalem. Holmes has ably demonstrated his main contention: the major source of Chrétien's poem is to be found in St. Paul. This demonstration stands, regardless of any speculation about Chrétien's racial origins. For Levy, Chrétien's racial origin is the gravamen of the debate.

1950 Urban T. Holmes, Jr., "The Arthurian Tradition in Lambert d'Ardres," *Speculum*, XXV, 100-03.

1951 Jean Marx, *La Légende arthurienne et le graal* (Paris), believes that the very subject of the Grail story is of pagan origin. According to Marx, the Procession of the Holy Grail is nothing more than the ancient rites of initiation and investiture in the royalty conformable to the notions of Celtic mythology.

1951 Mme Rita Lejeune, *Studi Medievali*, XVII, 8: "Or, dans quel calice, dans quel ciboire pourrait-on loger un saumon ou une lamproie, qui ne passent pas précisément pour des alevins?" Mario Roques answers this question (see *infra*, 1955), as does Mme Lot-Borodine (*infra*, 1956).

1951 Sister M. Amelia Klenke, O.P., "Liturgy and Allegory in

Chrétien's *Perceval*," *University of North Carolina Studies in the Romance Languages and Literatures*, XIV.

1952 W. A. Nitze, "The Fisher King and the Grail in Retrospect," *Romance Philology*, VI, 15: "As for the grail, there is little to commend Loomis's idea [*Arthurian Tradition and Chrétien de Troyes*, p. 172] that Chrétien was 'drawing upon a tradition concerned with a horn (nom. *corz* or *cors*; oblq. *cor*).' Chrétien's *graal* was a 'dish' or platter, and to connect it with a 'horn' requires steps that I am unable to follow."

1952 Alexandre Micha, "Deux Etudes sur le Graal," *Romania*, LXXIII, 462 ff.: Building on Mme Lot-Borodine's premises (see *supra*, 1931), Micha conceives of the *graal* as a pyxidium or pyx. He discusses at some length Chrétien's words *trestot descovert* (v. 3301) as applied to the grail. (See my article, "Chrétien's Symbolism and Cathedral Art," pp. 230, 233, 237-9.)

1952 Sister M. Amelia Klenke, O. P., "The Blancheflor-Perceval Question," *Romance Philology*, VI, 173-8.

1953 Helaine Newstead, "The Blancheflor-Perceval Question Again," *Romance Philology*, VII, 171-5, once more tries to prove that the relationship between these two characters was anything but chaste. We have criticized her arguments in the article, "The Spiritual Ascent of Perceval."

1953 Jean Frappier: "C'est faire fausse route que de chercher une correspondance précise entre le texte de Chrétien et les rites de l'Eglise.... J'admets que Chrétien a voulu garder ou créer autour du Graal une irradiation de sacré, un halo de religion, en faire le symbole d'un idéal à quêter.... mais une atmosphère religieuse assez vague, un peu floue, était plus propice à son dessein de romancier que l'imitation de rites réels—imitation qu'on découvre d'autant moins qu'on scrute davantage son texte.... Je ne boude pas la liturgie; j'estime simplement qu'elle n'explique aucune des énigmes du *Conte del Graal*" (*Romania*, LXXIII [1952], 92; LXXIV [1953], 367). "Le rapprochement entre l'énumeration des reliques dans *Le Pèlerinage de Charlemagne* et la description de la lance qui saigne et du Graal n'a vraiment rien de saisissant" (*Romania,* LXXIV [1953], 368). "Il est évident que les vers 6420-21 [Mes ne cuidez pas que il et Luz ne lamproies ne saumon] font allusion aux mets qu'on pourrait normalement s'attendre à voir portés dans un graal" ("Chrétien de Troyes: *Perceval ou le conte du Graal*," in *Les Cours de Sorbonne* [Paris, 1953], p. 90). Mario Roques has commented on this last statement (see *infra,* 1955).

1953 Flavia Anderson, *The Ancient Secret* (London, 1953). As the publishers say on the flap of the book-jacket: "This study of the origins of the legend of the Holy Grail is daring and original in its theme ... and imaginative in its development of the argument." Lady Flavia believes that the Grail was the holy object of a mystery cult not confined to Britain but so widespread as to be almost universal. She believes that this holy object was venerated because it demonstrated in symbolic fashion the mystery of the Trinity and that therefore both Jew and Gentile had some knowledge of the three-fold nature of God thousands of years before the Incarnation of Christ. According to Lady Flavia, the Grail is in fact the symbol of all earthly matter, including all natural generative powers, and the spear, a vital element in the legend, represents the entry of the divine into matter. She believes, however, that the Grail had a very definite material existence and that it was treasured in Glastonbury Abbey until the dissolution of the monasteries. Lady Flavia's theory is that the legend of the Grail had its origin in the almost universal cult of the sun, that the Grail was the "cauldron" or crystal which focused the sun's rays for the lighting of the fire. In developing her thesis, the author weaves a complex pattern of myth, hypothesis, and factual information: Egyptian burial customs, the Norse sagas, the alchemists' search for the philosopher's stone, the ritual of fire-making, the Grail-tree and the golden bough, the Grail-crystal and the apple of the Sun-god etc. "Lady Flavia seeks to clarify the profoundest problem of religion: God the sun, Mary (the 'virgin-vessel') as the lens, Jesus as the candle lit by the sun, and the rays from both sun and candle as the Holy Spirit."

1954 Mme Rita Lejeune, "La Date du *Conte du Graal* de Chrétien de Troyes," *Le Moyen Age*, LX, 51-79, places the composition of *Perceval* between August, 1179, and April, 1181. She draws ten parallels between the life of Perceval and the life of Philippe Auguste to show that Philippe d'Alsace sponsored the *Conte del Graal* as a pedagogical treatise "destiné à servir l'éducation chevaleresque de son royal filleul et élève." She points out that Chrétien de Troyes, who never mentions Jews in his other works, displays violent hatred toward them twice in his *Perceval:* "Lors de l'épisode du Vendredi Saint, c'est un véritable massacre des Juifs que les pieux pèlerins réclament en évoquant la mort du Christ." We have demonstrated *supra* that this hatred for the Jews was not a hatred harbored by Chrétien but a hatred which was reflected in the misguided zeal of many of the Crusaders (see chap. 7, pp. 121-22, and note 22). It was against just such hatred that Chrétien was apparently working when he wrote his *Perceval*, a tale whereby he sought the conversion of the Jewish Temple to offset further bloodshed of the Jews in France, Germany, and England.

1954 D. de Séchelles, *L'Origine du Graal* (Saint-Brieuc), p. 51: "Bien que le sujet du Graal soit d'origine chrétienne, c'est cet apport celtique qui lui confère non seulement son originalité et sa valeur poétique mais une grande part de sa portée morale. La religion ne saurait suffire à en expliquer le caractère." "Il faut avouer qu'il serait surprenant, pour expliquer un thème qui apparaît pour la première fois au XIIe siècle, que l'on soit obligé de remonter si loin dans le passé [à des rites païens celtiques]" (p. 7). *"Le Conte du Graal* ... fut écrit entre 1180 et 1185" (p. 9). "Ainsi, au début du XIIIe siècle nous nous trouvons en présence de deux oeuvres relatives au Graal ayant entre elles une ressemblance évidente, se situant l'une et l'autre dans le monde celtique, mais conçues dans un esprit très différent: d'une part celle de Chrétien de Troyes, de caractère à peine religieux, qui renferme des allusions inexplicables et qui possède un charme certain, d'autre part celle de Robert de Boron où le récit est transformé, le thème infléchi dans le sens chrétien mais qui n'a qu'un intérêt littéraire assez faible" (p. 14). "C'est un fait que Chrétien se plaît aux allusions et aux sous-entendus. En outre il a pu modifier à sa guise le récit que lui avait transmis Philippe de Flandres. Mais d'autre part nous savons qu'il était sensible à la poésie des contes celtiques et qu'il se souciait moins d'écrire un récit édifant que Robert de Boron et ceux qui l'ont suivi" (p. 21). (This statement we challenge. See *supra*, chap. 6.) "D'autre part de nombreux traits mythiques sont apparents dans l'aventure de Perceval et le graal lui-même évoque incontestablement le fameux chaudron d'abondance, symbole de fécondité et de puissance, que possèdent les divinités celtiques.... Il ne fait aucun doute par conséquent qu'il existe dans le thème du Graal tout un fond emprunté au paganisme.... Mais est-ce à dire que ces éléments d'origine celtique ont constitué plus qu'un milieu extrêmement favorable au développement de ce thème, un terroir particulièrement riche par suite du merveilleux qu'il apportait et qui pouvait s'y incorporer facilement? Le sujet lui-même est-il d'origine païenne? M. Jean Marx n'hésite pas à le croire et c'est ici où nous nous séparons quelque peu de sa manière de voir" (p. 25). "Qu'il y ait dans la littérature arthurienne et en particulier dans le thème du Graal bien des traits provenant de la mythologie celtique, c'est incontestable. Il est normal que les vieux rites païens qui ont déteint en quelque sorte sur les conceptions chrétiennes pendant les premiers siècles aient laissé des traces jusque dans la littérature. Mais de là à penser que le sujet lui-même du Graal soit d'origine païenne, il y a un espace considérable que l'on hésite à franchir surtout si l'on songe qu'il faut pour cela faire abstraction de dix siècles d'histoire"

(p. 28). "Il faut bien remarquer, en effet, que le cortège n'est pas une scène liturgique, mais une représentation symbolique. La différence est essentielle; on ne saurait trop insister là-dessus" (p. 29). The author is also to be commended for what he says (p. 32) concerning the Bleeding Lance.

"Dans l'*Historia Brittonum* [de Nennius, qui fut écrite au plus tard au IXe siècle], nous apprenons qu'il [Arthur] a gagné l'une de ses batailles grâce à l'effigie de la Vierge qu'il portait sur son armure, et autant que la renaissance de la Bretagne, ce qu'on attend de lui c'est le triomphe de la religion du Christ. Même après la conversion des Saxons, cette idée subsistera parmi les Bretons. A leurs yeux il fait donc figure de sauveur, on l'attend comme un messie" (pp. 40-41). "Il est certain que la légende du retour d'Arthur, étant d'origine essentiellement populaire, renfermait bien des éléments païens et l'on conçoit que le personnage du grand roi qui tendait à s'identifier au Messie n'ait pas été vu très favorablement par le clergé. C'est vraisemblablement sous l'influence du bardisme, héritier des traditions héroïques et païennes, qu'est née au sein du peuple breton la légende du retour d'Arthur. Renan, dans son célèbre essai sur *La Poésie des Races Celtiques*, a exprimé à ce sujet des idées qui gardent tout leur intérêt. Le VIe siècle, on le sait, a été la grande époque de la poésie bardique. Malheureusement nous ne connaissons plus que quelques noms des poètes de ce temps.... Si nous possédions leurs oeuvres elles nous éclaireraient vraisemblablement sur la naissance du mythe arthurien" (pp. 44-5). "Toutefois la profonde signification spirituelle et la complexité du thème du Graal peuvent laisser croire que l'Eglise n'a pas été étrangère à son origine. Il y a un fait important à cet égard: c'est qu'à partir de la fin du XIe siècle, c'est-à-dire de l'arrivée des Normands en Bretagne, le clergé s'est efforcé de lutter contre les croyances populaires concernant Arthur. ...On devait s'efforcer de le reduire à des proportions humaines et en premier lieu de détruire la croyance à son immortalité" (p. 46). This part of Séchelles' discussion is interesting to us, especially because of the tympanum at Modena and of Chrétien's symbolism which fits in so perfectly with it. For here, indeed, Arthur appears to be a symbol of Christ. It would seem to us that the Modena portal and Chrétien's poem are indicative of an effort on the part of the Church to put the Arthurian legend to the best possible advantage: to Christianize it thoroughly. There may have been some who mistook the symbol for the reality (just as there are many in the twentieth century who fail to understand twelfth-century symbolism). And it may have been partly on this account that ecclesiastics at Glastonbury decided to put an end to the worship of Arthur and to his immortality by "finding" his grave. We have long felt that the stir in Glastonbury had some connection with the writing of the *Perceval*. Séchelles has an interesting theory which deserves consideration: "Quant à l'œuvre de Geoffrey de Monmouth qui voit le jour peu après (en pays soumis à l'influence normande) il n'est pas sûr de tout, malgré les apparences, qu'elle ne procède pas de mêmes tendances. Car il était assez habile, il faut l'avouer, pour ruiner la croyance à Arthur et à son retour, d'en faire le héros d'une prodigieuse épopée, de le situer dans le domaine de la pure fiction en lui faisant conquérir une partie de l'Europe et de dépeindre sa cour sous des traits que tous les Bretons reconnaissent comme imaginaires" (p. 47). And the author concludes by thinking that it was an act of strategic politics on the part of Gautier of Oxford, Alexander of Lincoln, and other dignitaries of the Church of England of which Geoffrey of Monmouth was the protégé, before he himself became Bishop of St.-Asaph. What leads Séchelles particularly to this conclusion is the supposed discovery, in 1191, of the tombs of Arthur and of Guenevere in the Glastonbury Abbey. Thus the Church put an end to the superstitions which persisted among the Bretons concerning the immortality and the second coming of Arthur. This explanation seems much more plausible than that of

Ferdinand Lot, which makes of Glastonbury a veritable "officine de faux."

Again we agree with the author when he writes (p. 47): "Il semble donc qu'il y ait eu au cours du XIIe siècle une action, peut-être même un plan concerté, de la part du clergé de Grande-Bretagne pour lutter contre les traditions légendaires concernant Arthur. Et il est permis de penser que le thème du Graal a été imaginé d'après cette tendance." However, we do not hold with Séchelles when he says (pp. 14 and 21; see *supra*) that Chrétien's *Conte del Graal* was scarcely of a religious character and that Chrétien cared less than Robert de Boron and other continuators about writing an edifying tale. We hold that Chrétien used this Arthurian material to the best possible advantage, in a way most effective for the needs of the Church at that time: in an effort to convert the Jewish Temple and thus avert the further shedding of Jewish blood in France and elsewhere. This theory of ours gains added weight when it is recalled that Gautier de Châtillon, or de l'Isle, wrote a *Tractatus contra Judaeos* (Migne, *P.L.*, vol. CCIX, cols. 423-58) which was a dialogue on the theme of converting the Jews to Christianity and which compared the plight of the Synagogue awaiting its Messias to that of the Britons awaiting the second coming of Arthur. (See Margaret Schlauch, *Speculum*, XIV [1939], 461. Raphael Levy has referred to the *Tractatus* in "The Quest for Biographical Evidence in *Perceval*," p. 81.)

1954 Jean Marx, *Medium Aevum*, XXIII, 132: "Les explications par la symbolique ou la liturgie chrétienne ne rendent compte ni de la description du cortège du Graal, ni des objets merveilleux qui y sont portés, ni des caractères féeriques qui y sont attachés à ces mêmes objets.... Ces mêmes explications par le symbolisme et la liturgie ne peuvent rendre compte de la composition du conte du Graal avec ses énigmes et ses épreuves. Cette série de jeux n'a pu s'établir en partant des réalités les plus sacrées et les plus fondamentales du culte chrétien."

1954 Stefan Hofer, *Chrétien de Troyes—Leben und Werk* (Köln). The author claims that there is no Celtic tale which in structure, content, and sense, could come close to Chrétien's tale. Certain similarities in detail, he adds, are no proof at all for those who claim Celtic sources for the Champenois poet. The characteristic mark of Chrétien's spear—the bleeding—is totally lacking in all Celtic sources. And Hofer laughs at the idea of twelfth-century Frenchmen being interested in these imaginary Celtic heroes of the god Bran since there was no common bond between these strange Celtic heroes and twelfth-century Frenchmen. Hofer maintains that one cannot assume that the Anglo-Norman aristocracy in England or the Continental knighthood could have found the slightest degree of pleasure in ancient Celtic folklore with its primitive way of thinking and its culture based on the lowest of moral standards (pp. 196 ff.). He believes that Chrétien composed the *Perceval* between 1180-1197 (p. 201). He analyzes the hero's spiritual ascent culminating in charity (love of God), a theme the poet had stressed in his prologue. The author notes (pp. 214 ff.) the parallel which Chrétien has drawn between the worldly knight, Gornemanz, and the spiritual chivalry of the Crusaders. The poet's genius manifested itself, says Hofer, in his ability to blend the worldly Arthurian romance of adventure and courtly love with the deeply religious theme of the Passion relics. (Cf. Miss Newstead's review of this book in *Romance Philology*, X [1956], 56-61.)

1955 Sister M. Amelia Klenke, O. P., "Chrétien's Symbolism and Cathedral Art," *PMLA*, LXX, 223-43.

1955 Mario Roques, "Le Graal de Chrétien et la demoiselle au Graal," *Société de publications romanes et françaises*, L, studies the use to which Chrétien puts the Grail and the manner in which it is carried. By comparing these findings with illuminations in the twelfth-century *Hortus deliciarum* made for the Abbess Herrade, he concludes that Chrétien's *graal* could not have been anything but a chalice. He answers the objections raised by Mme Lejeune (see *supra*,

1951) and Jean Frappier (see *supra,* 1953) concerning Chrétien's verses 6420-1 ("Mes ne cuidez pas que il [le *graal*] et Luz ne lamproies ne saumon"): "On a conclu que le '*graal*' était assez grand pour pouvoir contenir des poissons de belle taille, comme les plats que nous voyons sur table dans des représentations figurées dont nous donnerons plus bas quelques exemples. Mais en fait ces poissons ne figurent dans les propos de l'ermite que par allusion, et rien ne permet d'affirmer que, s'ils avaient été réellement servis au vieillard, ils lui auraient été apportés justement dans ce graal ou dans un vase semblable" (pp. 2-3, note 3). The *tailleor* Roques identifies with the paten usually associated with the chalice; the Bleeding Lance is for him the lance of the Passion; the lance-bearer is Longinus; the maiden bearing the Grail is the Church Triumphant. The first four of these identifications (the chalice, the paten, the Lance of the Passion, and Longinus) I had made in 1951 ("Liturgy and Allegory in Chrétien's *Perceval*"). The fifth identification—that of the Church Triumphant— had been made by us in "Chrétien's Symbolism and Cathedral Art," submitted to *PMLA* in February, 1952, and printed in March, 1955. Mario Roques' booklet here discussed appeared the following month. That we have reached the same set of conclusions by means of a slightly different approach and each unknown to the other would seem to add validity to our findings.

1956 R. S. Loomis, "The Grail Story of Chrétien de Troyes as Ritual and Symbolism," *PMLA,* LXXI, 840-52. This detailed and severe criticism of my article, "Chrétien's Symbolism and Cathedral Art," is a not unexpected corollary to its author's loyal conviction (which he reaffirms, p. 850) that "it is the hypothesis of Celtic origin which answers the many riddles of the Perceval story and the Grail legend."

Concerning the relation between Perceval and Blancheflor (pp. 841-3), Loomis finds it impossible to believe that Chrétien could have written of love within the literary conventions of *courtoisie*, and at the same time remain "orthodox in his religious and moral outlook." Why not? The *tailleor d'arjant* (v. 3231) is disturbing to him as a symbol for the paten, but he overlooks the fact that the *tailleor* is described as *small* (v. 3567). Loomis's commentary suffers from several basic misapprehensions concerning the Liturgy. Troubled by the circumstance that the Grail is carried by a woman, he fails (unlike Roques and Mme Lot-Borodine) to consider her as an allegorical depiction of Ecclesia, often represented in mediaeval art as bearing a chalice. He is unaware of the fact that in twelfth-century religious art Synagoga was often represented with the Lance of the Passion. He is troubled by wingless angels, as even the ill-educated Perceval was not. Loomis does not mention the fact that the Fathers of the Church were almost unanimous in thinking that Our Lord partook of the Communion at the Last Supper: Chrétien could hardly have been unaware of this almost universal opinion. Loomis finds (p. 846) an implication in my paper that "Chrétien was reproducing the liturgical practices of Holy Week in the Grail procession." His quotations prove (p. 849) that the Procession was not a sacred rite, but my suggestion had been merely that this ceremony was inspired by liturgical ritual. Another misinterpretation is his assertion (p. 847) of my non-existent implication "that the only [mediaeval] vessels made of precious metals were chalices or wine-cups." And finally (p. 848) Loomis misrepresents me as having assumed that Synagoga was a vaslet in disguise.

So long as Grail disagreements continue (and they will) and so long as they remain informed with vigor and good feeling, scholarly interest will not be the loser. At several points in his article, Loomis graciously and urbanely points the way. For instance, he says: "No one, I suppose, would question that [Chrétien] was much concerned with the Grail and its many mysteries.... It may be granted, of course, that the life-sustaining host is a motif derived from current legends of the Eucharist and is not of Celtic origin."

1956 Raphael Levy, "The Motivation of *Perceval* and the Authorship of *Philomena*," PMLA, LXXI, 853-62. In his review of scholarship Professor Levy (p. 853) makes the crucial misrepresentation that "Holmes needs hypotheses (a) and (b) and (c) to support each other"—an idea which has never been Holmes's or mine. In fact, in the *PMLA* article which Levy is criticizing here, I have "brushed aside" the first hypothesis, Chrétien's possible conversion from Judaism, as Levy admits (p. 855). As far back as 1951, in my "Liturgy and Allegory" (p. 6), I was at pains to recall that "Holmes is careful to indicate that Chrétien's possible conversion is proposed only as a suggestion, and by no means a demonstrated fact." Yet, Levy still assumes (p. 854) that "the gravamen of the debate is whether to accept a biographical conclusion which is admittedly an assumption." It is not even so much as an assumption. It is merely a possibility which, incidentally, has unleashed unusual quantities of sometimes irrelevant speculation. Since Levy's title links motivation of *Perceval* with the *Philomena* authorship problem, precisely what does the speculation add to his discussion?

As a final word, I should like to acknowledge my indebtedness to Miss Helen Adolf for sending me a needed correction (p. 228 of my article, "Chrétien's Symbolism and Cathedral Art"). She points out that what I "describe as Wolfram's Grail Stone (vv. 233 20 ff.) is the *table* used by the Fisher King, wheras the Grail itself is described 234 20 ff."

1956 Mme Lot-Borodine, "Le *Conte del Graal* de Chrétien de Troyes et sa présentation symbolique," *Romania*, LXXVII, 235-88. In this long study, the author praises highly the findings of Mario Roques and Alexandre Micha and treats critically the theories advanced by R. S. Loomis, Jean Marx, and other Celticist scholars. "Elle [la théorie de Mario Roques] a au surplus l'avantage de bâtir un terrain vierge, c'est-à-dire en faisant abstraction de toute la littérature folklorique qui, de plus en plus touffue, foisonne depuis plusieurs générations autour du grand Mythe médiéval, en faussant délibérément son vrai sens. . . . Disons-le, une fois pour toutes: il y a pour nous impossibilité intrinsèque de la transmutation des valeurs propres d'une civilisation à l'autre quand ces valeurs, sociales, éthiques, religieuses surtout, restent foncièrement dissemblables. Des emprunts de motifs, quelques fictions poétiques; oui, jeux de surface uniquement, mais pas davantage car deux mondes hétérogènes ne peuvent fusionner. Un chaudron magique ne se transforme pas subitement en vase de la Grâce eucharistique, pas plus qu'un sorcier patenté ne deviendra un saint authentique. C'est ici l'erreur initiale de toute l'argumentation des critiques folkloristes qui combinent obstinément les données *matérielles* et jonglent avec des rapprochements purement extérieurs. Ceci tout particulièrement en ce qui concerne la 'senefiance' du Graal et de la Lance en tant que symboles *spirituels*. De même, lorsque Jean Marx dans son ouvrage de synthèse, *La Légende arthurienne et le Graal*, assimile le thème de la *transmission de la Souveraineté*,—qui reprend le thème du prêtre de Némi,—à la quête salvifique du vaisseau de la Grâce, il méconnaît l'inspiration originale, proprement chrétienne, *née* sous d'autres cieux, de cette Quête, humainement nostalgique et non sociologique. Un tel métissage des valeurs est inacceptable" (pp. 234-6).

The author accepts (p. 239) Mario Roques' identification of the Grail-bearer as Ecclesia and praises Roques' statement: "elle a recueilli ce sang qui la crée elle-même et qui fait sa mission permanente, et elle porte éternellement le vase où il se renferme." Speaking of the light emanating from the Grail, Mme Lot-Borodine writes (p. 240): "Aucune erreur n'est possible sur ce point pour un chrétien: voilà le *sol invictus* des Anciens,—le Christ de la Présence réelle—; c'est bien ce que nous révèle l'Hostie que le Graal contient. . . . Inutile donc d'invoquer les relents du culte solaire pour expliquer le rayonnement du Graal, comme le fait Jean Frappier (dans *Lumière du Graal*, Paris, 1952) [1951, pp. 175 ff.].... Le Graal, qui contient le *Corpus Domini*, ne saurait être, en effet, qu'un objet sacré, aux mains de la rayonnante graalophore, l'Eglise. Il semble impossible de ne pas s'incliner devant ce fait indubitable, patent, précis. Si l'on s'obstine quand même à voir en lui la séquelle d'un chaudron magique, le 'nourishing vessel' des légendes celtiques, ce n'est qu'en partant d'un *a priori* simplifié à l'extrême.—De fait, le viatique des chrétiens est aliment, nourriture par excellence, 'soustènement' du corps et de l'âme. Nous partons de là d'un pas ferme." Mme Lot-Borodine agrees that the Bleeding Lance is the Lance of the Passion, and that the Lance-bearer is Longinus: "Ce flot de sang...s'échappant du flanc transpercé, symbolise ... d'après l'antique croyance, les deux sacrements majeurs: le Baptême [necessary for the conversion of the Temple], naissance de la créature nouvelle; l'Eucharistie qui parachève cette rénovation, par l'énergie caritative de l'union divino-humaine. Voilà donc tout le cercle sacramentaire qui s'ouvre et qui se referme devant le regard du croyant" (pp. 247 ff.).

In connection with Holmes's theory that the Grail Castle is an allegorical representation of the Temple of Solomon, Mme Lot-Borodine adds an interesting point when she states (p. 249) that Wesselovsky considered the Oriental legends of Solomon as the sources of the prose romances of the Grail.

Mme Lot-Borodine differs from Mario Roques (and from us) by maintaining once again that the *graal* is a ciborium (or pyx) and that the *tailleor* is a vessel used to collect the Precious Blood. "Il semble que tout le monde soit d'accord aujourd'hui pour considérer ce porte-hostie [the Grail] uniquement comme un *ciboire* (ou pyxis), du moment qu'il sert à une communion à domicile.... Considérons la demoiselle qui porte ce *petit* tailloir d'argent comme un personnage symbolique, elle aussi. En ce cas, elle représente une des vertus théologales, très probablement 'la Foi en l'Eucharistie,' telle qu'on la trouve, dès la fin du siècle, dans les monuments figurés" (pp. 244-5). We have already criticized Mme Lot-Borodine's identification of the *graal* and Alexandre Micha's theories springing from this identification (see my article, "Chrétien's Symbolism and Cathedral Art," p. 233, and *supra*, pp. 172, 177). Suffice it to say that, in this allegorical procession, it would seem amazing for Chrétien—always so meticulously liturgical—to depart from the standard iconography of the Church by placing in the hands of Ecclesia a ciborium rather than a chalice. In ecclesiastical art from the earliest times, the chalice—rather than the ciborium or pyx—is associated with the host and/or the paten. We have spoken (chap. 7, pp. 111, 157) of Giovanni del Biondo's painting in which Ecclesia is depicted as holding in her left hand a chalice surmounted by a paten and a host. That the bearer of Chrétien's *tailleor* should be one of the theological virtues, as Mme Lot-Borodine suggests, seems very likely. However, since the Eucharist is the Sacrament of love and since the paten is so closely associated with both the chalice and the host, we suggest that the bearer of the *tailleor* may be Caritas. Moreover, as Stapper reminds us (*Catholic Liturgics* [Paterson, N. J., 1935], p. 232): "The chalice alone suggests the Heart of Jesus overflowing with the love of God (*caritas*).... The paten... likewise suggests the Heart of Jesus (*cor patens*) burning with love for mankind, but also the love of the disciples who surround Jesus.... Together they [the chalice and the paten] symbolize the new grave in which the disciples laid the body of the Lord." Webber (gloss) offers a reminder that the chalice symbolizes faith and as such was frequently put into the hands of the Virtue of Faith in mediaeval art; the paten is symbolical of the Eucharist and as such was essential to Chrétien's symbolical Blessed-Sacrament Procession.

Mme Lot-Borodine continues: "Le Graal ne contient que le *siccum sacrificium*, voir l'Hostie seule. Et c'est pour cette raison formelle... que la Lance, qui représente ainsi que le dit justement Mario Roques, le principe de *permanence, saigne perpétuellement* et qu'elle ouvre la marche au château du mystère eucharistique. Le voisinage—on voudrait presque dire le jumelage—du Graal et de la Lance ne se conçoit pleinement que dans cette perspective d'un symbolisme structural et réaliste" (p. 245). "Dans ce Cortège où tout est réel, mais toujours *sub velum*, la Lance-qui-saigne représente à la fois: le mémorial pathétique de la Passion, acte suprême de la Caritas, et le rappel réitéré du sacrifice *non sanglant*, perpétué *in corpore* par le vase de la Communion.... La permanence de cette Lumière, qui émane du Graal et enveloppe la Lance, témoigne à elle seule de la nature *théophanique* du défilé tout entier, véritable mimodrame sacral qui débute dans le temps avec l'Eucharistie, promesse et gage de la Résurrection" (p. 253). "Loin d'être, comme le veulent à tout prix les folkloristes, la coupe d'abondance païenne—chaudron magique ou autre objet de jouissance matérielle—le Graal de Chrétien représente le tabernacle-viatique d'une réalité toute spirituelle, éternellement subsistante." Mme Lot-Borodine is completely in accord (p. 258) with Mario Roques when he says: "Le Cortège du Graal est une exposition symbolique de la Foi chrétienne allant de la Rédemption à la Communion eucharistique." In a note (p. 262) she writes: "Il nous paraît incompréhensible que Brown (*Mod. Philo.*, t. XIV), et à sa suite Marx, aient pu supposer que 'le Poisson miraculeux pêché par le roi-Pêcheur soit servi pour son père ou pour lui-même *dans le Graal*' (p. 245). C'est presque aussi fort que l'hypothèse de Loomis sur le *cor-corps du Christ* chez Chrétien. De son côté, Mme Rita Lejeune, comme le signale en passant M. Micha (art. cit., p. 428), fait une singulière erreur, elle aussi, en supposant que le vieux roi 'se sert' des poissons énumérés (*cum grano salis*) par l'ermite (*Studi Medievali*, XVII, p. 8). Que de suppositions gratuites!" Mme Lot-Borodine discusses (pp. 263-80) the character of Perceval, his departure from the Faith, his basic chastity, and his spiritual ascent as presented by Chrétien, "le maître psychologue." (Cf. our "Spiritual Ascent of Perceval," p. 8.) She, too, is of the opinion that Perceval would have fulfilled his mission had Chrétien finished his tale. In a note (p. 272), she wonders how Loomis was led to identify the Hideous Damsel with the Graalophore in the *Perlesvaus*. Like Stefan Hofer, Mme Lot-Borodine is aware of the influences exerted on Chrétien by St. Bernard, by the founding of the Templars, and by the finding of the Holy Lance of Antioch which had been brought back to France after the First Crusade (pp. 287, 247). Like Hofer, Mme Lot-Borodine has noted the parallel which Chrétien has drawn between courtly chivalry and the celestial chivalry of the Crusaders, whose goal was Paradise (p. 287). Two of the author's most original ideas are that the Being of the Inner Room in the Grail Castle is Adam both before the Fall and after the Redemption (p. 257) and that the Inner Room represents the Garden of Eden (pp. 282 ff.). "Qu'est-ce donc que ce Château qui abrite entre ses murs évanescents à la fois le secret de la Révélation auquel se trouve lié le saint vieillard reclus, participant unique au Sacrement de vie, et cette cour fallacieuse, plongée dans la jouissance des biens matériels, combien précaires, et gouvernée par un seigneur impuissant qui n'attend son salut que d'une parole jamais prononcée? Force nous est de reconnaître ici le *thème du Paradis terrestre.*—Paradis perdu, en même temps que retrouvé, paradis toujours subsistant, celui même de l'immuable Foi et de la nostalgique Espérance."

1956 Sister M. Amelia Klenke, O. P., "The Spiritual Ascent of Perceval," *Studies in Philology*, LIII, 1-21.

1957 Jean Frappier, *Chrétien de Troyes, l'homme et l'œuvre* (Paris). Chapters I and VII of this useful survey are relevant for investigators of the *Perceval*. Frappier finds it "inutile de supposer, comme on l'a fait, qu'il [Chrétien] a voyagé en Angleterre ou en Armorique" (p. 56). "Il est juste de reconnaître la valeur de l'héritage celtique; mais cet apport n'était pas envahissant au point de gêner véritablement la liberté d'invention d'un Chrétien de Troyes" (p. 61). "Un auteur passé par la clergie n'ignorait pas l'Ecriture.... L'action exercée sur lui par la Bible demeure limitée.... La symbolique, dérivée en partie de l'exégèse biblique, n'est pas absente non plus de son oeuvre" (p. 21). "Il semble avoir usé volontiers d'une imitation composite et combiné des contes épars, en vertu d'un plan d'ensemble et en vertu du *sen*. Celui-ci a une valeur didactique" (p. 62). "Déjà le terme lui-même de *graal* est surprenant s'il s'agit de nommer un vase liturgique. Il ne convient en aucune façon à un ciboire ou à un calice" (p. 187). Frappier considers as "naturelle et nécessaire l'idée que le graal pourrait apporter de gros poissons" (p. 190) but overlooks the absurdity of Chrétien's placing a consecrated host in a vessel of such size. "La lance qui saigne est apparemment une lance composite, à la fois païenne et chrétienne" (p. 189). "Le recours aux personnifications et à l'allégorisme n'est pas dans la manière habituelle de Chrétien. Admettons toutefois, sans nous préoccuper de la seconde demoiselle du cortège, qu'il ait fait une exception en faveur de l'Ecclesia" (p. 195). Frappier's disagreement (pp. 193-6) with Roques is forced and unconvincing. "Il est vrai que Chrétien n'avait guère 'moralisé' dans ses romans antérieurs, bien qu'il eût toujours veillé à enrichir leur *matière* d'un *sen* original. Mais son *Conte du graal* marque un tournant" (p. 205). But is there any reason why Chrétien de Troyes should not have tried his hand at allegory? "Il reste que la juste interprétation de l'œuvre sera toujours difficile et en partie problématique, à la fois en raison de son symbolisme et de son inachèvement" (p. 208).

1957 Jean Marx, "Quelques Remarques au sujet de récents travaux sur l'origine du Graal," *Moyen Age*, LXIII, 469-80. This article, which restates certain of the critic's known theories, is primarily an attempt to refute Roques' findings about the *demoiselle au Graal* (cf. *supra*). "Pour ce qui est de l'identification de l'Eglise avec la demoiselle au

Graal, on peut s'étonner de la voir privée de la couronne qui ceint normalement sa tête.... Enfin le personnage barbu et vénérable, né d'une confusion légendaire entre le centurion de l'Evangile et le soldat qui perce le flanc du Crucifié n'évoque guère le jeune et beau valet qui porte la Lance dans ce conte." In the poem, the Lance is mentioned with no word of the bearer (vv. 3549-50, 4753-8, 6372-7, 6400-12). In vv. 3191 and 3200, where the Lance-bearer is mentioned, there is no qualifying adjective. What then is the origin of the epithets "young," "handsome," "beardless"? "A-t-il," continues Marx, "été jusqu'à pressentir l'analogie de la Lance magique et destructive avec la Sainte Lance dont une relique était conservée par Byzance et dont la découverte à Antioche eut tant de retentissement dans l'armée des Croisés et dans tout l'ensemble de la Chrétienté Occidentale? Je serais assez disposé à l'admettre ... Mais nous ne croyons pas que Celle qui portait le Graal était l'Eglise, ni que le valet fût Longin.... Cette ascension chevaleresque [de Perceval] s'accompagne d'une éducation morale, et d'un perfectionnement religieux.... Mais le conte reste toujours plaisant et souriant selon la manière du grand Champenois."

1957 Foster Erwin Guyer, *Chrétien de Troyes* (New York) concludes his preface (p. vii): "Whatever Celtic material may have found its way into these [Chrétien's] stories, the transmission is as yet unexplained, the amalgamation is still obscure, the main themes do not seem to me to be derived from the Celtic stories that we know today. For these reasons the Celtic side of the problem of Chrétien's sources is left aside for other scholars to pursue." Speaking of the *Perceval* (pp. 111-5), the author does little more than summarize the plot.

1959 Sister M. Amelia Klenke, O. P., "Some Mediaeval Concepts of King Arthur," *Kentucky Foreign Language Quarterly*, to be published.

1959 Sister M. Amelia Klenke, O. P., "The *Christus Domini* Concept in Mediaeval Art and Literature," *Studies in Philology*, to be published.

Alphabetical Key to the Symbolism of Chrétien's *Perceval*

"Les chrétiens du moyen âge avaient l'âme toute pleine de Jesus-Christ: c'est lui qu'ils cherchaient partout, c'est lui qu'ils voyaient partout. Ils lisaient son nom à toutes les pages de l'Ancien Testament. Ce genre de symbolisme donne la clef de beaucoup d'oeuvres du moyen âge, qui, sans lui, demeureraient inintelligibles. Nous ne parlons pas seulement des oeuvres d'art, mais de telle composition littéraire célèbre" (Mâle, *L'Art religieux du XIIIe siècle*, p. 159).

"The persistence of the higher meanings involved in poetic allegory gives to the thousand years of the mediaeval tradition a surprising unity and continuity. And this continuity is enforced by the attitude that Christ's New Law is the ultimate expression of truth and the only source of any real beauty" (D. W. Robertson, Jr., "The Doctrine of Charity in Mediaeval Literary Gardens," *Speculum*, XXVI [1951], 46).

N.B. It is inconceivable that any two evaluators could agree down to the last item in the following list of identifications. We call attention, therefore, to the four categories into which we have placed our identifications: (1) those which are virtually certain (***), (2) those which are very probable (**), (3) those which are plausible (*), and (4) those which are only a reasonable guess (†). Furthermore, one must bear in mind that it is not necessary, however possible, that every character and every stage prop had a specific symbolic meaning. After all, Chrétien was not writing for a research-minded audience. Note also that headings *In Old* and *New Testament* mean: on Old and New Testament levels.

*ANGUINGUERON. *In Chrétien:* Seneschal of Clamadeu.
In New Testament: The Vice of Lust.

***ARTHUR. *In Chrétien:* King of Britain, champion of oppressed natives against Angle and Saxon invaders. He is the type of perfect Christian knighthood. After the *Historia Brittonum* by Nennius (ninth century or earlier), the Britons of southwestern England began to look for the second coming of Arthur, thus bestowing upon him a sort of immortality. William of Malmesbury in his *De Gestis Regum* (I, xxviii) is explicit in giving a reason for this: "The sepulchre of Arthur is nowhere to be seen, whence ancient ballads fable that he is still to come." However, in his *De Antiquitate Glastoniensis Ecclesiae* (De nobilibus Glastoniae sepultis), the text of which is in a very corrupt state, a passage asserts that Arthur was buried at Glastonbury *inter duas piramides*. There are some scholars who think that this was an interpolation after Geoffrey of Monmouth's time (i.e., after 1154), when the Arthurian legend had reached its final form through that writer's fabrications. This may indeed have been the case. But the interpolation would seem to have been made before Chrétien's *Perceval*. There apparently was a concerted effort on the part of the clergy (English and Norman) to rectify in the minds of the people this superstition regarding the second coming of Arthur. Hence we have the "finding" of Arthur's tomb at Glastonbury and the Christianizing of the pagan belief to meet the needs of the Church: the conversion of the Jews who could profitably be used as powerful allies against the Turks in the capture of Jerusalem. See *supra*, "Partial List of Scholars," 1909, Hudleston, and 1954, Séchelles. The archivolt of the Modena portal in which Arthur and his knights are to be seen bears out this theory (see chap. 8). The *Tractatus contra Judaeos* by Gautier de Châtillon (or de l'Isle), in which the plight of the Synagogue awaiting its Messias is compared to that of the Britons awaiting the second coming of Arthur, is still further support (see Migne, *P.L.*, vol. CCIX, cols. 423-58). In mediaeval art King Arthur is usually represented with three crowns on his tunic and on his shield (see R. S. and L. H. Loomis, *Arthurian Legends*, Plates 11, 12, 13, 14). In Church iconography, three is a symbol of the Trinity and the crown is attributed to both David and Christ (see Webber, gloss). See Chapter 8, notes 22 and 48.

In Old Testament: King David, second king of Israel, consistently considered a type of the Messias. After conquering Jerusalem, he made it the capital of his kingdom. Hence he would have been looked upon by the Crusaders with special admiration. Like Christ, David was born in Bethlehem. Having led the life of a shepherd, he is a prototype of the Good Shepherd. His betrayal by a trusted counsellor and his passage over the Cedron are parallels of the Passion. (See *Catholic Encyclopedia.*) It will be remembered that when Arthur vows to set out to look for Perceval, he swears by St. David to do so (vv. 4133-40).

In New Testament: Christ, leader of the Church Militant. (See chap. 8, p. 136). The Virtue of Charity ("Deus est charitez," *Perceval,* v. 47; see also I John 4:16). Almost every time Arthur appears in the *Conte* he is made to rebuke Keu for his lack of charity. The Crusaders may have likened Arthur to Adhemar, who had been appointed by the Pope to lead the First Crusade. In him had been vested all moral authority. By his contemporaries Adhemar was likened to Moses (see John Hugh Hill and Laurita I. Hill, "Contemporary Accounts and the Later Reputation of Adhemar, Bishop of Puy," *Medievalia et Humanistica,* IX [1955], 32-7). In the Middle Ages, Moses was one of the most characteristic types of Christ (Mâle, *L'Art religieux du XIIIe siècle,* p. 158).

****Arthur's name.* Kemp Malone believes that the Welsh expression *aruthr,* meaning *terrible,* passed into use in Cornwall and from there back into Wales, undergoing regular phonological syncope to *arthur* (see *JEGP,* XXIII, 463-91). Does this explanation not make very good sense when placed side by side with Exod. 15:3, 11:

The Lord is as a man of war: Almighty is his name.
Who is like to thee among the strong, O Lord? who is like to thee, glorious in holiness, terrible and praiseworthy, doing wonders.

† *Arthur's court. In New Testament:* The Church Militant.

*** *Arthur's golden cup.* See chap. 8, pp. 136, 152.

In Old Testament: "My cup which cheereth me, how goodly is it!" (Ps. 22:5). This psalm was written for David.

In New Testament: Eternal priesthood (see Webber, gloss).

† *Arthur's knights.* Cf. Mrs. Laura Hibbard Loomis (*PMLA,* XLI, 771-84, and *MLN,* XLIV, 511-9), who proposes that the Round Table was taken from iconography, representations in stained glass windows and MS illuminations, of the Last Supper, suggesting "the exalted loyalty and equality of the first apostolic twelve."

In New Testament: The Apostles (with whom the most fervent Crusaders may have compared themselves).

* *Arthur rebukes Keu* for his sharp tongue. *In New Testament:* He manifests his love of Charity.

** *Arthur cares for Keu's wounds. In New Testament:* He manifests Christ's compassion for sinners.

** *Arthur grieves over Keu's treatment of Perceval. In New Testament:* He shows that converts are won through Charity, not by sarcasm and force.

*** *Arthur's affliction over Perceval's protracted absence* from the court and his determination to find him and lead him back to the court. *In New Testament:* Christ's sorrow over the loss of a soul and His efforts to bring it back to a life of grace.

** AVALON. *In Chrétien:* "Land of Apples," the Celtic underworld, the Land of the Blessed. (Holmes, *History of Old French Literature,* p. 162; cf. also Nitze and Jenkins, *Perlesvaus,* II, 55-9.)

In Old Testament: Sion.

In New Testament: Heaven.

*** BEING OF INNER ROOM in the Grail Castle. *In Old Testament:* Melchizedek.

In New Testament: Christ. There was almost universal agreement among the Church Fathers that Christ partook of the Sacrament at the Last Supper. "Verily, thou art a hidden God, the God of Israel, the saviour" (Isa. 45:15) and "Be converted to me, and you shall be saved" (Isa. 45:22).

***BELREPAIRE. *In Chrétien:* Abode of Blancheflor and of Religious (vv. 2941-4).

In New Testament: Haven of Chastity.

***BLANCHEFLOR. *In New Testament:* Virtue of Chastity.

****Blancheflor embraces Perceval. In New Testament:* She instills in Perceval a love for Chastity.

*** *Blancheflor inflames him with a desire to fight her foes. In New Testament:* She directs his will in line with the Virtues and opposed to the Vices.

***BLEEDING LANCE. *In Old Testament:* Probably the Rod of Aaron.

In New Testament: Lance of the Passion; Redemption.

***Lance's bleeding. In New Testament:* The renewal of the sacrifice of Calvary in the sacrifice of the Mass; religious persecution (see Roques, "Le Graal de Chrétien....," p. 18).

** *Lance will destroy the kingdom of Logres,* ancient land of the Ogres (vv. 6168-71; Foulet, p. 144). *In New Testament:* It is probable that Chrétien had already witnessed persecution of the Jews in France. Philip Augustus had banished them from France and confiscated their property in 1182. This may explain the pilgrim's words to Perceval, "the felonious Jews whom one should kill like dogs" (vv. 6292-3). Chrétien's poem is a protest against such persecution and a plea for conversion in order to spare the Jews further persecution which he foresees. In 1191, there was persecution in London and York.

*** *Lance-Bearer. In New Testament:* Longinus, the convert; conversion.

* CLAMADEU. *In Chrétien:* Enemy of Blancheflor.
In New Testament: The Vice of Covetousness.

** COTOATRE. Nitze and Williams (p. 291) accept Loomis's identification (*Arthurian Tradition*, p. 408), which is *Scottewatre* (Firth of Forth).

In Old Testament: Cateth (see Josue 19:15; and Holmes, "A New Interpretation," p. 17).
In New Testament: Galilee.

** CROWS, RAVENS. *In Chrétien:* Peck out eyes of Perceval's elder brother.

In Old Testament: "They have given the dead bodies of Thy servants to be meat for the fowls of the air," Ps. 78:2, incorporated in the Mass for certain martyrs.

In New Testament: The martyrdom of the saints.

** DAMSEL OF THE TENT. *In Old Testament:* "He hath set His tabernacle in the sun" (Ps. 18:6).

In New Testament: Mary as a symbol of the Church (see Mâle, *L'Art religieux du XIIIe siècle*, pp. 193-4). "God hath chosen her and preferred her: and He maketh her to dwell in his tabernacle," *Little Office of the Blessed Virgin.*

*** *Perceval's shameful treatment of her. In New Testament:* Saul's persecution of the early Church.

DINASDARON. *** *In Old Testament:* Castle of Aaron.

† *In New Testament:* Possibly interpreted by Crusaders as Heavenly Jerusalem.

* EAGLE. *In Chrétien:* On top of tent of sleeping damsel.

In New Testament: The writings of St. John the Evangelist, from which Chrétien drew inspiration.

* EMERALD RING. *In Chrétien:* Stolen by Perceval from damsel of the tent.

In New Testament: Virginity; Hope.

ERMINE. See GORNEMANZ

† ESCAVALON. *In Chrétien:* Where Perceval's brothers had been knighted. Name "probably from *Ex-* and *Avalon*" (Nitze and Williams, p. 272).

In New Testament: Crusaders may have associated it with Ascalon, where the Templars had distinguished themselves by their extraordinary valor.

*** FISHER KING. Cf. Nitze and Williams, pp. 288-9; and E. Brugger, "Die *Nodons-Nuadu* Hypothese als Erklärung des Namens 'Fischerkönig,'" *Romance Philology*, IX (1956), 285-97, which refutes Vendryes' hypothesis and Nitze's claim that this hypothesis is sound. According to Nitze, "He [Vendryes] derives the expression [roi pescheor] from Ir. *Nuadu* (W. *Nudd*, OF. *Nu*), cognate of Goth. *nuta, nutans*, and signifying 'fisher.' ... I have consistently sought to uphold this derivation. It helps to explain Chrétien's elaboration (esp. vv. 3516 ff.) of the name. It connects the character—through Nuadu—with the Irish Tuatha Dé Danann and the Dagda. And it identifies Nuadu with Nodons or Nodens, a maritime deity, the remains of whose temple exist today at Lydney on the Severn" (*Romance Philology*, VI, 14). Brugger asserts (p. 295) that *nuta* has no connection with fish. He asks furthermore (p. 297): "Warum haben denn gewisse Anhänger der keltischen Theorie die Bran-Hypothese erfunden? Ich kann mir keinen andern Grund denken als den Wunsch, ein keltisches Element in den Gralstoff einzuführen, um denselben nicht den Gegnern zu überlassen."

In Old Testament: Jacob, who was lame after wrestling with the angel. Had Perceval asked the vital questions, Jacob would have been converted and his lameness healed. He is a symbol of the High Priest of the Jewish Temple.

In New Testament: With the conversion of the Temple, Jacob will give way to Peter, the "fisher of men." Mme Lot-Borodine writes (*Romania*, LXXVII, 261, note): "D'après le maître Vendryès, le nom Nuadu dont la racine désigne la pêche, se retrouve dans la Bible gothique d'Ulfilas et signifierait *Pêcheur d'hommes*. ... Alors que conclure sur l'origine *païenne* de ces divinités maritimes?"

*** *Lameness and sorrow of the Fisher King. In Old Testament:* "But they shall serve the Lord their God, and David their king, whom I will raise up to them. Therefore fear thou not, my servant Jacob, saith the Lord. ... Jacob shall return, and be at rest. ... For thus saith the Lord: Thy bruise is incurable, thy wound is very grievous. There is none to judge thy judgment to bind it up: thou hast no healing medicines. ... For I have wounded thee with the wound of an enemy, with a cruel chastisement: by reason of the multitude of thy iniquities, thy sins are hardened. Why criest thou for thy affliction? thy sorrow is incurable: for the multitude of thy iniquity, and for thy hardened sins I have done these things to thee. . . . I will close up thy fear, and will heal thee of thy wounds, saith the Lord. Because they have called thee, O Sion, an out-cast: This is she that had none to seek after her. Thus saith the Lord: Behold I will bring back the captivity of the pavilions of Jacob, and will have pity on his houses, and the city shall be built in her high place, and the temple shall be founded according to the order thereof" (Jer. 30: 9-18).

† *The Fisher King bestows a mystic sword upon Perceval.* *In Old Testament:* Jacob rejects the Faith (symbolized by the sword) for himself and the Israelites.

† *The scarlet cloak is placed on Perceval* by four servitors. *In New Testament:* Perceval receives the Charity of the Gospels (?).

*** Fox. At Modena and Otranto.
In Old Testament: Ps. 62:9; Cant. 2:15.
In New Testament: The "spoiler of the vines"; Satan (see Webber, gloss).

† Gaste Forest. *In New Testament:* Solitude necessary for religious contemplation.

** Gawain. "Noted [i.e., in Chrétien's poems] for his *sens* or understanding" (Nitze and Williams, p. 273).
In Old Testament: Job. His patience under suffering is a type of Christ's sufferings at the hand of those who accused Him before Pilate (see Webber, p. 249). "So patiently enduring, he obtained the promise" (Heb. 6:15).
In New Testament: The Virtue of Patience. "The patient man is better than the valiant" (Prov. 16:32). This quotation may explain why Chrétien has offset Gawain (Patience) and Perceval (Fortitude). "Faith and patience shall inherit the promises" (Heb. 6:12).

† *Gawain's two swords or shields. In New Testament:* Hope and Charity, which complement Perceval's sword of Faith.

† *Gawain's encounter with the lions.* *In Old Testament:* "The roaring of the lion, and the voice of the lioness, and the teeth of the whelps of the lions are broken" (Job 4:2; also 5:22).

*** GORNEMANZ DE GOORT. Cf. Nitze and Williams, p. 275.

In Old Testament: Gamaliel, tutor of Saul. He was celebrated for his purity, piety, and wisdom.

In New Testament: Worldly Chivalry as opposed to the Christian Knighthood of Arthur's knights and of the Templars. According to Christian tradition, Gamaliel was baptized by Saints Peter and Paul.

* *Gornemanz's ermine cloak.* *In New Testament:* Purity of Gamaliel (see Webber, gloss).

* *Gornemanz's wand.* *In New Testament:* Authority (see Webber, gloss).

*** *Gornemanz advises Perceval against quoting his mother* at every turn, so as not to be taken for a fool. *In New Testament:* He caters to human respect. By following such a precept, Perceval fails to ask the vital Grail questions and thus fails to cure the lame Fisher King.

*** GRAAL. Nitze and Williams, p. 276, speak of "Chrétien's obvious meaning, 'serving-dish.'" This is reaffirmed on p. 294.

In Old Testament: The vessel containing the manna of the Old Law. In ecclesiastical art, it is in the hand of Melchizedek.

In New Testament: Chalice of the Last Supper; symbol of the Eucharist and Love. The Chalice with the Host symbolizes the Church with its sacramental system (see my article in *PMLA*, LXX [1955], 238).

*** *Oiste in the Grail.* *In Old Testament:* Manna of the Old Law.

In New Testament: The Blessed Sacrament, the Eucharist. It symbolizes the Sacrifice of Calvary and of the Mass.

*** *Light emanating from the Grail.* *In Old Testament:* The *sol invictus.*

In New Testament: Symbol of the Real Presence of Christ in the Eucharist.

*** *Maiden carrying the Grail. In Old Testament:* Synagoga with a vessel of manna.

In New Testament: Ecclesia carrying the Chalice with consecrated Host.

*** *Quest of the Grail. In New Testament:* Spiritual ascent through prayer and sacramental grace; an attempt to convert the Temple.

*** GRAIL CASTLE. *In Old Testament:* Temple of Solomon.

In New Testament: Had Perceval asked the vital Grail questions, the Temple would have been converted. The Templars probably associated the Grail Castle with their own quarters in Jerusalem, on the site of the old Temple of Solomon.

*** *The Inner Room of the Grail Castle. In Old Testament:* The Holy of Holies in which were kept the Vessel of Manna and the Tables of the Law.

In New Testament: The Christian Sanctuary in which takes place the Sacrifice of the Mass.

† *The mournful festival. In Old Testament:* "The fishers also shall mourn, and all that cast a hook into the river shall lament" (Isa. 19:8).

In New Testament: The *Agape* (?).

** GUINLOIE. *In Chrétien:* The maiden whom Gawain sets out to free. She is not named specifically as she is in the Modena archivolt, where she is called *Winlogée*.

In New Testament: The Truth which shall set men free (John 8:32). See also John 14:6: "I am the way, and the truth, and the life: no man cometh to the Father, but by me." This helps to explain why the sculptor has placed Winlogée on the spot usually reserved for the Crucified. If she is to be identified with Guenevere, as Loomis believes, she would be the Church—the Bride of Christ—described in the Canticle of Canticles.

** *Her castle. In Chrétien:* "au pui est soz Montescleire"

(*Perceval*, v. 4706; "sur une colline que domine Montesclaire," Foulet, p. 111).

In New Testament: The Dolorous Tower of Calvary. (See Mâle, *L'Art religieux du XIIe siècle*, p. 269, and Loomis, *Arthurian Legends*, pp. 34-5; see also chap. 8, pp. 132, 147).

* *Her jailer, Burmaltus. In Old Testament:* "They prophecied in Baal, and deceived my people Israel" (Jer. 23:13).

In New Testament: Satan; Ungodliness; False Prophecy. "And the Lord shall destroy out of Israel the head and the tail . . . and the prophet that teaches lies, he is the tail" (Isa. 9:14-5).

* *Battle-axe of Burmaltus. In New Testament:* Warfare (see Webber, p. 359); "The life of man . . . is a warfare" (Job 7:1).

* *Her jailer, Caradoc. In Old Testament:* Judas (?). "Even so are the ways of all that forget God, and the hope of the hypocrite shall perish" (Job 8:3).

In New Testament: Ingratitude of God's chosen people, symbolized by Judas's betrayal of Christ with a kiss. Judas also symbolizes Hypocrisy, Treachery, Deceit.

* *Mardoc*, mother of Caradoc. *In Old Testament:* Jezabel (?). Elijah accused falsely by Jezabel is also a type of Christ's sufferings at the hands of those who accused Him before Pilate (see Webber, p. 249).

In New Testament: Injustice.

For an understanding of this section of the Modena portal, see St. Paul to the Romans I, 18, 29-30: "For the wrath of God is revealed from heaven against all ungodliness and injustice of those men that detain the truth of God in injustice. . . . And they liked not to have God in their knowledge: God delivered them up to a reprobate sense. . . . Being filled with iniquity, malice, fornication, avarice, wickedness, full of envy, murder, contention, deceit, malignity . . . detractors, hateful to God." See also Apocalypse 3:8-10: "I know thy works. Behold I have given before thee a door opened which no man can shut: because thou hast a little strength and hast kept my word, and hast not denied my name. Behold, I will bring of the synagogue of Satan, who say they are Jews and are not, but do lie: Behold, I will make them to come and adore before thy feet: and they shall know that I have loved thee, Because thou hast kept the word of my patience. . . ." It will be recalled that we would identify Gawain with the Virtue of Patience.

† HEADLESS KNIGHT. *In New Testament:* St. James, one of the favorite saints of the Middle Ages as attested by the popularity of his shrine at Compostella. The martyrs of the Faith.

*** HERMIT PRIEST. *In Old Testament:* Abraham. "I say then: Hath God cast away his people? God forbid. For I also am an Israelite of the seed of Abraham, of the tribe of Benjamin" (St. Paul to the Romans 11: 1); "They are Hebrews, so am I. They are Israelites, so am I. They are the seed of Abraham, so am I" (II Cor. 11:22). "The book of the generation of Jesus Christ, the son of David, the son of Abraham" (Matt. 1:1).

In New Testament: St. John the Evangelist; the Virtue of Temperance. St. Paul, in opposing his enemies in Galatia, names John explicitly along with Peter and James the Less, as a "pillar of the Church," and refers to the recognition which his apostolic preaching of a Gospel free from the law received from these three, the most prominent men of the old Mother-Church at Jerusalem (Gal. 2: 9). It should also be recalled that Perceval, while with his mother, while visiting the damsel of the tent, and while with Blancheflor, as well as at the Grail Castle, had been much interested in bodily food. It is while he is at the hermitage that for the first time he manifests a longing for spiritual food which far surpasses his interest in food for the body.

** *Secret prayers which the hermit teaches Perceval. In New Testament:* Divine revelations received by St. Paul.

Abraham (see *Catholic Encyclopedia*) is one of the three Old Testament figures whose name appears most frequently in the Liturgy; and of the three (Abel, Abraham, and Melchizedek), his name is found far oftener than that of the other two. He is looked upon as the starting point of Old Testament religion. This explains why Chrétien speaks of the intimate relationship between the Hermit Priest, "la sore pucelle" (Mary), Perceval's mother (Faith), and the Being of the Inner Room (Melchizedek: Christ). In the Canon of the Mass of the Roman rite, Abraham is one of the three Old Testament names which appear. As the priest extends his hands over the Consecrated Species, he says: "Upon which do Thou vouchsafe to look . . . and accept them, as Thou didst vouchsafe to accept the gift of Thy just servant Abel, and the sacrifice of our Patriarch Abraham. . . ." (It will be remembered that the sacrifice of Abel is prominently portrayed in the Mosaic at Otranto, near the figure of King Arthur.) Here the Canon insists on the idea of sacrifice, a fact common to the Western liturgies, while those of the East, except the Maronite, omit in their *epicleses* all reference to the typic sacrifices of the Old Testament and appear concerned with impressing the faithful with the idea rather of sacrament and communion. This is esteemed a fact of capital importance towards a classification of the liturgies. In the Martyrology of October 9, Abraham is called "Patriarch and Father of all believers"—an apt choice for one who is to lead Perceval, the unbeliever, back to God. Abraham is also mentioned in the daily recitation of the Divine Office. But it should be noted particularly that in the third of the Prophecies of Holy Saturday, which is read silently by the priest at the altar and simultaneously chanted in a loud voice by a cleric, Abraham's name occurs again. Perceval was visiting the hermitage on Good Friday, Holy Saturday, and Easter Sunday. St. John the Evangelist is the Apostle of the Eucharist. Perceval received his Easter Communion from the hands of the saintly Hermit Priest whom we would identify with Abraham—St. John the Evangelist.

At this point, it will be rewarding to examine Mâle, *L'Art religieux du XIIIe siècle*, p. 156 and Fig. 83, which shows the celebrated bas-relief of a standing knight receiving Holy Communion. Mâle has captioned the picture "Melchisédech et Abraham" and says of it:

L'artiste de Reims a encore été plus audacieux [que celui de Chartres]: il nous montre Melchisédech présentant à Abraham le pain sous la forme d'une hostie (fig. 83). Je ne crois pas qu'on puisse douter que le prêtre qui fait communiquer un guerrier (statues intérieures de la cathédrale de Reims, portail du milieu, dans le bas) ne soit Melchisédech. Il ne faut pas s'étonner de voir Abraham vêtu comme un chevalier du XIIIe siècle. Le psautier de saint Louis (Bibl. Nat., ms. lat. 10525) nous le montre sous cet aspect.

In view of the popularity of Chrétien's *Perceval* and in view of the proximity of Reims to Troyes, it seems more probable to us that the warrior is St. Paul (Perceval), and that the priest is Chrétien's Hermit Priest—Abraham on the Old Testament level, St. John the Evangelist on the New. This supposition is all the more plausible since in the Middle Ages, St. Paul was patron saint of knights. No one will deny that twelfth-century Champagne was vitally interested in the Crusaders and the Knights Templar. Furthermore, as we have seen, Henry of Troyes (the Liberal), in 1179, had founded the Hospice of Saint-Abraham at Troyes, for pilgrims on their way to the Holy Land. He bestowed this hospice upon the Bishop of Hebron, in the Holy Land, whose cathedral was also called Saint-Abraham. The Jews claim that it is at Hebron that Abraham is buried.

In speaking of the Hermit Priest whom we would identify with Abraham-St. John the Evangelist, and the Virtue of Temperance, it is pertinent to note the following. In the Mass for the Saturday of the autumn Ember Week, one of the prophecies read at the Epistle side of the altar is taken from Mic. 7:14-20:

Feed thy people with thy rod, the flock of thy inheritance, them that dwell alone in the forest.... He will turn again, and have mercy on us: he will put away our iniquities, and he will cast all our sins into the bottom of the sea. Thou wilt perform the truth to Jacob, the mercy to Abraham: which thou hast sworn to our fathers from the days of old.

Shortly after, there occurs the following prayer: "Praesta, quaesumus Domine, sic nos ab epulis abstinere carnalibus; ut a vitiis irruentibus pariter jejunemus...." There then follows the reading of a prophecy by Zach. 8:14 ff. Verse 19 makes one think of the archivolt at Modena, where Truth may be represented by Guinloie (the French translation is more telling than the English):

Ainsi parle le Seigneur des armées: Les jeûnes du quatrième, du cinquième, du septième et du dixième mois, deviendront pour la maison de Juda des jours de réjouissance et d'allégresse, des solennités joyeuses. Aimez seulement la vérité et la paix, dit le Seigneur des armées.

Guinloie (Truth) was the *amie* of Gawain (Patience), who is depicted on the Modena archivolt.

The Epistle is taken from St. Paul, Heb. 9, which starts out by describing the Temple of Solomon with its Holy of Holies, candelabra, the table with its loaves of proposition, the veil, the golden altar, the Arc of the Covenant, the golden urn with the manna, the rod of Aaron which had blossomed, the tables of the Law, and the cherubim. Then St. Paul goes on to tell why the sacrifices of the Old Law were far inferior to the sacrifice of the New. And finally he refers to the second coming of Christ with which the Church supplanted the superstitious belief in the second coming of Arthur. The Gospel is taken from Luke 13 and tells of Christ healing "the daughter of Abraham whom Satan hath bound, lo, these eighteen years."

Once again the Liturgy has offered an abundance of material to Chrétien: the Hermit Priest (Abraham), who remits Perceval's sin, teaches him lessons of abstinence, and gives him his Easter Communion; the Lord of Hosts (Arthur), who seeks Truth (Guinloie); the second coming of Christ, which is used to replace the superstitious belief in the second coming of Arthur; the symbols of the Grail Procession and the conversion of the Temple symbolized by the lame Fisher King (Jacob).

** Hideous Damsel. *In Old Testament:* "I am become as a beast before thee" (Ps. 72:23).

In New Testament: False Prophecy of Synagoga. See Roques, "Le Graal de Chrétien...," pp. 14-5.

* *Her yellow mule. In Old Testament:* The ass of Balaam.

In New Testament: Jews who obstinately refused to accept the doctrine of Christ. "Do not become like the horse and the mule who have no understanding" (Ps. 21:9). See Mâle, *L'Art religieux du XIIIe siècle*, p. 142.

† *Hideous Damsel upbraids Perceval for his silence in the Grail Castle*—for not having spoken in the proper time and place.

210   *Appendix*

In Chrétien: "An mal eür tant te teüsses" (v. 4669)—"Quel malheur pour nous que ton silence!" (Foulet, p. 110).

In New Testament: Is this not Chrétien's way of complaining that the Christians, catering to human respect, had not worked hard enough to convert the Jews? Had the latter been converted, they could have been used as allies in saving Jerusalem from falling into the hands of the infidel. Saladin entered the city in 1187. It is too late to mend matters: "Fortune est chauve derriers et devant chevelue" (vv. 4646-7). See also Foulet, p. 110.

This passage may indicate a rather late composition for the *Perceval*, perhaps after 1184 when the *vetusta ecclesia* or *lignea basilica* had burned at Glastonbury and when funds were being collected to build a bigger and better church on its site.

* HIND, RUNNING. *In Old Testament:* Naphtali (see Webber, gloss).

In New Testament: Perceval's (Paul's) Hebrew ancestry?

* *Land of the running hind* where Perceval was reared. *In Old Testament:* Land of Naphtali. "And leaving the city of Nazareth, He [Christ] came and dwelt in Capharnaum, in the sea coast, in the borders of Zabulon and of Naphtali; That it might be fulfilled which was said by Isaias the prophet: Land of Zabulon and land of Naphtali, the way of the sea beyond the Jordan, Galilee of the Gentiles: The people that sat in darkness hath seen a great light: and to them that sat in the region of the shadow of death light is sprung up" (Matt. 4:13-6).

In New Testament: Palestine, battleground of the Crusaders.

† JESTER. *In New Testament:* Virtue of Joy (?).

† KEU. *In New Testament:* Vice of Anger (?).

† MAID WHO HAD NOT LAUGHED FOR SIX YEARS. *In New Testament:* Virtue of Humility (?).

† MAID WITH HEADLESS KNIGHT. *In New Testament:* Virtue of Charity (?).

*** MONT DOULOUREUX. *In Chrétien:* V. 4724; Foulet, p. 112.
In New Testament: Calvary.

† MONTESCLEIRE. *In Chrétien:* V. 4706; Foulet, p. 111.
In New Testament: Thabor (?).

† ORGUEILLEUX, LI. *In New Testament:* Vice of Pride; Heresy (Ps. 26:4; 72:6).

† *Chastel Orgueilleux. In Chrétien:* To which Hideous Damsel repairs (vv. 4689-90; Foulet, p. 111).
In New Testament: Abode of Heresy; Hell (?). The Crusaders may have thought of it as Palestine.

*** PERCEVAL. *In Old Testament:* Saul, "an Hebrew of the Hebrews" (Phil. 3:5) of the tribe of Naphtali.
In New Testament: St. Paul; the Virtue of Fortitude. For Chrétien, he would complement Gawain, the Virtue of Patience. St. Paul was patron saint of mediaeval knights, hence the ideal hero in a tale of Christian knighthood.

*** *Perceval's name. In New Testament:* He who "pierces the veil." See chap. 7, pp. 118-19.

*** *Perceval's father. In Old Testament:* Jacob, ancestor of the Twelve Tribes of Israel, third great patriarch.
In New Testament: Virtue of Justice; the priesthood of Jacob which gives way to that of Christ.

*** *Perceval's mother. In Old Testament:* Rachel, ancestress of the Jewish race.
In New Testament: Virtue of Religion.

*** *Perceval prefers bodily food* to his mother's admonitions. *In Old Testament:* Saul prefers food for the body to that of the soul.

† *Poor garments given to Perceval by his mother. In New Testament:* Poverty of the Christian Church in Jerusalem. The opening words of the Prologue are from St. Paul, II Cor. 9, where the Apostle begs alms for the Christians in Jerusalem.

*** *Perceval's mother is desolate at his departure. In Old Testament:* "A voice in Rama was heard, lamentation and great mourning; Rachel bewailing her children, and would not be comforted because they were not," taken from the Mass of the Holy Innocents.

In New Testament: The Church sorrowing over the death of her martyrs.

*** *Perceval departs from his mother. In Old Testament:* Heedless of the voice of the Church, he departs from the teachings of the Church and thus commits his mortal sin.

*** *Death of Perceval's mother. In Old Testament:* Saul is without Faith and about to persecute the Church, symbolized by the damsel of the tent.

*** *Perceval's naïveté. In Old Testament:* "When I was a child, I spoke as a child, I thought as a child" (I Cor. 13:11).

*** *Perceval beholds the Grail Procession. In New Testament:* As a "vessel of election," Paul is given extraordinary graces.

*** *Perceval's silence. In Old Testament:* "I revealed myself to those who made no inquiry" (Isa. 65:1 and Rom. 10:20).

In New Testament: Saul is converted without having made inquiries.

He is upbraided by the Hideous Damsel. See HIDEOUS DAMSEL

*** PROCESSION OF THE HOLY GRAIL. *In New Testament:* The Church will triumph when Israel is converted and persecution shall be at an end.

QUINQUEROI FOREST. *In Chrétien:* Home of the Red Knight.
In New Testament: Hell (?).

***RED KNIGHT. *In Chrétien:* Arthur's worst enemy (vv. 945 ff.).
In Old Testament: The Jews who envied Christ's kingdom and plotted His death. See chap. 8, p. 152.
In New Testament: Vice of Envy. Dissension among the leaders of the Crusades was one of the chief causes of their failure.

** SAGREMOR. *In Chrétien:* "estoit Desreez apelez," v. 4221; Foulet, pp. 98-9.

In New Testament: Vice of Anger.

** SNOW. *In New Testament:* Purity, Virginity (see Webber, gloss).

** STAG HUNTED. *In New Testament:* Persecution of the early Christians (comparable to the plight of the Church in Jerusalem in the twelfth century). See Webber, gloss.

* SUN. *In Chrétien:* Beating on gilded eagle gracing tent of sleeping damsel.

In Old Testament: This symbol appears also in the Otranto mosaic above Abel with his sacrificial lamb.

In New Testament: God the Father (see Webber, gloss).

** SWORD. *In Chrétien:* Given to Perceval by the Fisher King.

In Old Testament: The "sword not of man" (Isa. 27:1; 31:8).

In New Testament: Faith. Like Perceval's sword, Faith is a gift freely given.

** *If broken, Perceval's sword can be mended* by Trebuchet at Cotoatre. *In New Testament:* Faith, if shattered, can be restored by Christ of Galilee.

*** TAILLEOR. *In Old Testament:* Perceval, in his blindness, may have thought of it as the Table of the Law. "Let their table become as a snare before them, and a recompense, and a stumbling block" (Ps. 68:23). Cf. the Châlons window depicting Church and Synagogue (see chap. 7, pp. 111-13).

In New Testament: The paten used to cover the chalice. The paten together with the chalice represents the tomb of Christ sealed with a stone (see my article in *PMLA*, LXX [1955], 232 and note 13). "The stone, says the *Glossa ordinaria*, is the table of the Ancient Law" (Mâle, *L'Art religieux du XIIIe siècle,* p. 196).

* *Bearer of tailleor. In Old Testament:* Cherubim of Holy of Holies as understood by Perceval, or possibly Synagoga (?).

In New Testament: Angelic figure—"For an angel of the Lord descended from heaven: and coming, rolled back the stone and sat upon it" (Matt. 28:2). See also "Partial List of Scholars," 1956, Mme Lot-Borodine, pp. 187-90. Mme Lot-Borodine suggests that the bearer of the *tailleor* is one of the Virtues, probably Faith. We believe it is more likely that, if one of the Virtues, she is Charity. In mediaeval iconography, Faith was represented with the chalice.

** TENT OF THE SLEEPING DAMSEL. *In Old Testament:* Israel in the wilderness (see Webber, gloss).

In New Testament: The Church—"Deus! or voi je vostre meison" (v. 655); Foulet, p. 19.

** *Bowers surrounding tent.* *In Old Testament:* Feast of Tabernacles on which day Jews plotted the death of Christ (see Webber).

† THREE DROPS OF BLOOD ON SNOW. *In New Testament:* Paul's future martyrdom (?). See Webber, gloss.

* TREBUCHET. *In New Testament:* Christ; Virtue of Justice. See Holmes, "A New Interpretation," p. 22.

† UTERPENDRAGON. *In Chrétien:* Father of King Arthur.
In New Testament: God the Father (?).

*YONET. *In Chrétien:* Helps Perceval don the armor of the Red Knight whom he has just killed.

In New Testament: Virtue of Prudence (one of the four Cardinal Virtues).

Bibliography

The following works are those referred to in this book.

Adams, Henry. *Mont-Saint-Michel and Chartres.* Boston and New York, 1936.

Allen, D. F. "Irish Bracteates: Two Little Known Hoards in the National Museum of Ireland," *Numismatic Chronicle*, II, 6th series (1942), 80.

——. *A Catalogue of English Coins in the British Museum, the Cross and Crosslets ... Type of Henry II.* London, 1951.

Anderson, Lady Flavia. *The Ancient Secret.* London, 1953.

Anscombe, A. "Local Names in the Arthuriana in the *Historia Brittonum*," *ZCPh*, V (1905), 103 ff.

Arnaud, Anne-François. *Voyage archéologique et pittoresque dans le département de l'Aube et dans l'ancienne diocèse de Troyes.* Troyes, 1837.

Aubert, Marcel. *Suger.* Paris, 1950.

Aucassin et Nicolette, ed. Suchier. 9th ed. Paderborn, 1921.

Bell, Mrs. Arthur. *The Saints of Christian Art.* London, 1901.

Blenner-Hassett, Roland. *A Study of the Place-Names in Lawman's Brut.* Stanford, Calif., 1950.

Bles, Arthur de. *How to Distinguish Saints in Art.* New York, 1925.

Boutiot, Théophile. *Annuaire administratif et commercial du département de l'Aube*, XLI (1866).

——. *Histoire de la ville de Troyes et de la Champagne méridionale.* 5 vols. Troyes, 1870-80.

Brial, M. J.-J. In *Histoire littéraire de France* (Paris, 1869), XIV.

Brooke, George C. *English Coins.* London, 1932.

Brugger, E. "Die *Nodons-Nuadu*-Hypothese als Erklärung des Namens 'Fischerkönig,'" *Romance Philology*, IX (1956), 285-97.

Brut, ed. Arnold. 2 vols. Paris, 1938-40.
Callan, Charles J. *The Psalms.* New York and London, 1944.
Carré, Gustave. *Histoire populaire de Troyes et du département de l'Aube.* Troyes, 1881.
"La Cathédrale de Strasbourg," *Encyclopédie Alpina Illustrée.* Paris, 1939.
Cathédrales de France. Editions des Deux Mondes. Paris, 1950.
Catholic Encyclopedia:
    "Abraham," J. A. Howlett
    "Abraham (in Liturgy)," H. T. Henry
    "Angels, Early Christian Representations of," Maurice M. Hassett
    "Cardinal Virtues," John Rickaby
    "David," John Corbett
    "Glastonbury Abbey," G. Roger Hudleston
    "Grail, The Holy," Arthur Remy
    "Lance, The Holy," Herbert Thurston
    "Rachel," James F. Driscoll
    "Symbolism," Herbert Thurston
    "Templars," Charles Moeller
Cézard, Pierre. "Périodiques," *Romania,* LXXVIII (1957), 274-5.
Chapin, E. *Les villes de foire de Champagne des origines au début du XIVe siècle.* Paris, 1937.
Chrétien de Troyes. *Der Percevalroman (Li Contes del Graal),* ed. Alfons Hilka. Halle, 1932.
———. *Erec et Enide,* ed. Wendelin Foerster. 3rd ed. Halle, 1934.
———. *Perceval le Gallois,* français moderne par Lucien Foulet, introd. par Mario Roques. Paris, 1947.
City of Jerusalem, trans. C. R. Conder. Palestine Pilgrims' Text Society, VI, No. 2. London, 1888.
Connick, Charles J. "Windows of Old France," *International Studio,* LXXVIII (1923), 187-95.
Corrard de Bréban. *Les rues de Troyes anciennes et modernes.* Troyes, 1857.
Courtalon-Delaistre, Jean-Charles. *Typographie historique de la ville et diocèse de Troyes.* 3 vols. Troyes, 1783-84.
Delbouille, Maurice. "Genèse du conte del Graal." Editions du Centre national de la Recherche scientifique (1956), pp. 83-91.
Dieudonné, A. *Manuel de numismatique française.* Paris, 1936.
Dillon, Myles. *Early Irish Literature.* Chicago, 1948.
Faral, Edmond. "Chrétien de Troyes et les romans arturiens," in

Joseph Bédier and Paul Hazard, *Littérature française* (2 vols.; Paris, 1923), I, 18 ff.

———. *La Légende arthurienne*. 3 vols. Paris, 1929.

Ferguson, George. *Signs and Symbols in Christian Art*. New York, 1954.

Foerster, Wendelin. *Kristian von Troyes: Wörterbuch zu seinen sämtlichen Werken*. Halle, 1914.

Frappier, Jean. "Sur l'interprétation du vers 3301 du *Conte du Graal*," *Romania*, LXXI (1950), 240-45.

———. "Du 'Graal trestot descovert' à la forme du Graal chez Chrétien de Troyes," *Romania*, LXXIII (1952), 82-92.

———. "Du 'Graal trestot descovert' à l'origine de la légende," *Romania*, LXXIV (1953), 358-75.

———. "Chrétien de Troyes: *Perceval* ou *Le Conte du Graal*," *Les Cours de Sorbonne*. Paris, 1953.

———. *Chrétien de Troyes, l'homme et l'œuvre*. Paris, 1957.

Gaster, Moses. *Studies and Texts*. London, 1925-28.

Gerald the Welshman. "Itinerarium Kambriae," ed. Dimock, *Opera* (London, 1868), VI.

———. "Speculum Ecclesiae," ed. J. S. Brewer, *Opera* (London, 1873), IV.

———. "De principis instructione," ed. George Warner, *Opera* (Rolls Series; London, 1891), VIII.

Gilbert, J. T. *Historic and Municipal Documents of Ireland*. Rolls Series. 1870.

Green, Richard H. "Alain of Lille's De Planctu Naturae," *Speculum*, XXXI (1956), 651 ff.

Grodecki, Louis, ed. *The Stained Glass of French Churches*. London and Paris, 1948.

Gross, Heinrich. *Gallia-Judaica, dictionnaire géographique de la France d'après les sources rabbiniques*. Paris, 1897.

Gsteiger, Manfred. *Die Landschaftsschilderungen in den Romanen Chrestiens de Troyes*. Bern, 1958.

Guyer, Foster E. *Romance in the Making*. New York, 1954.

———. *Chrétien de Troyes*. New York, 1957.

Héliot, P. "Résidences princières bâties en France," *Moyen-Age*, LXI (1955), 37-38.

Hill, John Hugh and Laurita L. "Contemporary Accounts and the Later Reputation of Adhemar, Bishop of Puy," *Medievalia et Humanistica*, IX (1955), 30-38.

Hofer, Stefan. *Chrétien de Troyes—Leben und Werk des altfranzösischen Epikers.* Köln, 1954.

———. "Bemerkungen zum Perceval," *Romanische Forschungen,* LXVII (1955), 36-54.

Holmes, Urban T., Jr. *History of Old French Literature.* New York, 1948.

———. "A New Interpretation of Chrétien's *Conte del Graal*," *University of North Carolina Studies in the Romance Languages and Literatures,* VIII (1948). This is a revised and fuller version of an article of the same title, *Studies in Philology,* XLIV (1947), 453-76.

———. "The Arthurian Tradition in Lambert d'Ardres," *Speculum,* XXV (1950), 100-03.

Huon de Bordeaux, ed. F. Guessard and C. Grandmaison. Paris, 1860.

Jackson, Kenneth. "Les sources celtiques du Roman du Graal." Editions du Centre national de la Recherche scientifique (1956), pp. 215-27.

Jocelyn. *Life of Abbot Samson.* ed L. C. Jane. London, 1907.

Jullian, René. *L'Eveil de la sculpture italienne.* 2 vols. Paris, 1945.

Kittredge, G. L. *Study of Gawain and the Green Knight.* Cambridge, Mass., 1916.

Kleist, James A., and Lilly, Joseph L. *The New Testament,* rendered from the original Greek with explanatory notes. Milwaukee, 1954.

———, and Lynam, Thomas J. *The Psalms in Rhythmic Prose.* Milwaukee, 1954.

Klenke, Sister M. Amelia, O. P. "Liturgy and Allegory in Chrétien's *Perceval,*" *University of North Carolina Studies in the Romance Languages and Literatures,* XIV (1951).

———. "The Blancheflor-Perceval Question," *Romance Philology,* VI (1952), 173-8.

———. "Chrétien's Symbolism and Cathedral Art," *PMLA,* LXX (1955), 223-43.

———. "The Spiritual Ascent of Perceval," *Studies in Philology,* LIII (1956), 1-21.

———. "Some Mediaeval Concepts of King Arthur," *Kentucky Foreign Language Quarterly.* To be published.

———. "The *Christus Domini* Concept in Mediaeval Art and Literature," *Studies in Philology.* To be published.

Köhler, Erich. *Ideal und Wirklichkeit in der höfischen Epik—Studien* zur Form der frühen Artus- und Graldichtung. Beihefte zur Zeitschrift für Romanische Philologie, Heft 97. Tübingen, 1956.

Lalore, Charles. Collection des principaux cartulaires du diocèse de Troyes. 7 vols. Paris, 1870-90.

Lanson, Gustave. Histoire de la littérature française. Paris, 1922.

———, and Tuffrau, Paul. Manuel d'histoire de la littérature française. Paris and Boston, 1932.

Larousse. Histoire de France, ed. Marcel Reinhard and Norbert Dufourcq. 2 vols. Paris, 1954.

Lasteyrie, R. de. Miniatures inédites de l'Hortus deliciarum de Herrade de Landsberg (XIIe siècle). Paris, 1885.

Lejeune, Mme Rita. "Préfiguration du Graal," Studi Medievali, XVII (1951), 277-302.

———. "La Date du Conte du Graal de Chrétien de Troyes," Moyen Age, LX (1954), 51-79.

———. "Encore la date du Conte du Graal de Chrétien de Troyes," Bulletin Bibliographique de la Société Internationale Arthurienne, IX (1956), 85-100.

Levy, Raphael. "The Quest for Biographical Evidence in Perceval," Medievalia et Humanistica, VI (1950), 76-83.

———. "The Motivation of Perceval and the Authorship of Philomena," PMLA, LXXI (1956), 853-62.

Lewis, C. S. The Allegory of Love. Oxford, 1948.

Lloyd, Sir John. In English Historical Review, LVII (1942).

Longnon, A. Documents relatifs au comte de Champagne et de Brie. Documents inédits. 2 vols. Paris, 1901-14.

Loomis, Laura Hibbard. "Arthur's Round Table," PMLA, XLI (1926), 771-84.

———. "The Table of the Last Supper in Religious and Secular Iconography," Art Studies, V (1927), 71-96.

———. "The Round Table Again," Modern Language Notes, XLIV (1929), 511-9.

Loomis, R. S. Celtic Myth and Arthurian Romance. New York, 1927.

———. Arthurian Tradition and Chrétien de Troyes. New York, 1949.

———. "The Grail Story of Chrétien de Troyes as Ritual and Symbolism," PMLA, LXXI (1956), 840-52.

———. Wales and the Arthurian Legend. Cardiff, 1956.

———, and Laura H. *Arthurian Legends in Medieval Art*. London and New York, 1938.

Lot-Borodine, Myrrah. "Autour du saint graal à propos de travaux récents (II. Les rites eucharistiques)," *Romania*, LVII (1931). 147-205.

———. "Le *Conte del Graal* de Chrétien de Troyes et sa présentation symbolique," *Romania*, LXXVII (1956), 235-88.

Mabillon, John. *Life and Works of Saint Bernard*. London, 1899.

McSorley, Joseph. *An Outline History of the Church*. St. Louis and London, 1943.

Mahoney, John. "The Evidence for Andreas Capellanus in Re-examination," *Studies in Philology*, LV (1958), 1-6.

Mâle, Emile. *L'Art religieux du XIIe siècle en France*. Paris, 1928.

———. *L'Art religieux du XIIIe siècle en France*. Paris, 1948.

Malone, Kemp. "The Historicity of Arthur," *Journal of English and Germanic Philology*, XXIII (1924), 463-91.

Martin, Henry. *La Miniature française*. Paris and Brussels, 1923.

Marx, Jean. *La Légende arthurienne et le Graal*. Paris, 1951.

———. In "Correspondance," *Medium Aevum*, XXIII (1954), 132.

———. "Quelques remarques au sujet de récents travaux sur l'origine du Graal," *Moyen Age*, LXIII (1957), 469-80.

Mergell, Bodo. *Der Gral in Wolframs Parzival*. Halle, 1952.

Micha, Alexandre. "Encore le 'Graal trestot descovert,'" *Romania*, LXXII (1951), 236-8.

———. "Deux Etudes sur le Graal (I)," *Romania*, LXXIII (1952), 462-79.

———. "Deux Etudes sur le Graal (II)," *Romania*, LXXV (1954), 316-52.

Migne, J. P., ed. *Patrologia Latina*. 221 vols. Paris, 1879-90.

Mommsen, Theodor. *Chronica Minora*. 3 vols. Berlin, 1892-98.

Morey, Charles F. *Mediaeval Art*. New York, 1942.

Morgan, Raleigh, Jr. "Old French *jogleor* and Kindred Terms," *Romance Philology*, VII (1954), 279-325.

Mot, G.-J. *Les Vitraux de Saint-Nazaire de Carcassonne*. Toulouse, 1954.

Musée des Arts Décoratifs. *Vitraux de France*. 23rd ed. rev. and cor. Paris, 1953.

Nelli, René. "Le Graal dans l'ethnographie," *Lumière du Graal* (Paris, 1951), pp. 1-36.

Newstead, Helaine. "The Besieged Ladies in Arthurian Romance," *PMLA*, LXIII (1948), 803-30.

———. "The Blancheflor-Perceval Question Again," *Romance Philology*, VII (1953), 171-5.

———. Review of Stefan Hofer, *Chrétien de Troyes—Leben und Werk* (Köln, 1954), *Romance Philology*, X (1956), 56-61.

———. Review of R. S. Loomis, *Arthurian Tradition and Chrétien de Troyes* (New York, 1949), *Speculum*, XXXIII (1958), 105-12.

Nitze, William A. "How Did the Fisher King Get His Name?," *Mediaeval Studies in Honor of J. D. M. Ford*. Cambridge, Mass., 1948.

———. "Perceval and the Holy Grail," *University of California Publications in Modern Philology*, XXVIII, No. 5 (1949), 281-332.

———. "The Fisher King and the Grail in Retrospect," *Romance Philology*, VI (1952), 14-22.

———, and Cross, T. P. *Lancelot and Guinevere*. Chicago, 1930.

———, and Dargan, E. Preston. *A History of French Literature*. New York, 1938.

———, and Jenkins. *Le haut livre du graal; Perlesvaus*. Chicago, 1932-37.

———, and Williams, Harry F. "Arthurian Names in the *Perceval* of Chrétien de Troyes, Analysis and Commentary," *University of California Publications in Modern Philology*, XXXVIII, No. 3 (1955), 265-97.

d'Outremeuse, Jean. *Ly Mireur des histors*, ed. A. Borgnet. 7 vols. Bruxelles, 1864-80.

Paris sous Philippe le Bel. Documents inédits. 1837.

Parks, George Brunner. *The English Traveler to Italy*. Stanford, Calif., 1954.

Parry, J. J. Review of R. S. Loomis, *Arthurian Tradition and Chrétien de Troyes* (New York, 1949), *Modern Language Quarterly*, XIII (1952), 99-101.

Pauphilet, Albert. *Le Legs du Moyen Age*. Melun, 1950.

Ponsoye, Pierre. *L'Islam et le Graal*. Editions Denoël. Paris, 1957.

Poole, A. L. *From Domesday Book to Magna Carta*. Oxford, 1950.

Pope, Arthur U. "Persia and the Holy Grail," *The Literary Review*, I (1957), 57-71.

Porter, Arthur Kingsley. *Lombard Architecture.* 4 vols. New Haven, 1917.
La queste del saint Graal, ed. Albert Pauphilet. Paris, 1923.
Regnaldi Monachi Dunelmensis Opera. Surtees Society, I. London, 1835.
Rickard, Peter. *Britain in Mediaeval French Literature.* Cambridge, Eng., 1956.
Riquer, Martín de. "Perceval y Gauvain en Li Contes del Graal," *Filología Romanza,* IV (1957), 119-47.
Ritchie, R. L. Graeme. *Crétien de Troyes and Scotland.* Oxford, 1952.
———. *The Normans in Scotland.* Edinburgh, 1954.
Roach, William. "The Modena Text of the Prose Joseph d'Arimathie," *Romance Philology,* IX (1956), 313-42.
Robertson, D. W., Jr. "The Doctrine of Charity in Mediaeval Literary Gardens," *Speculum,* XXVI (1951), 24-49.
Le roman de Flamenca, ed. P. Meyer. Paris, 1901.
Romanesque Art. Victoria and Albert Museum. Ipswich, 1957.
Roques, Mario. "Le Graal de Chrétien et la demoiselle au Graal," *Société de publications romanes et françaises,* L (1955). This also appeared with the same title in *Romania,* LXXVI (1955), 1-27.
Cahiers de civilisation médiévale. 2 nos. Poitiers, 1958—.
Runciman, Steven. *A History of the Crusades.* 3 vols. Cambridge, Eng., 1951-55.
Schlauch, Margaret. "The Allegory of Church and Synagogue," *Speculum,* XIV (1939), 448-64.
Seaby, W. A. "Mediaeval Coin Hoards in North-East Ireland," *Numismatic Chronicle,* 6th Ser., XV (1955), 161-71.
Séchelles, D. de. *L'Origine du Graal.* Saint-Brieuc, 1954.
———. "L'Evolution et la transformation du mythe arthurien dans le thème du Graal," *Romania,* LXXVIII (1957), 182-98.
Simson, Otto von. *The Gothic Cathedral.* Bollingen Series XLVIII. New York, 1956.
Siren, Oswald. *A Descriptive Catalogue of the Pictures in the Jarves Collection Belonging to Yale University.* New Haven, 1916.
Stapper, Richard. *Catholic Liturgics,* trans. and adapted from the German by David Baier. Rev. ed. Paterson, N. J., 1938.
Studies Presented to R. L. Graeme Ritchie, ed. F. Mackenzie, R. C. Knight, and J. M. Milner. Cambridge, Eng., 1949.

Tatlock, J. S. P. "The Dates of the Arthurian Saints' Legends," *Speculum*, XIV (1939), 345-65.
Vigneras, L. A. "Chrétien de Troyes Rediscovered," *Modern Philology*, XXXII (1934-35), 341-2.
Walpole, Ronald. "The *Pèlerinage de Charlemagne:* Poem, Legend, and Problem," *Romance Philology*, VIII (1955), 173-86.
Webber, F. R. *Church Symbolism*. Cleveland, 1938.
Weston, Jessie L., trans. *Wolfram von Eschenbach's "Parzival."* London, 1894.
Ziltener, Werner. *Chrétien und die Aeneïs*. Köln, 1957.
Zimmer, H. "Bretonische Elemente in der Arthursage des Gottfried von Monmouth," *ZFSL*, XII (1890), 253-6.
Zingerle, I. *Reiserechnungen Wolfgers von Ellenbrechtskirchen*. Heilbronn, 1877.

Index

Abraham, symbol, 101, 102, 119, 126, 206-9
Ackerman, Phyllis, 73n
Adam and Eve, symbol, 134, 141, 149, 150, 151, 161, 192
Adams, Henry, 119, 136
Adam Scot, 80n
Adèle de Champagne, 14
Adhemar of Le Puy, 130, 131, 197
Aelesdes de Marolio, 18
Ailred of Rievaux, 29
Alain de Lille, 79
Alfred, King, 15, 53
Allen, Derek F., 40n
Andreas Capellanus, or de Luyères, 16, 17, 35, 36, 43
Aneurin, 27
Anglo-Saxon Chronicle, 14-15
Angoulême Cathedral, portal, 129, 130, 133, 137, 156
Anscombe, Alfred, 31
Appellations, 52-55, 60-61
Arnaud, Anne-François, 4n, 6n, 16n, 49n
Arnould of Guines, 75
Arthur, battles of, 14, 31, 32; legends about, 15, 25n, 26, 27-28, 29, 30, 38-39, 77, 140-41; in *Cligés*, 23-24, 41; tomb of, 33-34, 159; in *Conte del Graal*, 65, 66, 67, 70, 128, 138-39; as Christ, 72, 87, 95, 125, 132, 133, 136, 137, 145, 148, 149, 151, 152, 154; name, 132; mentioned, 35, 43, 44, 49, 59, 63, 80, 84, 107, 143, 153, 157
Artusius, 123, 140
Aube river, 15, 16, 31
Auberon, 40

Aubert, Marcel, 120
Aucassin et Nicolette, 48
Augustinians, 6, 15, 51
Aumonière of Saint-Estienne at Troyes, 48-49
Autun, 31
Avallon, 38

Bari, San Niccolà, 124, 131
Bar-sur-Aube, 9, 15, 16, 58, 59, 81
Beauvais, 40
Becket, St. Thomas, 53
Bell, Mrs. Arthur, 99n
Beneëit de Sainte-More, 30
Benjamin of Tudela, 76n
Benton, John, 18n, 58
Bern, woodcut, 157, 160
Bernard, Georges, 58
Beroul, 36
Bible, 36, 134-35
Birds, symbol, 133
Blancheflor of Belrepaire, 67-68, 71
Bleeding Lance, not for Gawain, 66-67; mentioned, 69, 71, 80, 84, 95, 96n, 109, 110, 116, 132
Bles, Arthur de, 99n
Bourges Cathedral, Passion window, 111
Boutiot, Théophile, 13n, 55
Bretons, 10-11, 22, 23, 25, 28, 29, 83, 128, 155, 156
Brial, dom Michel J.-J., 13n
Brittany, 23, 24, 25, 28, 30
Broce as Juis, 5-6, 12
Burmaltus, 125, 139, 152
Bury-St.-Edmunds, 20, 22, 48
Byzantium, 14, 42, 49, 166

Index

Caerleon, 34, 38
Cain and Abel, symbols, 134-36, 149, 151
Caino, 32
Carcassonne, Saint-Nazaire of, 149, 150-51
Castle of Troyes, 5, 6
Catalogue of knights, 37-38, 48
Cathedrals. *See specific ones*
Catte street, 25
Celts, 22, 23, 25, 28, 36, 37, 48, 77, 83, 94n, 136, 149, 152, 154. *See also* Bretons, Welsh
Cézard, Pierre, 106
Chalice, 80, 96n, 98, 109, 116
Châlons-sur-Marne window, 18, 61, 76, 107n, 109, 111-14, 115, 119, 120, 121
Champagne. *See* Chrétien de Troyes, and Troyes
Chansons de geste, 39, 51n. *See also* Chanson de Roland
Chanson de Roland, 49, 97, 98, 131
Charity, theme, 22, 62, 63, 67, 77, 78, 84, 91, 94, 125, 137, 138
Charlemagne, 132. *See also Pèlerinage de Charlemagne*
Chartres, window, 132, 133, 157
Chrétien de Saint-Maclou, 58, 83
Chrétien de Troyes, and Troyes, 4, 5, 6, 7-8, 14, 17, 32, 41-61, 81, 91, 94, 95, 96, 97, 102, 106, 115, 119, 122, 158; content and sources of works, 11, 37, 39, 62, 63, 66, 68, 73, 74, 75, 79, 82, 85, 86, 92, 98, 99, 100, 103, 104, 105, 107-11 *passim*, 113, 116, 118, 125, 127, 128, 130-33 *passim*, 136, 137, 138, 145, 146, 147, 152-55 *passim*, 157, 159, 160, 161; life of, 18, 19-22, 83-84, 87; and England, 23-25, 29, 34, 64, 83; *matière*, 35-36, 40; and the Jews, 71, 121; death, 78
Christ, as knight, 97, 104n, 148
Christianus, physician, 54
Church Pre-Triumphant, 106-7
Church Trumphant, 73, 84, 87, 106, 109, 110, 113
Church-Synagogue. *See* Synagoga-Ecclesia
City of Jerusalem, 75
Clercs, 15, 17, 22, 50
Clermont-Ferrand, Notre-Dame-du-Port, 156

Cligés, 14, 19, 23, 24, 39, 40-42, 46, 48, 82
Cluny, 14
Coins, 32n, 40n
Cologne, Rathaus, 154
Color symbolism, 46, 82
Connick, Charles J., 109, 113
Constantinople, 49. *See* Greece *and* Byzantium
Conte del Graal, quoted, 6-7, 21, 62, 77-78, 116, 127-28, 158, 161; *livre* of, 22, 59-60; parallels with previous works, 46; Gawain adventures in, 63-76, 72-73; Perceval adventures in, 67-71, 72-73, 136; compared to *Queste del Saint Graal*, 84-87; prologue, 91-107, 122, 137; mentioned, 35, 36, 50, 51, 81, 109, 119, 125, 146, 152. *See also* Chrétien de Troyes
Conversion, 52, 63, 77, 78, 86, 91, 93, 96, 97, 106, 154, 159
Cornish place-names, 36
Courtly love, 43, 50, 167
Cowper, Frederick A. G., 111
Cressac, chapel of Templars, 97n, 130, 133
Crestiens li Gois, 21
Crows and ravens, symbol, 104, 106n, 152
Crusade, First, 114, 120, 124, 130, 131, 156
Crusaders, sought to convert, 97; popularize Arthur in Italy, 128; Arthur is their "high-priest," 137; and the Apostles, 131; mentioned, 12, 94n, 97, 130, 133, 147
Cumbria, 83
Cyfarwddion, 27-28
Cynfeirdd, 27

Dampierre-sur-Aube, 16, 51, 52
Daniel, prophet, 144, 147
Dargan, E. P., 110n
David, King, as Arthur and therefore Christ, 142, 143, 145
David, King of Scotland, 37
Delbouille, Maurice, 28n
De Lombardo et lumaca, 128
Demoiselle au Graal, 106n-7n, 110
Deschamps, Paul, 124, 157
Dillon, Myles, 33n
Dinasdaron, 137
Dream of Rhonabwy, 28, 38

Dublin, Castle Register, 54
Dumbarton Rock, 37

Ecclesia, carries Chalice, 110, 111, 114, 117, 157; mentioned, 76, 77, 80, 86, 106. *See also* Synagoga-Ecclesia
Ederyn, son of Nudd, 28, 38, 156
Education, 17, 22
Eleanor of Aquitaine, 17, 43, 119
Eliduc, 28, 29
Enide, name, 34-35
Erec, name, 38; mentioned, 34, 35, 39, 59
Erec et Enide, 11, 19, 21, 34-35, 36, 37, 38, 39, 52, 59, 81, 82, 83
Ermine, symbol, 115n
Estorie des Englés, 15n, 35n
Estregales, 36
Ezechiel, 114, 136, 141-43, 144, 147

Fairs of Troyes, 9-10, 11
Faral, Edmond, 30n, 39n
Ferguson, George, 115n, 143, 144, 152
Fisher King, as Jacob, 102-03, 125, 140; mentioned, 77, 85, 99, 125
Flamenca, 11, 23
Flemings, 10, 26
Foerster, Wendelin, 23
Fox, symbol, 133, 135, 136
Francis, Elizabeth, 49
Frappier, Jean, 57

Gaels, 40
Gaimar, Geoffroi, 14, 15, 35
Galaad, 85
Galloway, 37, 64, 65
Galterus Christiani, 57, 58, 59, 83-84
Gamaliel, 115
Gaster, Moses, 74
Gaufridus, 25
Gautier de Châtillon-sur-Seine, 77, 95, 106, 122, 124, 147, 154, 157
Gautier de Coincy, ii
Gawain, equated with Perceval, 72-73; mentioned, 7, 43, 44, 63, **82, 84,** 85, 87, 127, 128
Geoffrey of Monmouth, 14, 15, 24, 25, 26, 28, 29, 30, 31, 33, 34, 35, 37, 39, 46, 47, 123, 155
Gerald the Welshman, 3, 34, 38, 77
Gerbert de Montreuil, 21, 78
Gildas, 15
Giovanni del Biondo, 111, 157
Glastonbury, 14, 25, 34, 38, 39

Godefroi de Laigny, 20, 22
Gododdin, 27
Gold cup, symbol, 137
Goliards, 10
Gornemanz, as spiritual knighthood, 100; as Gamaliel, 115n; mentioned, 67, 70
Gorre, 44-45, 46, 59, 66
Grace, 59, 76, 84, 86, 101
Grail, Castle of, 63, 73-76, 77, 78, 81, 99, 115; meaning, 96, 99, 110, 114. *See also* Procession of Grail
Greece, 40. *See also* Byzantium
Green, Richard H., 79
Gregory of Tours, 32
Griffin, symbol, 152, 155
Grodecki, Louis, 96n, 112, 113, 114, 115
Gsteiger, Manfred, 69n
Guenevere, tomb of, 33-34; mentioned, 43, 44, 46, 47, 82, 85
Guglielmo, at Modena, 124; his associates, 125-26
Guillaume d'Angleterre, 9n, 20, 22, 49-50, 56, 59
Guyer, Foster E., 51n

Hansa, 9, 132
Hebrews, Epistle to the, 76, 77, 102, 145
Héliot, Pierre, 6n
Henry I (Liberal) of Troyes, library, 16, 80, 119; marriage, 18; mentioned, 7, 11, 12, 15, 17, 43, 50, 55, 59, 63, 75, 81, 83, 100, 102n
Henry of Blois, Bishop of Winchester, 14, 24, 25, 32, 50, 96
Henry of Huntingdon, 30
Herman, or Judas le Juif, 78n
Hermit Priest, symbol, 101, 102
Hideous Damsel, 46, 71, 72, 166, 192, 209-10, 212
Hind, symbol, 103, 105, 108
Historia Regum Brittaniae, 30, 35. *See also* Geoffrey of Monmouth
Hofer, Stefan, 94n, 100, 131, 147
Holy of Holies, 74, 76, 80, 137
Hortus Deliciarum, 144, 159
Hound of Heaven, motif, 106, 139
Hugues, Count of Troyes, 7, 13
Huon de Bordeaux, 76
Huon de Méry, 51, 53
Huy, Godefroid de, 76

Ider, son of Nuth, 28, 38, 39, 156. See also Ederyn
Inner Room. See Grail, Castle of
Innocent III, Pope, 5n
Ireland, 40
Irois, 40
Isaias, prophet, 134, 139-40, 144
Isles de Mer, explanation of, 72; mentioned, 59, 67, 68, 71, 80, 81, 84, 166
Italy, 3, 9
Iwenus, son of Urianus, 31, 47-48. See also Yvain

Jackson, Kenneth, 27, 28, 33
Jacob, wrestles with Angel, 103, 134, 140; on old Testament level, 104; mentioned, 76, 77, 78, 125
Jaucourt, 15, 16, 58
Jeremias, prophet, 103, 140, 147
Jews, in Troyes, 11-13, 16; called dogs, 71, 121; banished, 96; handbooks for, 122; to be converted, 121-22, 154; incredulity of, 133; idolatry of, 142; envious, 152; mentioned, 51, 52, 54, 59, 74, 76, 77, 80, 81, 84, 86, 91, 106, 120, 124, 159
John, King, 24
Johns, John L., 81
Judaeo-Christian interpretation of Grail, in brief, 73, 77-78, 103
Jullian, René, 123-24, 125-27, 131, 145-46, 148, 156, 157

Kei, 27-28
Keu, 32, 37, 39, 43-44, 71, 82, 128, 137, 138
Kittredge, George Lyman, 123
Knight as saint, 98, 104, 130-31. See also Christ
Köhler, Erich, 79n-80n, 161, 165-67
Kulhwch and Olwen, 27

Lady in the tent, 67, 70, 105, 152
Lambert d'Ardres, 53, 75
Lance. See Bleeding Lance
Lancelot, name, 46-47
Lancelot, or *Le Chevalier de la Charrette*, discussed, 42-45; similarity to *Conte del Graal*, 59-60, 84; mentioned, 20, 21, 36, 38, 39, 48, 59, 63, 72n, 84, 119

Lancelot, prose, 85, 128
Lang, Andrew, 48
Langres, 15, 32
Laon Cathedral, 157
Legends, of Britain, 14, 15, 25; mentioned, 19-40 *passim*, 48, 83, 142, 149, 154, 157. See also Arthur, legends about
Levels of interpretation, 100-01. See also *Sens et matière*
Levy, Raphael, 106, 183
Lewis, Clyde S., 79
Lincoln, Jewish massacre, 96
Livre, cited by Chrétien, 60, 62, 71, 132
Loomis, Laura Hibbard, 107, 161. See also Loomis, Roger S.
Loomis, Roger Sherman, 25n, 27, 28, 94n, 105, 107, 123-24, 125, 126, 128, 131, 140-41, 144, 148, 149, 153, 154, 155, 156, 157
Lot-Borodin, Mme, 131, 147, 155
Louis VII, of France, 17
Luyères. See Andreas Capellanus

McSorley, Joseph, 96n
Mahoney, John, 16n, 81n
Malcom, King of Scotland, 37
Mâle, Emile, 95n, 114, 121, 124, 126, 128, 129, 131, 146, 151n, 157
Marie de Champagne, 17, 18, 20, 21, 42, 43, 45, 50, 58
Marie de France, 28, 29, 38
Marx, Jean, 26
Mathilda of Carinthia, 13-14
Matthew Paris, 3
Mediaeval practice, 23, 25-26
Melchizedech, Being in Inner Room, 118; mentioned, 137, 203
Mergell, Bodo, 166-67
Merlin, or Myrddin, 26, 27
Messiah, 77, 84, 103, 124, 125, 143, 159
Midrashim, 51, 73n
Minstrels, 10-11, 23, 34
Modena Cathedral, main portal, 95, 106, 144-45; combat, 126-27, 134, 139-40; archivolt, 153, 154, 156; helmets, 156-57
Moissac, 126, 127
Moneyers, 54. See also Coins
Mont Douloureux, 31, 126, 127, 132, 147
Montesclaire, 132, 204-5

Mont Saint-Michel, 31, 32
Mordred, 14, 24
Morey, Charles, 109, 117
Morgan, Raleigh, 11n
Morgan la Fee, 33, 34, 38
Mot, Georges-J., 149-51

Nelli, René, 98n, 100n
Nennius, 31
New Law, 77, 78, 86, 116, 145
Newstead, Helaine, 156
Nine Heroes Tapestry, 160. *See also* Paris Tapestry
Nitze, William, 110n
Noah, symbol, 134, 149, 150, 151, 161

Old Law, bloody sacrifices, 111; figures of great faith, 117-18; mentioned, 39, 77, 78, 86, 116, 145, 157
Orders, in the Church, 23, 57, 59
Orgeuilleus, 64, 65, 72
Otranto mosaic, discussed, 140-45, 148-49; date, 157; mentioned, 132, 133, 135, 151, 153, 154
Ovid, 19, 21, 22, 51, 83
Owen of Bath, 28, 47. *See also* Iwenus

Palace of Troyes, 6-7, 8, 10, 13, 16, 17
Palis, 16, 17
Paris, Gaston, 23, 42
Paris, Louis, 18n
Paris Tapestry, 60-61, 145
Parzifal, 73n, 78
Pèlerinage de Charlemagne, 98, 121n
Perceval, name and meaning, 70, 81, 82, 84, 119; symbol of St. Paul, 99; as a Jew, 108; oath of, 115; Communion of, 153; mentioned, 14, 63, 85, 86, 87, 109, 116, 136, 138, 152, 158
Perceval. *See Conte del Graal*
Petrus Comestor, 17
Philip Augustus, King, 17, 96n
Philip of Flanders, 22, 55, 59, 62, 75, 78, 81, 84, 91, 92, 94, 97, 106
Philippe de Harveng, 55, 56, 81
Philomena, 19, 21, 56
Pigmy king, 141, 153
Pilgrims, Perceval meets, 116; mentioned, 13, 75
Poncius of Saint-Loup, 56-57
Ponsoye, Pierre, 73n
Pope, Arthur U., 73n

Porta della Pescheria, dating, 123-25, 157; figures on it, 125, 128; their inspiration, 134; waves for mountain, 126, 133, 151; lower part, 133-34; mentioned, 137, 140, 146, 149, 151, 152. *See also* Modena Cathedral, archivolt
Porter, Arthur K., 123, 134, 157
Premonstratensians, named Chrétien, 81; mentioned, 13, 16, 55, 56, 58, 59, 80n, 81
Procession of Grail, 63, 69-70, 73, 95, 96n, 99, 106n, 113-14, 145, 153. *See also* Grail

Queste del Saint Graal, 84-86

Rabbenu Tam, 12, 52
Rachael, symbol, 103, 104, 106
Ram, symbol, 143-45
Ramerupt, 12, 15, 51, 76
Rashi, 12
Reciprocity of Old and New Testaments, 96, 116
Reims, the standing knight, 153, 207-08
Remy, Arthur, 153-54
Reynolds, Robert L., 53
Rhys, Sir John, 62
Rickard, Peter, 8n, 23, 62
Rion, King of Isles de Mer, 67, 72
Riquer, Martín de, 47, 63n
Ritchie, R. L. Graeme, 31, 36, 37, 48
Roach, William, 146-47
Roman de Flamenca, 11, 23
Roman de la Rose, 106
Roman de Thèbes, 51n
Romans, 15, 31-32, 64n
Roques, Mario, 38, 45, 73, 95n, 106, 110, 111, 131, 147
Round Table, 33, 35, 37, 47, 161
Runciman, Steven, 94n

St. Abraham, Hospice of, 102, 158
Saint-Amand de Boixe, tympanum, 160
St. Bernard, 14, 16, 63, 84, 96, 100, 120, 158
St. Bonaventure, 151
Saint-Denis, 7, 114, 115, 117, 119, 132, 133
Saint-Estienne Church, 6, 7, 11, 15, 16
Saint-Etienne, Auxerre, 97n, 104n, 148
Saint-Frobert, 12, 97
San Geminiano, 129, 160

St. John, on Charity, 93, 94; mentioned, 137, 153
St. John the Baptist, statue at Modena, 146
Saint-Loup, Abbey, 5, 6, 11, 12, 15, 16, 56, 57, 59, 115
Saint-Martin d'Ainay, at Lyons, 124
Saint-Pantaléon, 12, 97
St. Paul, conversion of Jews, 78, 96; begs for poor in Jerusalem, 97; sword of, 99; symbolically expressed, 101; read by Chrétien, 109; patron of Templars, 137; statue at Modena, 146; mentioned, 77, 91, 93-94, 102, 105, 115n, 145, 153, 159
Saint Pierre Cathedral, 5, 6, 15, 17
Saladin, 97, 122
Salomon, 76, 113
Salter, Henry E., 24, 25n
Schools, 17, 22; Jewish, 76
Scotland, 23, 30, 31, 36, 37, 40, 47, 49, 83
Sens et matière, xiii, 19, 21, 35. See also Levels of interpretation
Serfs, 11, 12
Shield devices, 38n, 47
Sower, motif, 22, 92-94, 105
Stag, motif, 103, 105, 106n, 152. See also Hind
Stavelot, portable altar, 76, 109, 117, 119, 121, 151
Stephen, King, 14, 25-26
Stirling, 49-50
Strasbourg Cathedral, 105n, 106n, 109
Strasbourg Symposium, 26-27
Suger, Abbot, window, 109, 114, 119; travels, 115; *vase du trésor*, 116; mentioned, 76, 77, 91, 95, 98, 107, 117, 120, 121, 122, 131, 159
Symbolism, 95-107
Synagoga, return to by Perceval, 86; awaits Messiah, 95; blindfolded, 111, 118-19, 144, 159; baptized, 157; mentioned, 59, 76, 77, 80, 86, 109, 117, 145
Synagoga-Ecclesia motif, 73, 76, 84, 96n, 97, 99, 101, 109, 111, 145

Tailleor, 70, 80, 96n, 111
Taliessin, 26, 27
Talmudists, 12, 13, 51, 52
Tatlock, James S. P., 155-56
Templars, oath of, 99-100, 134; compared with Arthur's conquered, 139; mentioned, 13, 121, 158
Temple of Solomon, Veil of, 82, 159; as heaven, 114; mentioned, 74, 75, 76, 77, 78, 84, 98, 102, 116n, 189
Thibaut, knight, *quondam Judaeus*, 52
Thibaut II, Count of Troyes, 7, 13, 24
Tour Douloureuse, 138. See also Mont Douloureux
Tree of Life, symbol, 149, 160
Tristan and Iseut, 34, 36, 39, 42
Troyes, discussed, 3-18; Oppidum, 5, 15, 155; Chapel of Saint-Estienne, 6-7, 16, 115; Chapel of Saint-Frobert, 12, 97; Jewish synods in, 13, 158; Chapel treasury, 49; people's names in, 55; synagogues, 97; mentioned, 23, 36, 42, 51, 53, 56, 58, 63, 81, 84, 87. See also Chrétien de Troyes, and Troyes

Venice, San Marco, 131, 135
Verona Cathedral, portal, 131
Victoria and Albert Museum, enamel, 96; German reliquary altar, 109
Vigneras, Louis A., 57n
Von Simson, Otto, 77, 95n, 97, 98, 99n, 114n, 118, 130-31, 147

Wace, 29, 33, 35, 37, 38, 39, 46, 47
Wagner, Anthony, 47n
Walpole, Ronald H., ii, 121n
Walter, Archdeacon, 29-30
Walther von der Vogelweide, 10
Webber, F. R., 141, 145
Welsh, Cath Palug of, 140; mentioned, 22, 23, 25, 26, 27, 28, 30, 31, 32, 35, 47, 48, 142, 149, 153, 157
William of Malmesbury, 25, 28, 29, 30, 38-39, 56, 83, 128, 159
Winchester, font, 14; Bible, 14; enamel plaque, 96; mentioned, 23-24, 25, 34. See also Henry of Blois
Winlogée, 124, 125, 126, 133, 147, 152, 156, 160
Wolfger von Passau, Bishop, 10

Yvain, name, 37, 44, 47-48. See also Iwenus
Yvain, or *Chevalier du lion*, 20, 21, 39, 45n, 47-49, 59

Zacharias, prophet, 148, 151-52
Ziltener, Werner, 34, 37, 51n

www.ingramcontent.com/pod-product-compliance
Lightning Source LLC
Chambersburg PA
CBHW020301010526
44108CB00037B/324